APR 1 1 1983	DATE DUE		
OCT 0 2 1991			
SEP 2 4 1991			
DEC 1 1 1991			
JAN 0 2 1992			
JAN 0 3 1992			

CARR McLEAN, TORONTO FORM #38-297

THE VOYAGE THAT NEVER ENDS

THE VOYAGE THAT NEVER ENDS

MALCOLM LOWRY'S FICTION

SHERRILL E. GRACE

UNIVERSITY OF BRITISH COLUMBIA PRESS
VANCOUVER

THE VOYAGE THAT NEVER ENDS
Malcolm Lowry's Fiction

© The University of British Columbia 1982
All rights reserved

This book has been published with the help of a grant from the Canadian Federation for the Humanities, using funds provided by the Social Sciences and Humanities Research Council of Canada.

Canadian Cataloguing in Publication Data
Grace, Sherrill E., 1944-
　　The voyage that never ends

　　Bibliography: p.
　　Includes index.
　　ISBN 0-7748-0154-9 (bound). — ISBN
　　0-7748-0159-X (pbk.)

　　1. Lowry, Malcolm, 1909-1957 — Criticism and interpretation. I. Title.
PS8523.097Z67　　　　　C813'.52　　　　　C82-091245-X
PR6023.096Z67

ISBN-0-7748-0154-9 (hardcover edition)
ISBN-0-7748-0159-X (papercover edition)

Printed in Canada

For John
No se puede vivir sin amar

Contents

Acknowledgements ix
Note on Editions and Abbreviations xi

Introduction xiii

1. The Voyage That Never Ends 1

2. Outward Bound: Early Stories, *Ultramarine, Lunar Caustic* 20

3. The Luminous Wheel: *Under the Volcano* 34

4. Withdrawal and Return: "La Mordida" and *Dark as the Grave* 59

5. Beginning Yet Again: *October Ferry to Gabriola* 74

6. Symbols of Tenuous Order: *Hear Us O Lord* 79

Conclusion 118
Appendix: Conrad Aiken 123
Notes 129
Selected Bibliography 144
Index 149

Acknowledgements

This study of Malcolm Lowry has passed through various stages of research, writing, and revision over a period of nine years. For permission to reprint and recast material from articles I have published during this time, I am grateful to *The Journal of Canadian Fiction, Studies in Canadian Literature,* the British and American publishers of *The Art of Malcolm Lowry,* edited by Dr. Anne Smith, and to *Canadian Literature* which in 1973 published the study of *Ultramarine* much as it now appears in chapter 2. Complete references appear in the bibliography.

Although all Lowry readers and scholars owe a special debt to Margerie Lowry, without whom Lowry would have published far less, I would especially like to thank her for permission to quote from both published and manuscript material and for the interviews she gave me in the spring of 1975. Anne Yandle, Head of The University of British Columbia Library Special Collections, which houses the Lowry manuscripts, has been extremely helpful in many ways, as has Sara Hodson, Assistant Curator of Literary Manuscripts at The Huntington Library, San Marino, where I was able to study the Lowry papers in the Conrad Aiken collection in 1981; to both my sincere thanks. For assistance with films, I am indebted to the Film Centre of the New York Museum of Modern Art, the National Film Library in Ottawa, and to William Everson of New York University who kindly gave me a screening of *Mad Love.* My special thanks also go to Albert Erskine for his help in locating a copy of Lowry's 1951 "Work in Progress" statement. I am grateful, as well, to Samuel Weiser, Inc., for permission to reproduce material from Frater Achad's *Q.B.L.* or *The Bride's Reception* and to the University of California Press for permission to use the print of *The Hands of Orlac* from Lotte Eisner's *The Haunted Screen.* Every effort has been made to contact authors and publishers to obtain permissions. If the publisher is made aware of any errors which may have been made in obtaining permissions, the publisher will take steps to ensure that proper credit be given at that time.

A Canada Council Research Grant in 1975 enabled me to interview Mrs. Lowry, study films, and work on the manuscript of this book, and travel grants from McGill University and The University of British Columbia made it possible for me to do further research and to present papers on aspects of this book at conferences and thus to benefit from colleagues' comments.

Indeed, my thinking on Lowry has been influenced at various times, over several years, by so many different students, colleagues, and friends that it is impossible to single out every contribution. My deepest thanks go to other Lowry critics, in particular Bill New, whose work on Lowry has been both stimulating and useful and whose advice I have appreciated. My debt to others such as Dale Edmonds, Muriel Bradbrook, and Brian O'Kill will be clear from the numerous references to their work in my notes. For help in the preparation of the manuscript, it is my great pleasure to thank Professor Alec Lucas for his comments and support, Professor Peter Buitenhuis, who supervised my doctoral work on Lowry, Shirley Lumpkin, who patiently typed what Lowry would have called the "whole bolus," Doreen Todhunter who helped me prepare the final typescript, and my editor, Jane Fredeman, whose keen eye and intelligence have saved me from many a *barranca*. Errors which persist are my own. I am grateful, as well, to the Canadian Federation for the Humanities for their reviewers' helpful comments on the manuscript and for their grant in aid of publication.

Two special acknowledgements remain: to Madame Berthe McKibbin, who helped me loyally for five years, and most important, to my husband, who discussed the manuscript with me, accompanied me through Mexico, and to whom the book is dedicated.

S.E.G.
VANCOUVER, 1981

Note on Editions and Abbreviations

First editions of major texts have been used throughout; *Selected Letters of Malcolm Lowry* and *Psalms and Songs* are cited as *Selected Letters* and *P & S*. Manuscript material from The University of British Columbia Library is indicated parenthetically by box, folder, and page, except for the 1951 "Work in Progress" statement which is cited as "WP" followed by the page number. Silent changes in manuscript material quoted occur only when there has been an obvious spelling error, when Lowry has forgotten to add the slash to Sigbjørn, and when he has clearly crossed out one word and replaced it with another.

The extensive Lowry Collection includes letters, manuscripts of published and unpublished work, books from Lowry's personal library, and other materials. Copyright is held by Margerie Lowry, and material reprinted in this study is by permission of Literistic, Ltd.

The flowering past

There is no poetry when you live there.
Those stones are yours, those noises are your mind,
The forging thunderous trams and streets that bind
You to the dreamed-of bar where sits despair
Are trams and streets: poetry is otherwhere.
The cinema fronts and shops once left behind
And mourned, are mourned no more. Strangely unkind
Seem all new landmarks of the now and here.

But move you toward New Zealand or the Pole,
Those stones will blossom and the noises sing,
And trams will wheedle to the sleeping child
That never rests, whose ship will always roll,
That never can come home, but yet must bring
Strange trophies back to Illium, and wild!

        SELECTED POEMS OF MALCOLM LOWRY

Introduction

The Malcolm Lowry legend rests upon two foundations, *Under the Volcano* and alcohol. Because Lowry is most often seen as a one-book author who exhausted his genius in the creation of a single masterpiece, his other fiction is neglected and relatively unknown. However, this aspect of the legend needs emphatic qualification because, for a variety of reasons, *Under the Volcano* is best viewed as the magnificent Popocatapetl among lesser, but by no means uninteresting, peaks. In fact, Lowry had planned his novels as parts of an opus entitled "The Voyage That Never Ends," and he never intended *Under the Volcano* to stand alone. One of the aims of this study, therefore, is to modify the idea of Lowry as a one-book author by examining his fiction as a whole and by relating *Under the Volcano* to its "Voyage" companions — *Ultramarine, Lunar Caustic, Dark as the Grave Wherein My Friend Is Laid,* and *October Ferry to Gabriola.*

The other aspect of the Lowry legend, his alcoholism, began well before his death, just before his forty-eighth birthday, in 1957, and it is rather more difficult to qualify. However, the popular picture of Lowry as a suffering, guilt-ridden drunk, lost in the whirl of his own cerebral chaos, has unfortunate consequences. No doubt Lowry himself fostered this image, but in its most pernicious guise it leads to devaluation of his work — either on the ground that he was too drunk to write or that he was preoccupied with the single subject of dipsomania. An alcoholic he most certainly was, as were many writers of his generation, but somewhere amidst the anguish and liquor he worked hard at his writing, read extensively, played both ukelele and piano, became a knowledgeable film-buff, travelled widely, made many life-long friends, and enjoyed seventeen years of a devoted, if tempestuous, marriage.

Particularly during the years from 1940 to 1954, which he spent on the beach at Dollarton with his second wife, Margerie Bonner, Lowry enjoyed long periods of work, interspersed with swimming and reading. He wrote notes to Margerie regularly — love notes, progress notes, or simply morning greetings. Margerie helped him in a variety of ways, from typing to editing his manuscripts. Her sense of narrative pace and her descriptive powers are evident in the manuscripts and in the published work.[1] Without her faith in his genius and her practical advice, Lowry would have published far less. The other side of this idyll was undeniably infernal. Trouble plagued Lowry, even at his Dollarton paradise, in the form of fire, eviction threats, and fame. His poem "After publication of *Under the*

Volcano" illustrates the precariousness of his happiness and the depth of his despair:

> Success is like some horrible disaster
> Worse than your house burning, the sounds of ruination
> As the roof tree falls following each other faster
> While you stand, the helpless witness of your damnation.
>
> Fame like a drunkard consumes the house of the soul
> Exposing that you have worked for only this —
> Ah, that I had never suffered this treacherous kiss
> And had been left in darkness forever to founder and fail.[2]

Lowry was a man of astonishing extremes. He dwelt either in heaven or hell, and the two realms existed side by side for him, so that when the faulty neon sign from the Shell refinery across the bay lit up the night to spell "HELL," he saw it flashing him an amusing reminder of his position. And yet, despite his dislike of the vengeful Protestant God and his rejection of much from his strict Methodist upbringing, he was always a deeply religious man who acknowledged the religious springs of his life and art in a prefacing quotation to *Under the Volcano:* "Whoever unceasingly strives upward . . . him can we save." He was also a man with a wry sense of humour, sensitive in the extreme, dismayed by man's destruction of the natural world, and deeply enmeshed in the puzzle of man's purpose on earth. The years after the Lowrys left Dollarton brought him deeper despair and illness culminating in his death, but the end cannot be allowed to overshadow earlier years. Nor can the Lowry myth be allowed to supersede the work.

In the following chapters, I do not discuss Lowry's life in any detail or provide an introduction to his work, for this has already been ably done by Douglas Day, Muriel Bradbrook, Richard Hauer Costa, David Markson, and William New.[3] Previous acquaintance with Lowry's fiction is assumed, and although I have attempted to offer fresh insight into *Under the Volcano*, my primary concern is with Lowry's fiction as a whole. Questions of influence from other writers, from his reading, or from films and music are examined where they seem most relevant. Of these influences only a few, such as Nordahl Grieg, Conrad Aiken, German expressionist film, and American jazz, truly stand out. Lowry was not a scholar. His tastes were catholic; therefore, he enjoyed third-rate fiction as well as the classics, works of popular mysticism as well as serious philosophy.[4] Little-known writers such as Ralph Bates and Claude Houghton were as important to him as Yeats, Eliot, or Joyce, and he never forgot either Henry James, who was much in vogue during Lowry's Cambridge years (1929-32), or his respect for the nineteenth century.[5]

The aims of this book spring from my belief in Lowry's art. If his works are to continue to be regarded as important, as I believe they shall, it must be on their merits alone and not because of the gruesome or tragic stories surrounding his life — stories which his brother, Russell Lowry, claims are false or exaggerated.[6] Interpretation and analysis of Lowry's fiction has, in fact, suffered from overly partisan and heavily biographical approaches, but there are other, equally fruitful, critical ways to examine his art.

In order to understand the nature of Lowry's fiction, what influenced him and led him to develop his own philosophy and aesthetics must first be considered. A formal critical approach to the novels, one that examines the complex of narrative point of view, structure, style, and symbol, not only helps in assessing Lowry's achievement, but it is also the best way to illuminate themes in specific novels and to gain an appreciation of Lowry's overall vision. Although Lowry does not invite his reader, as Robbe-Grillet does, to co-create the text, like Joyce, Faulkner, Fowles, and many other modern writers, he does insist that the reader participate actively in the fiction, and his novels often contain comments on the way they should be read. Chapter 1, then, is devoted to a general discussion of his aesthetics and his elaborate plans for "The Voyage That Never Ends" sequence. Here, the manuscript material, most notably Lowry's 1951 "Work in Progress" statement, has been invaluable. Lowry's plan to write a novel sequence has been widely known since the publication of *Selected Letters* in 1965, but Douglas Day was the first to mention the existence of this more detailed plan.[7] Chapters 2 to 5 offer discussions of the individual novels as parts of "The Voyage That Never Ends" and provide close readings of the texts themselves. Chapter 6 is devoted to *Hear Us O Lord from Heaven Thy Dwelling Place*, which stands largely outside the "Voyage" itself. However, this collection of stories, carefully articulated like a novel, is a perfect Lowry microcosm and epitomizes his voyage concept. In the Conclusion, I have tried both to summarize and reiterate points of importance and to locate Lowry within the context of twentieth-century fiction.

Throughout my discussion, I use Lowry's concept of voyage as continuous withdrawal and return and his circle symbolism as touchstones to his work because Lowry frequently associates examples of the withdrawal/return pattern (such as the swing of perception between extremes of subjectivity and objectivity, the ambiguous relationship of writer to work, or simply man's repeated victories and defeats in the journey of life) either with vicious circles of destruction or, alternately, with the beneficent cycles of stars and sea. Furthermore, he had intended *Under the Volcano* to be the "centre" of the "Voyage" cycle with, in turn, the perceiving mind of its creator as the centre of an ever-expanding perimeter of experience. Equally important, and inextricably bound up with this pattern and symbolism, is Lowry's belief in temporal process and his superb control of the temporal and spatial dynamic of his narratives; therefore, in much of what follows it has been necessary to examine his use of "spatial form" in detail.

Together, the withdrawal/return paradigm, circle symbolism, and "spatial form" provide a kind of *vade mecum* for Lowry's work, but they should not be seen as rules which delimit his vision so much as the elements in a literary enterprise which was evolving up to the time of his death. They are the means whereby he continued to explore the possibilities of his art and to deepen and refine his vision in the never-ending voyage of creation.

1

The Voyage That Never Ends

Malcolm Lowry was many things—a poet, an incorrigible drunk, a weaver of impossible "biographical" legends, a syphilophobe, one of the great novelists of this century, a charming, sly, humorous man, and an interesting thinker. Because he was first and foremost an artist, he was not concerned with rigorous treatment of abstract theories, logic, or intellectual systems, and it is useless to search for a tightly argued philosophical position in his works. Nevertheless, Lowry was very much a product of the modern age—the age of Heisenberg, Gombrich and Wittgenstein—and he wrestled constantly with epistemological questions about the nature of perception and consciousness. These questions, in turn, led him to probe his understanding of temporal and spatial reality, as well as the ability of language and narrative structure to express that reality. In a 1953 letter to his editor, Albert Erskine, he wrote that he was looking for "a new form, a new approach to reality itself" (*Selected Letters*, 330); that "new form" was to be created in "The Voyage That Never Ends."

Lowry's philosophical reflections appear in both his manuscripts and published work. For example, in a fascinating story, "Ghostkeeper," Lowry writes that "it is a pity I have no philosophical training for I unquestionably have some of the major equipment of a philosopher of sorts."[1] This late story, a species of biographical metafiction about a writer, Tom Goodheart, who is trying to write a story, is in many ways an excellent place to begin an investigation of Lowry's theories. Interspersed with parts of the "Ghostkeeper" story proper are some of Lowry's personal observations on what he described to Erskine as "reality itself":

> Life is indeed a sort of delirium perhaps that should be contemplated however by a sober "healthy" mind. By sober and healthy I mean of necessity limited. The mind is not equipped to look at the truth. Perhaps people get inklings of that truth on the lowest plane when they drink too much or go crazy and become delirious but it can't be stomached, certainly not from that sort of upside-down and reversed position. Not that the truth is "bad" or "good"; it simply *is,* is incomprehensible, and though one is part of it, there is too much of it to grasp at once, or it is ungraspable, being perpetually Protean. (*P&S,* 224)

The single most important aspect of this "reality" is its dynamism. For Lowry, the universe was in a constant process of change akin to the Nietzschean state of becoming that underlies romanticism and expressionism. His affinity with a worldview based upon perpetual movement and possibility led him to philosophers like Bergson and Ortega y Gasset, to a mystic like Charles Stansfeld-Jones (the Cabbalist, Frater Achad, whom Lowry met in Dollarton in 1942), and to quasi-philosophers like J.W. Dunne, Annie Besant, P.D. Ouspensky and Hermann Keyserling.[2] For example, in his notes for the unpublished "La Mordida," Lowry supports his belief in process with quotes from Keyserling's *Recovery of Truth:*

> Those who regard the harmony of the celestial spheres as an ideal state and hold it up to the living, therefore acknowledge death to be their life-ideal.... We came to the conclusion that only states of perfection of a kind that are fruitful, that continue motion, that offer the promise of higher development, are compatible with the meaning of life. (12:27, 1)

Viewed in these terms, the cycles and recurrences which play such important symbolic and structural roles in Lowry's fiction can be seen to represent subsidiary aspects of reality, the wheels within wheels of an eternal flux.

Another outstanding feature of Lowry's world is its signification. Once again, in "Ghostkeeper," Lowry comments upon the complexity of life and art:

> In fact, no sooner did poor Goodheart come to some sort of decision as to what line his story should take than it was as if a voice said to him: "But you see, you can't do it like that, that's not the meaning at all, or rather it's only one meaning—if you're going to get anywhere near the truth you'll have twenty different plots and a story no one will take." And as a matter of fact this was sadly true. For how could you write a story in which its main symbol was not even reasonably consistent, did not even have consistent ambiguity? Certainly the watch did not seem to mean the same thing consistently. It had started by being a symbol of one thing, and ended up—or rather had not yet ended up—by being a symbol of something else. (*P&S,* 219)

To Lowry it seemed as if nothing could be explained away as mere accident. Everything connects or corresponds to form a highly significant whole; everything has meaning. Lowry gives creative form to his sense of interconnection and significance by using journeys, metaphors of paths, ladders, wheels, and fresh and intriguing symbols like that of the Panama Canal. Even in the strange books of Charles Fort, whose data on fires Lowry used in *October Ferry*, he found a fascinating collection of "facts" which he could draw upon to suggest that the visible world contains signs and connected events which logic cannot explain.

By 1928, when he first read Conrad Aiken's "House of Dust" and *Blue Voyage*, Lowry was already interested in questions about individual consciousness and perception (the influence of Aiken on Lowry is discussed in the Appendix). Like the symbolists, he was unwilling to allow mechanistic limitations to the human psyche, and his obsession with the creative and intuitional power of the mind is symptomatic of early twentieth-century neo-romanticism. Moreover, Lowry came to believe that the development of consciousness is never complete; therefore, his "Voyage That Never Ends" is, on one level, the never-ending effort of the individual to develop consciousness and thereby achieve understanding of a dynamic universe.

The fusion of opposites was another of Lowry's central ideas through which he related his concept of active, evolving consciousness to his picture of a many-levelled, intricately connected world. Influenced by his reading of P. D. Ouspensky (*Tertium Organum* and *A New Model of the Universe*, originally published in 1920 and 1931 respectively), Jones, and Coleridge (in particular *Aids to Reflection*), Lowry viewed life in terms of polarities that must be balanced. He felt that the activity of unifying or balancing opposites reflects the vitality of the universe and illustrates the creativity of the mind. Because Lowry believed man could penetrate deeper and deeper into the mystery of reality by means of an ever-expanding consciousness, he was convinced that to misuse this power would quickly render a potentially paradisial existence infernal.

Briefly, then, Lowry's philosophy, although eclectic, achieves a degree of unity through the considerable synthesizing powers of his imagination. Most importantly, he believed that reality must be understood as being in constant motion, "perpetually Protean," and that a man's moral duty is to live in harmony with this universal motion through constant psychic growth. The past, while it threatens to enclose and paralyse the movement of the mind, he viewed as synonymous with the self created thus far in time; therefore, by understanding the past, a man understands the self he has created and becomes free to continue his growth. From this Lowry concluded that the writer's task is to strive constantly to capture in art the protean nature of reality. In practical terms, of course, he set himself an impossible task because the artist must select, begin, and end, but the effort to achieve this goal explains much about Lowry's narrative strategies, style, and what he called the rhythm of "withdrawal and return" that characterizes his work. Even his creative method, his way of writing, is congruent with these beliefs and artistic goals.

Lowry's manuscripts and notes offer valuable insight into the way he wrote. Very rarely did he cut material from his manuscripts without incorporating it, in another form, elsewhere in the text so that his work continued to expand. The extant notes for each of his novels indicate that he began with a central episode for the book, as well as for each chapter, and then built upon this foundation by adding blocks of descriptive and narrative material at either end. Frequently, he would shift the position of whole passages. In *Under the Volcano*, for example, paragraphs which he had first placed in one chapter were later moved to another. He never seemed satisfied with the symbolic resonance or, to keep the architectural analogy, with what he called the "churrigueresque," or overloaded, façade of his work.[3] His imagination continually discovered new connections and unexplored resemblances among words, images, and events. Symbols, allusions, motifs, were constantly inserted—almost like mortar—at strategic points in the manuscripts. Even individual sentences illustrate the way he added phrase after phrase, adjective after adjective to his initial idea as if to probe, develop, and expand every nuance of meaning.[4] Nevertheless, the writing was never careless or hurried: he rewrote sentences and paragraphs many times, and marginal notes indicate that he had complicated reasons for every punctuation mark.

Two features of Lowry's creative method stand out as especially significant. Firstly, he put a book together passage by passage almost as if it were a house or a pier; secondly, his work never seemed, to his eyes, complete. Even *Under the Volcano* was unfinished, because, for Lowry, a work of art was like a building that was constantly being built. Despite the hopelessness of the attempt, the fact that the work could never be finished or made permanent was its greatest source of value. In *Dark as the Grave,* Sigbjørn Wilderness emphasizes that the artist must constantly rebuild his ever-changing work of art, and he goes on to explain that

> "Part of the artist's despair . . . in the face of his material is perhaps occasioned by the patent fact that the universe itself—as the Rosicrucians also held—is in the process of creation. An organic work of art, having been conceived, must grow in the creator's mind, or proceed to perish."[5]

The key to Lowry's art, then, the unifying idea of his metaphysics and aesthetics and the insight upon which he based his vision of life and his masterwork "The Voyage That Never Ends," is that "an organic work of art . . . must grow in the creator's mind, or proceed to perish." Because symbols, images, and words are constantly expanding, Lowry's attempt to capture this activity in art becomes absurd. Commenting upon this absurdity in "Ghostkeeper," he writes:

> The minute an artist begins to try and shape his material—the more especially if that material is his own life—some sort of magic lever is thrown into gear, setting some celestial machinery in motion producing events or coincidences that show him that this shaping of his is absurd, that nothing is static or can be pinned down, that everything is evolving or developing into other meanings, or cancellations of meanings quite beyond his comprehension.... In any case the average short story is probably a very bad image of life, and an absurdity, for the reason that no matter how much action there is in it, it is static, a piece of death, fixed, a sort of butterfly on a pin.... But the attempt should be—or should be here—at least to give the illusion of things—appearances, possibilities, ideas, even resolutions—in a state of perpetual metamorphosis. (*P&S,* 223-24)

The attempt must be made because, in Lowry's terms, the most realistic work of art is the one that imitates the flux of noumenal and phenomenal reality.

Lowry founded his aesthetic upon a belief in the infinite variation and movement of life. Just as his universe is an intricately connected, supremely meaningful structure, so his fiction is a multi-levelled world in which time and space are unlimited. By penetrating the future or reliving the past, by interpreting coincidences and events as signs and portents, by travelling mentally and physically, the Lowry protagonist inhabits and *becomes* a dynamic, mysterious universe. Finding watches, crossing borders under the scrutiny of customs officials, riding in buses, ferries, boats and planes, looping-the-loop, visiting the ruins of Pompeii, even contemplating the stacks of polished glasses in a bar, becomes, within Lowry's artistic system, a metaphor for a mystical journey, a metonymy for a larger reality.

Lowry clearly stands apart from the main body of Western philosophic and aesthetic thought. So convinced was he of the goal-less motion of life that he could not envision a final static eternal heaven any more than he could imagine "a perpetual spiritual orgasm."[6] Time could not be spatialized in Platonic terms, and art, mirroring reality, must not hypostasize life. He also stands somewhat outside Leavis's "great tradition," although the experimental quality of certain of his texts does not make him either an "anti-realist" or a thoroughgoing "modernist." As Malcolm Bradbury makes clear, Lowry shares much with the Romantics,[7] and yet his increasing interest in metafictional forms points to his affinities with some post-modernist writers. I will return to this question of fictional mode in the Conclusion because it is important to place Lowry in this wider context, but for the moment, it is enough to point out that Lowry was moving away from traditional realist concepts of plot, character and language.

In *October Ferry,* for example, Ethan reflects on the "reality" of films or novels and decides:

> A novelist presents less of life the more closely he approaches what he thinks of as his realism. Not that there were no plots in life, nor that he could not see a pattern, but that man was constantly in flux, and constantly changing.[8]

The only artistic form which Lowry felt could possibly embody his vision and offer "a new approach to reality itself" was the cyclical voyage ever-renewed. Lowry's need for constant creative activity is manifest in the "never-ending" aspect of the voyage, for the protagonist's quest, like that of the artist or any individual, lacks a final goal—unless it be the knowledge that the voyaging must continue. His "realism" lies in the artist's endeavour to recreate in the very form of his art the "perpetually Protean" nature of life. In the effort, according to Lowry, the artist would continuously create himself. Or perhaps, to be more realistic, the artist would destroy himself. Without doubt Lowry's vision of reality, his desire to pack everything in and to keep everything moving, helped to destroy him.

"The Voyage That Never Ends" developed slowly in Lowry's mind, and his plans for the work were never finalized. To trace the evolution of the "Voyage," it is necessary to go back to 1940 when Lowry conceived of a Dantean trilogy to follow on from *Under the Volcano.*[9] Later, in 1946, he described his plan to the publisher Jonathan Cape:

> [I] conceived the idea of a trilogy entitled *The Voyage That Never Ends* for your firm (nothing less than a trilogy would do) with the *Volcano* as the first infernal part, a much amplified *Lunar Caustic* as the second, purgatorial part, and an enormous novel I was also working on called *In Ballast to the White Sea* . . . as the paradisal third part, the whole to concern the battering the human spirit takes . . . in its ascent towards its true purpose. (*Selected Letters,* 63)

Certainly, *Lunar Caustic,* in its present form, is at least as infernal as it is purgatorial, and it is difficult to imagine how Lowry would have altered its ambiguous, if not downright dark, vision simply by amplifying. As he later came to see, the novella belonged to a later stage in the "Voyage." In fact, the early Dantean conception of the sequence has a finality and a naiveté about it which could not possibly have suited Lowry's complex evolving system, and this is no where more clear than in the story of the "paradisal third part." The one-thousand page manuscript of "In Ballast to the White Sea" was destroyed (except for a few charred fragments) when the Lowry cabin burned in 1944. According to Lowry, it was to have told the story of a young man's salvation from inertia through a coincidental meeting with an older writer for whom he has a mysterious affinity (*Selected Letters*, 63 and 255). That older writer was modelled on the Norwegian, Nordahl Grieg (1902-43).

Some time before his arrival at Cambridge in 1929, Lowry had discovered Grieg's novel (*Skibet Gaar Videre*), translated in 1927 as *The Ship Sails On*. The nineteen-year-old Lowry, who had been to the Far East in 1927 on the *Pyrrhus* and was writing a novel (to be called *Ultramarine*) about his experiences, was shaken by Grieg's portrayal of young Benjamin Hall's first voyage and by Grieg's grimly moralistic picture of a sailor's life. Despairing of news from his girl at home and disillusioned by the brutality and boredom of the ship, Hall has his first sexual experience with a prostitute, contracts syphilis, and nearly commits suicide. Grieg's book, written in a straightforward realistic mode, reveals a profound philosophical pessimism in scattered remarks such as — "Life had played one of its scenes over again, a new spiral had wound its way upward, and now he found himself looking down into it" — and in the underlying suggestion that time repeats itself inexorably and that life is a maelstrom of meaningless change—that life, like the ship, moves on oblivious of private pain.

The influence of *The Ship Sails On* is most obvious in the subject of *Ultramarine*.[10] Lowry's fascination, however, was not simply with the congruity of Grieg's book with his own experience. It is a minor step from the idea of "the ship sails on" to "the voyage never ends." In the summer of 1930, Lowry had signed aboard a tramp steamer bound for Norway in order to meet Grieg, and it was from this voyage, and the eerie significance of discovering *The Ship Sails On* while he was working on *Ultramarine*, that he conceived "In Ballast to the White Sea." Nordahl Grieg had provided Lowry with the first evidence for his Pirandellian belief that he was, in a sense, a character in someone else's novel. This idea became both an obsession and a basic premise in "The Voyage That Never Ends."

Despite the loss of "In Ballast to the White Sea," plans for a major opus grew. Although the Dantean parallel became too restrictive, Lowry continued to talk about his work in terms of hell, purgatory, and paradise. It was characteristic of his creative method and aesthetic beliefs that his evolving plan should attempt to include every new idea. In the autumn of 1951, he wrote to his agent, Harold Matson, that his reconstituted literary continuum would include

> five, perhaps six interrelated novels, of which the *Volcano* would be one, though not the best one by any means, the novel you suggested I should write some years back, a sort of *Under Under the Volcano,* should be ten times more terrible (tentatively it's called *Dark as the Grave Wherein my Friend Is Laid*) and the last one *La Mordida* that throws the whole thing into reverse and issues in triumph. (The Consul is brought to life again, that is the real Consul; *Under the Volcano* itself functions as a sort of battery in the middle but only as a work of the imagination by the protagonist.) Better still: some years back I was not equipped to tackle a task of this

nature: now, it seems to me, I've gone through the necessary spiritual ordeals that have permitted me to see the truth of what I'm getting at and to see the whole business clearly. (*Selected Letters*, 267)

On 22 November 1951 he sent Matson the detailed description of his ambitious plan. "Work in Progress" contains a thirty-four page discussion of "The Voyage That Never Ends" and twenty-nine pages devoted to *Hear Us O Lord* and "Forest Path." Although Giroux was deeply impressed, Harcourt Brace was unable to support Lowry. Happily, Random House offered Lowry a contract enabling him to work with his former editor and friend, Albert Erskine. The 1951 outline in "Work in Progress" is as follows:

THE VOYAGE THAT NEVER ENDS[11]

THE ORDEAL OF SIGBJØRN WILDERNESS 1

UNTITLED SEA NOVEL
LUNAR CAUSTIC

UNDER THE VOLCANO   The Centre

DARK AS THE GRAVE WHEREIN MY FRIEND IS LAID ⎫
ERIDANUS   ⎬ Trilogy
LA MORDIDA   ⎭

THE ORDEAL OF SIGBJØRN WILDERNESS 2

The untitled sea novel is, of course, *Ultramarine*, which Lowry felt needed considerable rewriting. *Lunar Caustic,* instead of functioning as a purgatorio in a trilogy, now precedes *Under the Volcano*, which assumes a focal position midway in the "Voyage." By this time Lowry thought of *Dark as the Grave,* "Eridanus," and "La Mordida" as a "trilogy" within the "Voyage" and worked on them concurrently. This ordering, however, was far from final. During the 1950's —in fact, until his death—Lowry struggled with *October Ferry,* which gradually consumed the material for "Eridanus," thereby causing another major shift in the "Voyage." According to Margerie Lowry, he later altered the position of "La Mordida," putting it before "Eridanus" (now called *October Ferry to Gabriola*). The "Voyage" would therefore proceed thus:

"Ordeal 1"

Ultramarine
Lunar Caustic

Under the Volcano

Dark as the Grave
"La Mordida"
October Ferry to Gabriola

"Ordeal 2"

This order seems logical because "La Mordida" is a continuation, in time and place, of *Dark as the Grave* whereas *October Ferry* leads on into the future. There are other indications in the manuscripts, discussed below, which further corroborate these late changes, but Lowry would no doubt have revised his plan still further had he lived.

Lowry held high hopes for his ambitious masterwork. The "Voyage" was to be an image of life, viewed as "primarily (among other more pleasant factors) ordeal, a going through the hoop an initiation, finally perhaps a doing of God's will" ("WP," 3), and a genuine portrayal of life in all its monotony and simple joy. It was to be many other things as well: a great love story, a quest for faith, and certainly Lowry's own testament to the wonder of man and universe. Towards the end of "Work in Progress" he declared: "He who, even in extreme youth, turns to page 870 passim of the Voyage That Never Ends, such is my ambition, will not go on unrewarded, or uncomforted, or empty away" ("WP," 30). Incredible as it sounds, given the fact that *Under the Volcano* took ten years, he actually estimated that the entire "Voyage" might require five years to complete!

Without doubt, "The Ordeal of Sigbjørn Wilderness" is the most fascinating of the "Voyage" fragments. In July 1949 Lowry injured his back in a fall from his Dollarton pier, and during a brief stay in hospital, he experienced hallucinations and visions and heard voices.[12] Lowry was deeply moved by this experience, not least because it related to work he was doing at the time (*Selected Letters*, 183). Art had seemed to influence life. Lowry in turn used the hospital experience to provide a setting for both parts of the "Ordeal" and, thereby, a framing device for the entire "Voyage."

"The Ordeal of Sigbjørn Wilderness" consists of a very raw draft—notes, Lowry's discussions with himself, and quotations from Arthur Lovejoy and Annie Besant (13:7, 151 pages). The intention was for the protagonist, like Lowry, to injure himself in a fall and to hear voices from his past while he was confined to hospital. Among the voices is that of a college friend, James Travers, who had committed suicide. The typescript contains frequent references to Lowry's other novels, and the Travers scenes foreshadow *October Ferry to Gabriola*. As Muriel Bradbrook points out, the suicide of his Cambridge friend, Paul Launcelot Charles Fitte, haunted Lowry all his life, causing him recurrent feelings of guilt and responsibility.[13] Consequently, he wove the event into the "Voyage." As far as the "Voyage" is concerned, however, Fitte (as Travers or

The Ordeal of Sigbjorn Wilderness

ATOMIC RHYTHM

I Then like the Pit and the Pendulum

(Also see
description
in Dark as
the Grave)

In the old hospital of St. Nicolas de Bari's, on the ground floor, upon a stretcher, a man lay with a broken back. etc. The feeling the ground floor is the basement. The log rolling in; the sense of it being like Euston station, lamps like veiled incandescent lamps, and the sense of their being something wrong; description as per on m.s. paper.

2 describe the hospital, its dissimilarity from other hospitals, that it is a Catholic hospital, but make point that most Catholic hospitals are good.

Description of the accident - as it were thrown from his own creation, the pier - and also of how the days were spent since Primrose's departure. His telegram. He imagines he sees Primrose. But as if in answer to this hallucination a telegram is brought from Primrose herself saying that she is going to arrive on the morrow. (Also some account of their having built thei pier, so that it is placed as his creation) This makes him happy and he clutches the telegram in his hand. For what has happened he is sorry only on Primrose's account. For it was as if there had been something important in his being there at the airport; it would have cancelled out perhaps, that other unpleasantness, so much of his past untrustworthiness, growing worse during the last years since the fire. But he wished to god she were here now. (It was as if, since she went, he had been suffering from a chronic case of abulia - yes, the word, a bad one. Martin did not think of this in a usual connotation of a rather obsolete psychological term meaning loss of will power.

Lowry's typescript notes for the beginning of the *Ordeal* (13:7, 29)

Cordwainer, as he would be called in *October Ferry*) was not to be dead in any final sense, but passed on to another plane from which he could commune with the living. Sigbjørn Wilderness himself was to cross the border from life into death after the accident because "the Ordeal of Sigbjørn Wilderness is the ordeal of death itself . . . albeit in fact . . . the protagonist, who has suffered a near fatal accident, does not actually die" ("WP," 1). During this death-in-life crisis Sigbjørn reviews his entire existence, not haphazardly, but with events carefully selected and edited. This "transcript," giving form and meaning to his life, comprises the novels of "The Voyage That Never Ends"; "the action properly speaking begins with the second novel, the untitled sea novel, i.e., with an actual voyage" ("WP," 1).

The "Ordeal" involves one of the most unusual and challenging concepts in modern fiction. Part 1 was to take Wilderness from the accident to the threshold of death and the beginning of the novel sequence. Part 2, emerging from the last novel, was to bring the protagonist back to life, back to his wife, back to his home, back to a balanced existence. Lowry's summary of the "Ordeal" in "Work in Progress" places the entire project in context:

> Should the plan as I now conceive it be carried out the end of La Mordida would merge into Sigbjørn Wilderness' recovery in hospital after his near fatal accident, though this, far from banal as it sounds, is actually one of the most original scenes in the Voyage. Wilderness has been placed (the accident is in Eridanus from his own self-built pier, and the opening passage of the whole work describes the flux and flow of the inlet as portrayed in the Forest Path to the Spring) shortly after the book opens in a Catholic hospital. After he has been there some days and seems to be recovering there is evidence of the most extraordinary psychic phenomena in his cell as a consequence of which—though he has injured his spine—he is considered possessed by the devil, people are removed from the adjacent wards, and he is transferred to the Protestant City Hospital. It is during this period, already beyond life, and as if he is trying to present to God some meaning in his ways on earth, that the other books, starting with the sea voyage which merges into the other hospital experience of Lunar Caustic, the Volcano, etc., and ending with La Mordida are as it were dreamed, or lived through, merging in turn again into the psychic experiences. As he wakes, certain in his own mind that he has had among other things direct evidence of life beyond the grave and the survival of the soul . . . he slowly realises that no one will believe him should he try to convince anyone of the supernatural side of his experience, not even his wife. . . . On the other hand he has been given his life and his health back as by a miracle, and he determines to spend the rest of it more wisely and unselfishly and usefully and the book closes once more, as it began (and as it is portrayed in the Forest Path to the Spring) on a note of happiness, with the Wildernesses

watching the tide bearing the ships out upon its currents that become remote, and which, like the Tao, becoming remote, return.[14] ("WP," 31-32)

This passage clearly demonstrates Lowry's desire to contain the delirium of life within a literary form capable of dramatizing the necessary process of spiritual growth. On its simplest level, that form represents the patterned narrative of Wilderness' mind as he withdraws from the hospital situation into the wider reality of his imagination, finally to return to life "as by a miracle." Control or balance is all. Even at the moment of death, man must shape "his-story" because, according to Lowry, it is this shaping of life-into-art-into-life that gives meaning to existence: "Not only the editor, but man himself is a cutter and a shaper; indeed as Ortega observes, a sort of novelist" ("WP," 2). Sigbjørn Wilderness is both the author reliving his life in *Under the Volcano, Dark as the Grave* and the other novels, and the protagonist in the "Ordeal," where his life is being written; therefore, he is contained not only within his own books but also within the imagination of the writer of the "Voyage." This concept of fabulation as a metaphor, not only for the activity of the human mind, but also for life is the cornerstone of Lowry's "Voyage."

Describing the "real protagonist of the *Voyage*" in his letters as "not so much a man or a writer as the unconscious," Lowry goes on to say that

> Wilderness is not, in the ordinary sense in which one encounters novelists or the author in novels, a novelist. He simply doesn't know what he is. He is a sort of underground man. Also he is Ortega's fellow, making up his life as he goes along, and trying to find his vocation. . . . According to Ortega, the best image for man himself *is* a novelist, and it is in this way that I'd prefer you to look at him. . . . Moreover he is disinterested in literature, uncultured, incredibly unobservant, in many respects ignorant, without faith in himself, and lacking nearly all the qualities you normally associate with a novelist or a writer. . . . His very methods of writing are absurd and he sees practically nothing at all, save through his wife's eyes, though he gradually comes to *see*. I believe I can make him a very original character, both human and pathetically inhuman at once. I much approve of him as a doppelgänger. (*Selected Letters*, 331-32)

Lowry approves of Sigbjørn as a *Doppelgänger* because this character is more than a conventional persona; he is a double, Lowry's other self. But his inspiration for this concept of man as novelist comes from José Ortega y Gasset's *Toward a Philosophy of History*, which he discovered in 1950 (*Selected Letters*, 210). According to Ortega, "body and soul are things: but I am a drama, if anything an unending struggle to be what I have to be."[15] Wilderness, then, is a dramatization of the unconscious of the master-creator of the "Voyage," and as such he represents humanity in the process of creating history. If Lowry had lived to complete more of the "Voyage," the position and importance of the Wilderness protagonist would have imparted, as Barry Wood suggests, a strong metafictional quality to the entire "Voyage,"[16] and for this aspect of the fiction the protagonist's (or Lowry's) autobiography is immediately relevant, not because it is of personal significance but because it is the type of the general human story. Through Wilderness and the "Ordeal," Lowry was deliberately moving the "Voyage" novels further and further away from conventional realist narratives of three-dimensional, consistent characters (an aspect of fiction which he claims—in his famous letter to Cape about *Volcano*—never greatly interested him) and ever closer to the depersonalized centres of consciousness found in *Tristram Shandy*, *Finnigans Wake* and *Gravity's Rainbow*, as well as some recent metafiction.

Lowry's description of the "Voyage" proper begins with a discussion of *Lunar Caustic*. The relationship between the sea novel and *Lunar Caustic* was to be like that between *Volcano* and *Dark as the Grave*—the protagonist in *Lunar Caustic* was to be the author of the sea-novel. Lowry foresaw the finished *Lunar Caustic* as "a novel of almost total blackness" ("WP," 4). At the same time, it was to be purgatorial, hell being set aside for subsequent novels: "in one way—though originally designed to succeed it—it will be seen to lead up inevitably to Under the Volcano" ("WP," 5). There is little further description of the book in "Work in Progress," but Lowry expatiated upon his *grand guignol* plans in complementary notes (36:5).

Apparently Lowry wished to incorporate as much material from the lost "In Ballast to the White Sea" into *Lunar Caustic* as possible. The hero, now named Thurstaston (another Wilderness projection), dreams of his university days and his youthful fixation on an older writer.[17] All this was to occur in a flashback while Thurstaston lies in hospital suffering from *delirium tremens*. Futhermore, he fears he has been contaminated by a homosexual, that his only son is dead, and that his wife has been unfaithful! The projected *Lunar Caustic* was to contain many parallels with Lowry's other novels, among them the hospital setting, which links it with the "Ordeal," and the fact that the insane asylum, though like a "marathon of the dead," has windows which connect it with more propitious locales:

> But what is below is like what is above. The window that gives on the East River is the counterpart of the window that gives on Eridanus inlet when we have at long last, as it were, emerged into Paradise! (36:5, 8)

At this point he planned that the ending of *Lunar Caustic* should be set in a Catholic church (not the bar where Plantagenet withdraws in the published novella), "thus paralleling the end of Dark as the Grave" (36:5, 17).

Lunar Caustic, as published, suffers from the lack of convincing explanation for the hero's suffering, but *Lunar Caustic* rewritten along the horrifying lines sketched in the notes would have run the risk of becoming grotesquely melodramatic. Perhaps sensing these problems, Lowry devised an etiology for his protagonist: Thurstaston was to be a murderer (which is hardly surprising when one remembers the guilt of Ethan Llewelyn and Geoffrey Firmin, and the fantasies of Dana and Sigbjørn):

> I had better explain this so-called murder (which will involve another flashback) because it is a key to the whole Voyage, and it is also the key to the Consul's character and his guilt. It must be remembered that Thurstaston will turn out to be, like the Consul, Wilderness' "creation".... But we shall learn in Dark as the Grave that it is Wilderness that has really committed the murder. (36:5, 10)

This "murder" is the suicide of a young Cambridge student for which Thurstaston feels responsible. Subsequently, Thurstaston/Sigbjørn's life has been one long atonement. In this way *Lunar Caustic* would double back on the "Ordeal" and dovetail into *Volcano* and *October Ferry:*

> In the Ordeal of Sigbjørn Wilderness, the first part, the man he thinks he has murdered actually speaks to him . . . and forgives him, telling him that his, Wilderness', atonement has long been made but that his continuing remorse is forcing him, the dead man, to follow him everywhere.[18] (36:5, 12)

Lowry quickly dismisses *Under the Volcano* in "Work in Progress" and moves on to his plans for *Dark as the Grave Wherein My Friend Is Laid.* For the most part, the plot is identical with the published version, but there is one interesting exception. Lowry wanted to incorporate a new major character, M. L'Hirondelle, who was to be a film-maker and owner of the tower in Quauhnahuac where the Wildernesses stay. L'Hirondelle spots Sigbjørn in the airport on the way to Mexico and retrieves the manuscript, which Sigbjørn left in the bar, of *The Valley of the Shadow of Death* (the title for *Under the Volcano* in *Dark as the Grave*). L'Hirondelle, who knew Sigbjørn as a young man, turns out to be the prototype of Jacques Laruelle. Once all the characters have arrived in Quauhnahuac, "M. Laruelle and the Consul meet . . . in the person of M. L'Hirondelle and Sigbjørn Wilderness, quite near the ravine of the Consul's demise" ("WP," 14). Sigbjørn was definitely to live within his own book. Despite eight pages of analysis and description, "Work in Progress" does not substantially clarify the many problems surrounding *Dark as the Grave.* Lowry reiterates what is obvious from the published text—that the novel is "a quest for faith"—but it is impossible to see how his plans, as set forth in "Work in Progress," would have significantly improved it. As far as I am aware, the proposed sections involving L'Hirondelle were never written.

Lowry devotes only one page of "Work in Progress" to an outline of

"Eridanus," which was to be the next novel in the sequence. Briefly, the Wildernesses, still in their tower in Quauhnahuac, have invited L'Hirondelle to dinner, and the evening is spent "invoking" their happy life in Eridanus. Although the framing device of the dinner party seems never to have been started, the descriptive passages in "Eridanus" grew into *October Ferry*. Lowry's intention in 1951 was to use the idyllic "Eridanus" material as an "intermezzo" between the hells of *Dark as the Grave* and "La Mordida." The trilogy would thus have had a brief breathing space in the middle as well as an emphatic reminder of what the characters stood to lose. The three books, *Dark as the Grave,* "Eridanus," and "La Mordida," were to span seven months (seven being an important Lowry number) from November 1945 to May 1946.

"La Mordida" "is a continuation in time of *Dark as the Grave* and a resumption of that story" ("WP," 23). The work, a sprawling 422-page typed draft (12:9-26), exists as a collection of notes, quotations, and prose passages scarcely approximating a novel. Recorded is a thinly fictionalized account of the Lowrys' misadventures in Mexico in 1946 and their ultimate deportation. (See additional discussion in chapter 4.) Sigbjørn and Primrose leave Quauhnahuac for a holiday in Acapulco where they are placed under hotel-arrest for a breach of visa regulations and for an unpaid fine. The remainder of their stay is spent in futile visits to the authorities while Sigbjørn withdraws to the bottle. His drinking signals yet another stage in the ordeal of life, another withdrawal before the next successful return to equilibrium. This withdrawal, however, was intended to be still more hellish than either *Volcano* or *Dark as the Grave.* Once again, the "mordida" in question is Sigbjørn's personal remorse and guilt.

The book was not to be the unrelieved nightmare that this synopsis suggests. The drama of the story—and Lowry believed it would be "an extremely exciting story, more so than Under the Volcano" ("WP," 29)—was to arise first from a sense of ironic contrast and, second, from a quality of "self-cancelling melodrama" (WP," 29). Constant contrasts, amounting to counterpoint, would be created by the repetition of scenes from the other novels within the distorted, all-threatening context of "La Mordida"—scenes in prison, in a church, by the sea, in a bottle, and on the inevitable buses. The "La Mordida" bus rides were to outdo anything previously portrayed, as Lowry suggests in this description of the sense of melodrama he was seeking:

> the suspense, which seems to build up and up and up during the time of their ordeal, reading through my notes for this part, seems to me to hint of something new, or something old, that has not been thought worth developing in literature—I believe, from something I read recently, that Howells would have given me full marks—which is the drama of actual life, of stagnation, hopelessness, of monotony, the awful suspicion added to day after day, that they are never going to get their passports back at all, the self-cancelling melodrama of D. W. Griffith-like last-moment arrivals at

the Consul's office—having almost every day either by bus or car climbed the 10,000 feet up to the Tres Marias, and descended the 4,000 from Quauhnahuac to Mexico City—only to find that the Consul [not Geoffrey but the American Consul helping them] has let them down again, that no one is there: and yet they are under arrest, and are deprived of all freedom, the withdrawals and returns repeating themselves endlessly, more and more wearily, without apparent meaning. ("WP," 29).

Despite these elaborate plans and high hopes, "La Mordida" remains a tedious venture. However, Lowry's notes for the novel refer to two dream chapters that were to operate as escapes from the reality of his characters' incarceration (36:7, 1). One was to be "Through the Panama," the other was to be a story with a Haitian setting called "Battement de Tambours," which Lowry never began, and these chapters might have alleviated the monotony of the plot. The ending, in which the protagonists escape across the American border, fuses the story with the "Voyage." Beneath a brilliant night sky, Sigbjørn, with his wife in his arms, realizes that his soul has been reborn from all "these weavings to and fro, these treacheries, these projections of the past upon the future, of the imagination upon reality. . . . These dislocations of time" (12:26, 345). He has a "vision of absolute joy" and knows he will now return to rebuild his Canadian paradise.

October Ferry to Gabriola does not appear as a part of the "Voyage" in the 1951 "Work in Progress," but because of later developments and its eventual importance within the continuum, a few points should be made here. (The genesis of *October Ferry* is discussed in chapter 5.) The published text elaborates Lowry's concept of withdrawal and return first by examining Ethan Llewelyn's paralysing obsession with guilt, remorse, and disaster, and then by portraying Llewelyn's desperate struggle toward faith, psychological and emotional equilibrium, and the promise of joy. Although the story repeats this fundamental "Voyage" theme, it offers, with the exception of "Forest Path to the Spring," Lowry's most convincing portrayal of harmony. Links with the "Voyage" are obvious and numerous, from the ubiquitous "Frère Jacques" melody to the haunting presence of Peter Cordwainer.

The Cordwainer material is the most important link with the "Voyage" for it includes the identical psychic situation that Sigbjørn experiences in the "Ordeal," and as previously noted (p. 14 above), Lowry was determined to introduce the suicide-guilt configuration from the "Ordeal" into *Lunar Caustic*. The Cordwainer theme, although clearly stated in the published *October Ferry*, lacks nuance and significance, but in an unpublished letter to Erskine (see p. 76-77), Lowry mentions that he planned to have Cordwainer appear to Ethan in a dream. When completed, this scene of communion with the dead would echo that in the "Ordeal" and further unify the "Voyage."

More interesting still is the draft of a dream chapter in which Ethan experiences his own death. The chapter, entitled "The Perilous Chapel," exists in a

rough pencil draft which was apparently never typed. This heavily annotated manuscript (20:15) of twenty-six pages, most surmounted by a plea to St. Jude for help, was in no condition to be included in the published text. Nevertheless, in addition to illuminating an underdeveloped aspect of *October Ferry*, it reveals Lowry grappling with the terrors of recalcitrant prose and attempting to orchestrate his multifarious themes, motifs, and images.

"The Perilous Chapel" holograph bears scant resemblance to chapter thirty-five in the published *October Ferry*, which has the same title. The manuscript presents Ethan's dream of climbing the cliff to a mysterious chapel at its summit. A dog accompanies him on his "monumental ascent" as he battles with "death itself"—both the dog and the ascent recalling mythic and religious references in the *Volcano* while the entire scene parallels and reverses the scene of Geoffrey's death. Ethan reaches the chapel and prostrates himself before the altar upon which a single candle is burning, and here the dream acquires a nightmare quality as he experiences his dark night of the soul. Finally, the nightmare abates, and he begins his descent with the realization that reprieve from evil and death requires change: "The change had to be made now, to be made in Gabriola, or they would lose their future, as well as any but the most disastrous meaning in their past" (21:15, Q). He reaches the beach at the foot of the cliff amidst visions of angels drawn from Swedenborg, and having awakened from his ordeal, he is ready—like the Ancient Mariner—to bless and to love. Not only has Lowry conceived of a striking parallel to Geoffrey's final vision, but also the chapel with its single candle recalls the planned propitious close of *Dark as the Grave*, and the overall sense of withdrawal and return intensifies and recapitulates the central dilemma of the "Voyage." Here, the protagonist has died in order to be reborn, and he is reborn into the knowledge that the voyage never ends. With this movement of the protagonist from dream to waking, from death to rebirth, Lowry would have merged the end of *October Ferry* with part two of "The Ordeal of Sigbjørn Wilderness," from where the voyaging would have continued, ever renewed, always outward bound.

As Robert Giroux predicted, "The Voyage That Never Ends" did promise to be an outstanding literary project, not only for the fifties, but also for the century. The fragmentary remains of Lowry's masterwork provide a clear sense of the scope and unity of Lowry's system through configurations of symbols, recurring allusions and motifs, repetition of events (such as visits to bars and churches, bus rides, lighting candles, dreams, ascending mountains, and so on), and the inescapable presence throughout of an encyclopaedic perceiving consciousness. Lowry's unifying principle of repetition is nowhere more obvious, however, than in the repeated narrative pattern of withdrawal and return, and whether the movement of withdrawal from reality occurs on an epistemological or a psychological level, or more simply on the level of ordinary personal relationship, it is always a negative state characterized by narrative and stylistic stasis and by a character's emotional, spiritual, or physical death. Return from this state, like the flow of the tides, brings movement, clarity, balance, and joy—"as by a miracle."

Each of the "Voyage" novels creates a stage in Sigbjørn Wilderness' journey through life—the initiation, repeated ordeals with failure and retreat, followed by success and development, that in turn give way to fresh defeat. At each stage the same lessons recur: man must learn to change and evolve by courageously accepting his past and joyously creating his future. With *Ultramarine* the voyage begins. In *Lunar Caustic* the hero descends into a hell of self that climaxes in the apocalyptic vision of *Volcano*. In *Dark as the Grave,* a new effort begins that, with constant setbacks, will be renewed in *October Ferry to Gabriola.* Together Lowry's novels express his myth which is "his-story" of life repeated over and over again in "The Voyage That Never Ends."[19]

2

Outward Bound[1]:
Early Stories, *Ultramarine, Lunar Caustic*

The nature and the form of Lowry's metaphysical and experiential quest begins to develop in his early writings.[2] Lowry quickly discovered that finding is making—the quest is the constant making and remaking of self and reality—and the characteristic Lowry method for the fabrication of self and world is present in this early work as a process of encircling and containing. In other words, the self expands in the constant effort to surround experience, and the poetic act itself becomes an imaginative analogue for the encircling of time and space. In *Ultramarine,* if not before, Lowry is clearly aware of fiction's structural potential to surround time and space, to enfold it verbally, and to make the reader repeat the process. With *Ultramarine* he begins to use the resources of narrative structure and of language in order to show the reader how to read his text.

Throughout the work of the late twenties and thirties, the influence of Aiken, Grieg, Bergson, Dunne, and Ouspensky is obvious. Because he had not yet learned to transform the techniques and ideas of others, Lowry's stories, and to a lesser degree *Ultramarine,* suffer from an obtrusive use of dreams, serialism, precognition, and elaborate metaphors for the expansion of consciousness. But these ideas, though more thoroughly assimilated in the later work, remain important to Lowry, as "Garden of Etla," published in 1950, reveals. In this essay, he was to remark that, according to Bergson, "the sense of time is an inhibition to prevent everything from happening at once,"[3] and that if everything happened at once, there could be no past and, more important, no future; the individual would be trapped in a static moment.

The story "China," dating from the early thirties, illustrates Lowry's early awareness of this dilemma.[4] In it, an ex-sailor reminisces about his voyage to China as a fireman aboard the *Arcturion* until, at the climax of this mental voyage through time-past, he declares that China did not and does not exist for him:

> What I want to convey to you is that to me it was not China at all but right here, on this wharf. But that's not quite what I wanted to say. What I mean is what it was not was China: somewhere far away. What it was was here....
> You see, I had worn myself out behind a barrier ... of time, so that when I did get ashore, I only knew it was *here*. (*P&S*,52)

Time and space have become totally internalized and fixed for the narrator, until there is here and then is now, and the individual exists in a solipsistic world without future or possibility. The form of the story conveys the paralysing force of this dilemma as the narrator, losing all sense of the present situation, discusses his strange experience in the past tense. Even when he ends his monologue with a direct address to the reader in the present tense, he emphasizes his sensation that the past is present, that nothing changes: "And you carry your horizon in your pocket wherever you are" (54). By doing so, he reveals the typically troubled Lowry sensibility. However, there is not yet any confrontation with the destructive potential (so dramatically realized in *Volcano*) of such a radical lack of differentiation between internal and external reality because the story's form, describing a closed circle within which time and space are suspended, provides no access to a social or psychological context in the narrator's present.

The significant feature of "Bulls of the Resurrection," also written in the early thirties, is the precognitive dream shared by the two main characters who are undergraduates vacationing in Granada.[5] After their girlfriend has left with another man, the students recount their dreams of the previous night, but these dreams, which both prefigure disaster for the girlfriend and her new lover, curiously interlock to form one dream. The first undergraduate observes the girl's new boyfriend arrested and beheaded for shooting someone; in his dream, he watches the murderer re-enact the shooting several times. The second undergraduate simultaneously dreams that he has seen the girl be shot, die, then rise to be shot over and over again.

The elements of prefiguration and repetition here suggest (with some help from the very verbal and analytic undergraduates) that the two men are "participating" in some kind of ritual. The first dreamer describes his vision in a striking image of perception caught in a nightmare of mechanical repetition:

> It was like El Greco gone mad.... It was as though a moving picture had

been projected onto a Greco instead of onto a screen. There was this fixed, timeless, haunted background, but this was not part of what was going on, this was only the relief against which it could be seen, the means by which it became visible. (8)

The mechanical movement in the dream is contained, frozen within the static frame of the El Greco painting.

The second dreamer, aware that he was about to see "*something* extraordinary which in some manner held the past and the present in its meaning," articulates the horror of the dream more clearly: "Only, in this dream, we seemed to have no individuality. We were shadows whirling together in the void of a nightmare" (10). Despite the obvious awkwardness of this dream phenomenon, it does foreshadow aspects of the characteristic Lowry consciousness. Lowry drops obvious dream mechanisms in favour of more subtle treatments in such later works as *Volcano, Dark as the Grave,* and *October Ferry,* but nightmarish loss of identity and whirling visionary shapes recur so frequently that they come to signal a necessary stage in the protagonist's ordeal. Furthermore, the second dreamer's way out of this infernal closed circle is effective for subsequent Lowry heroes:

Then I knew that unless I took action swiftly, Terry would be compelled for ever and ever to go on performing the fatuous dumb show of her own death. (11)

This is the lesson that Dana learns and the Consul rejects. With the example of Ouspensky's time-spirals and recurrence, Lowry began to dramatize his characters' need to act, move, interfere in order to break out of a totally internalized landscape or dreamworld.

"June the 30th, 1934", another early story, marks a considerable formal advance over "Bulls of the Resurrection" and "China."[6] Here Lowry develops his concept of the dynamic circle, a concept that underlies *Ultramarine* and is fundamental to the voyage theme. The story deals with the reflections and visions of a British clergyman, Bill Goodyear, during his return from an unsuccessful mission in the Far East. Accompanied by a fellow traveller named Firmin, he moves from one conveyance to another—from train, to boat, to train. Paralleling this physical movement, Goodyear's perception moves, as Ouspensky suggests, from one level to another until he achieves a vision of the heart of reality:

They were changing elements, but the idea struck him; no, it is more than this, something greater is being changed—(*P&S*, 40)

... a new cycle was beginning ... the face of the world was changing ... (*P&S*, 46)

Lowry employs two central metaphors to convey his idea of movement and change—the familiar one of the voyage and a more unusual one of alchemical transformation. The story takes the form of a voyage in which Goodyear travels closer toward his home at the same time as he moves toward an understanding of reality. Through repeated alchemical references to metals and alloys, Lowry suggests that a transformation of Goodyear's psyche takes place until he reaches a point where he is able to apprehend the meaning of life. The implications are that physical movement through time and space parallels psychic metamorphosis and that the elements of human consciousness may expand and change like physical reality.

During these moments of psychic metamorphosis (he even feels at one point that he has *become* Firmin), Goodyear has two visions. First, he sees a young boy racing through the fields, "charging alone, keeping up with the train." At one point, this boy is his own son Dick, but a moment later the boy appears to be Firmin as a youth. The boy, it seems, is Goodyear's vision of the future racing into the past, and as such he symbolizes the movement of time. The second vision comes during the third part of his journey, with Goodyear again on a train. Peering through "the steaming glass" of the window, he realizes that

> Chaos, change, all was changing: the passengers were changing: a sea change.
>
> Goodyear lay back in his seat. He could feel the change within him, somehow his thoughts were becoming longer: an insidious metallurgy was in practice within him as his ores, his alloys, were isolated. The titanic thunder of the night-shift hammered on his nerves, lacerating them as though it would draw out from him the fine wire of his consciousness.
>
> He knew that he had been altered by the true pattern, the archetype of the events, on the surface so trivial, of the journey. And he sensed that the other passengers . . . were even at a crucial point in their lives, turning towards another chaos, a new complexity of melancholy opposites. (*P&S*, 47)

The dramatic force of Lowry's story comes less from Goodyear's visions, marred as they are by the type of explication which Lowry sedulously avoided in the *Volcano*, than from the circular structure of the narrative. Throughout, the protagonist is encircled or contained in the boat and on trains, as well as in the intense all-enveloping space of his mind. However, this encircling, emphasized by references to the train's wheels and the wheels and levers of the boat's engines, is not static or closed, but dynamic. The circumference of the circle, symbolized by the encircling walls of train or ship, is moving, while the centre, Goodyear's consciousness, is expanding and changing.

"June the 30th, 1934" represents Lowry's first attempt to meet and overcome the everpresent physical and spiritual boundaries and crossroads which he perceived in life. Through the journey metaphor and the images of transformation, this story signals a character's release from the fixed circle of consciousness into a repeated shaping of new circumferences around an ever-expanding perceiving centre. Juxtaposed with a final image of time plunging into a future of war and chaos, "as the express screamed on like a shell through a metal world," is Goodyear's realization that —

> It's never too late, never too late. To start again. You bore in the earth. Silver and copper. Silver and gold. Man makes his cross. With crucible steel. Base metal; counterfeit; manganese; chromium; makes his iron cross; with crucible steel. (*P&S*, 48)[7]

As always with Lowry, the outcome is ambiguous; the transformation may be counterfeit or the true philosopher's stone. The most important point, as in *October Ferry*, is that change must be welcomed. One must be willing to begin again.

In "Seductio ad Absurdum," Lowry again develops the contrast between time and space, seen as suspended within the closed circle of the mind, and the flux of life. This short story was originally published in *Experiment* (Spring, 1931), under the intriguing title "Punctum Indifferens Skibet Gaar Videre" (Pointless Point The Ship Sails On), and later it became the major part of chapter 4 in *Ultramarine*.[8] The most significant feature of the story may be briefly stated. Listening to the crew discuss and abuse him, Dana repeatedly shifts from the inhospitable present to comforting memories of the past. Suddenly he decides to challenge his chief enemy. But time (as memory) and space (within the mind and ship), concentrated into one moment's hatred, become literally and metaphorically pointless because all Dana's efforts to hold time and space suspended in a long brooding stretch of anger lead to nothing. His challenge fails and the crew members disperse to their chores — the ship sails on. In *Ultramarine*, this persistent attempt to fix time and space within the closed circle of the mind is Dana's besetting sin, and Lowry successfully conveys Dana's crippling tendency to withdraw into himself through the structure of the narrative.

After a somewhat chequered career, *Ultramarine* was first published in 1933. Though it had been accepted by Chatto and Windus in 1932, the manuscript was subsequently stolen, sending Lowry, who vowed he had no copy, into a frenzied attempt to rewrite the book. When he failed, his friend Martin Case, at whose home he had worked on the manuscript, produced a copy from draft pages Malcolm had discarded. Now unsure of the book's worth, Lowry asked Chatto and Windus not to publish *Ultramarine* unless they thoroughly approved of it. Welcoming this release, the publishers promptly handed the book back. Luckily for Lowry, Jonathan Cape soon accepted it with enthusiasm.

Still, Lowry was never happy with *Ultramarine*, and he continued to tinker with it over the years. In 1963, Cape reprinted the book with the small changes that he had made, but the "rewritten" *Ultramarine*, which, according to Margerie Lowry's "Introductory Note," was to be "the first volume in ... *The Voyage That Never Ends,"* was never truly begun. The actual changes amount to little more than the cutting of gauche undergraduate remarks, cumbersome references to Eliot's *The Waste Land*, and ornate punctuation. He also added the Pat Murphy joke and changed the name of Dana's ship from *Nawab* to *Oedipus Tyrannus* in order to link *Ultramarine* to *Under the Volcano*, but in substance and structure the two editions are identical.[9]

In spite of its weaknesses, the book's structure illustrates the increasing control that Lowry was developing over his materials.[10] As with *Volcano* and *Dark as the Grave*, Lowry expands a short period of time, approximately forty-eight hours in *Ultramarine*, into the months and years of Dana's consciousness. Thus, nineteen years are compressed within the short span of two days passed in one place. The movement of *Ultramarine* is circular. Beginning in Dana's mind, the narrative circles repeatedly from external action and dialogue back into Dana's consciousness until the final line of the book places the reader within the hero's mind once more. Images of circles and encircling — the engines, wheeling birds, eyes, Dana's lost compasses — predominate, and the ship, the harbour of Tsjang-Tsjang, and the sea suggest further layers of encircling reality.

Within the first four chapters, which should be considered as a unit, Lowry juxtaposes two key points in Dana's voyage and consciousness: Liverpool and the past/ Tsjang-Tsjang and the present. As the book opens, the *Oedipus Tyrannus* nears her destination, in the port of Tsjang-Tsjang, but Dana tries desperately to reject the event by remembering the ship's point of departure; in his mind, the ship is still preparing to leave Liverpool. This critical moment of departure haunts him because it symbolizes his severance from past and youth and his initiation into life — an initiation from which he shrinks in dread. The second geographic and spiritual point of Dana's vicious circle is represented by the harbour of Tsjang-Tsjang, which symbolizes the abyss of his present self-indulgence. While the ship lies idle, Dana succumbs to an analogous passive state in which he explores the private hell he has created from his obsession with the past and his terrified refusal to confront present reality. Transfixed between these two points, Dana must recognize that his hell is self-inflicted, and that he must break free if he wishes to live in the present.

At the end of chapter 1, with the ship at the dock and night falling, Dana refuses to meet life by going ashore and, instead, retreats to his bunk and his regressive memories. His visions reflect his spiritual crisis, but the reader, who is drawn into the maelstrom of Dana's mind, also experiences the claustrophobia of a consciousness closed in upon itself. Believing that the ship "had a manifold security: she was his harbour; he would lie in the arms of the ship" (43), Dana glides into a sleep immediately filled with wheeling horror:

Above, the moon soared and galloped through a dark, tempestuous sky.

All at once, every lamp in the street exploded, their globes flew out, darted into the sky, and the street became alive with eyes; eyes greatly dilated, dripping dry scurf, or glued with viscid gum: eyes which held eternity in the fixedness of their stare: eyes which wavered, and spread, and, diminishing rapidly, were catapulted east and west; eyes that were the gutted windows of a cathedral, blackened, emptiness of the brain, through which bats and ravens wheeled enormously. (44)

Significantly, this vision is one of movement where enclosing circles break: lamps explode, their "globes" flying into the sky, eyes waver, and "diminishing" are "catapulted east and west"; even the enclosing glass of windows shatters, allowing bats and ravens to "wheel enormously" through their empty frames. Dana must eventually accept this vision of the chaotic flux; however, at this point in his voyage he is only capable of seeing chaos as nightmare. The closest he comes at this point to acknowledging his true position occurs in the dream which concludes the chapter — without his compasses (to draw continual circles or to locate his own centre) he is "Lost. Lost. Lost."

In chapter 2, Dana escapes the reality of present time and place by dredging up memories of time past and of pre-voyage places until they form a protective shell around his timorous psyche. The climax of his self-indulgent descent into the past comes with his distorted vision of the *Oxenstjerna*. Formerly the ship seemed a symbol of movement, life, and a positive growing past; it was the ox-star "that shines above the lives of men." Now he sees it grounded and oozing death:

It is the *Oxenstjerna* they are talking about, the *Oxenstjerna* that has gone aground. It is the *Oxenstjerna* which now turns over and sinks into the sand, while the oil spreads a mucous film over the Mersey; and now the white sea gulls . . . known by name to the dockers are dying by the score — (74)

With the power characteristic of *Under the Volcano*, this striking image of death functions like a magnet within the book. In one brief passage Lowry connects the cluster of motifs surrounding the *Oxenstjerna* with the various bird motifs in the novel. Even the haunting motif of eyes, "a mucous film" (like all the eye imagery, drawn from Lowry's personal sufferings), recalls the vision of eyes in chapter 1 and fuses with the general theme of Dana's spiritual blindness. Superficially, the image is simple, but in addition to echoing several motifs which can only be fully understood within the context of the whole work, the *Oxenstjerna* passage describes Dana's state of mind: like the ship, he "has gone aground" and "now turns over and sinks into the sand."

Dana reaches his nadir in chapter 3 as he stumbles about Tsjang-Tsjang in a drunken nightmare. In keeping with Lowry's concept of the fusion of opposites, this low point marks the beginning of his ascent as Dana grapples with the recognition and articulation of his position. His analysis remains exaggerated and maudlin, but at least he is aware of his self-dramatization, and enclosed within the rhetoric of his self-portrait is the further realization that he alone creates his heaven or hell:

> Tinfoil Jesus, crucified homunculus (who is also the cross), spitted on the hook of an imaginary Galilee! Who is the crown of thorns dripping red blossoms and the red-blue nails, the flails and the bloody wounds. The tears, but also the lips cupped to embrace them as they fall; the whips, but also the flesh crawling to them. The net and the silver writhing in the mesh, and all the fish that swim in the sea.—The centre of the Charing Cross, ABCD, the Cambridge Circle, the Cambridge Circus, is Hilliot—but every night, unseen, he climbs down and returns to his hotel—while the two great shafts, the propeller shafts, the shafts of wit, laced with blood, AB, CD are the diameters.
> Now with his navel as centre and half CD as radius, describe a vicious circle! (98-99)

Amidst a geometrician's paradise of circles, Dana sees himself as a cheap poseur, a Christ who climbs down from his self-inflicted cross to seek the shelter of a bed in a hotel room. The image of Dana as the centre of a circle with the four points on the circumference, marking the arms of a cross ABCD, crystallizes his physical and spiritual dilemma. The points are fixed, the radius is given, the circle is closed, vicious.

As he questions his entire purpose in making this voyage, Dana begins to articulate, and thus to comprehend, the nature of his problem. Challenging Janet's belief in him, he cries

> ... could you still believe in me, still believe in the notion that my voyage is something Columbian and magnificent? Still believe in my taking a self-inflicted penance; in this business of placing myself within impenetrable and terrible boundaries in order that a slow process of justification to yourself may go on. (99)

Because naming the names and saying the words are always magic with Lowry, Dana will soon be able to break free of the seemingly "impenetrable and terrible boundaries." As centre to his circle he will move and in moving transcribe an ever-new circumference.

In chapter 4, Dana's agonized attempts to re-inhabit the past bring him circling back to the point at which the book opened, the departure from England of the *Oedipus Tyrannus*. During this last retrospective view of his farewell with Janet, the Mersey strikes him as "like a vast camera film slowly and inexorably winding. Soon he will be entangled in her celluloid meshes, and wound out to the open sea" (142). And the image of the film "wound out to the open sea" signals his acceptance of that traumatic departure. In a sense, Dana has used his memory to trace a full circle around his own mental position, much as he does later with Andy, and he is now ready to live in the present. Though it is abortive, his challenge to Andy is his first decisive action on the voyage. What he has not yet realized is the profound truth that this intense moment of anger and frustration is, in fact, a *punctum indifferens*. Life (or Andy) cannot be seized and frozen in this way because it moves on, forever eluding the grasp.

As the ship sails on, or, at least as it prepares to leave port in chapter 5, the culminating crisis occurs. Norman's pet pigeon escapes from its cage and drowns—its death recalling the ethical and symbolic associations of the Ancient Mariner's albatross. Dana and the crew stand helplessly by watching it die while a nearby motor boat, "its occupant . . . spinning the easy wheel while it circled around gaily . . . turned on itself and rolled in its own swell" (162). Dana's inability to save the bird parallels the ship's immobility at the dock. Then, amidst rolling winches and coiling ropes, "the windlass clanking and racing around gladly" and the tiger "moulding its body to the shape of its cage," Dana thinks of Norman's grief at the loss of his pet and realizes that

> No, such things couldn't happen really. But Norman's words made a sort of incantation in his brain. "Time! Of course there would have been time. Time wouldn't have mattered if you'd been a man." (166)

This truth is without value, however, unless one knows how to use it, and Dana is still uncertain. In the renewed peace of the vessel under sail, he contemplates the roaring fires in the "pulsating and throbbing" engine room:

> Why was it his brain could not accept the dissonance as simply as a harmony, could not make order emerge from this chaos? . . . Chaos and disunion, then, he told himself, not law and order, were the principles of life which sustained all things, in the mind of man as well as on the ship. (169)

Being unable to accept chaos is Dana's failing, and thus far in his effort to order and contain reality, he has only succeeded in thwarting his own development and denying the processes of life.

Once he admits the priority of chaos, he is ready to move on to a reconciliation with Andy, who symbolizes the life into which Dana must be initiated. Clearly perceiving the meaning of the maelstrom and "a reason for his voyage," Dana peers down into the engine room once more. There he sees the fireman serving the very source of energy and chaos:

> The iron tools blistered his hands, his chest heaved like a spent swimmer's, his eyes tingled in parched sockets, but still he worked on, he would never stop—this was what it was to exist—(171)

Never to stop in the journey of life, this is Dana's discovery. Life is flux, chaos, energy; death, like a ship gone aground, like a fixed, transcribed circle, ABCD, is the cessation of motion. Paradoxically, life exists in the fiery abyss of the ship, and Dana cherishes this discovery while "somewhere," as if warning that this point of rest is a *punctum indifferens*, "a lantern clanged with eternal, pitiless movement" (172).

Significantly, *Ultramarine* does not end on this pinnacle of insight. Although the narrative rhythm reaches fulfilment by the end of chapter 5, the novel continues with a sixth chapter, mirroring in its structure what Dana has still to learn. In this sense, *Ultramarine* was an ideal prologue for Lowry's intended "Voyage That Never Ends." Dana Hilliot, prefiguring the restless voyaging of subsequent Lowry heroes, realizes that he has "surrounded Andy's position" and must move on: "outward bound, always outward, always onward, to be fighting always for the dreamt-of-harbour" (201).

Lest this solution of life's mystery appear too simple, Lowry charts the next stage in Dana's initiation. When a fireman falls ill, Dana is chosen to replace him and must descend into the "little hell" of the stokehold. During his last moments on deck, a strange ship drifts through the night mist "morseing" her name: *Oxenstjerna*. Like a voice from the past, this ship calls to him, reminding him that while he creates a new circle into the future he must take the past with him—as comfort and as threat. If he again makes the profound mistake of retreating from life and refusing to grow, he will destroy himself because life's voyage is "always outward, always onward."

Dana's descent into "the little hole" of the ship's furnaces prefigures the next stage in Lowry's "The Voyage That Never Ends." In *Lunar Caustic*, the protagonist "gliding over the cobbles lightly as a ship leaving harbour" searches frantically for "any harbour at all" until he finds that he is "outward bound" for hell. Consequently, the novella charts a further withdrawal from reality after the temporary respite and balance established at the end of *Ultramarine*.

Lowry was proud of *Lunar Caustic,* referring to it in 1952 as a "masterwork" (*Selected Letter,* 292). The published novella, however, represents the work of Earle Birney and Margerie Lowry, who combined and edited two different versions of the story to produce the existing text in 1963.[11] Lowry had planned to lengthen and alter the book considerably. (See chapter 1.) He began the story in 1935, and by 1936 he had completed a first version based upon his own brief visit to New York's Bellevue Hospital in 1934. Never published, this story was called "The Last Address," and in 1940 Lowry wrote a second version entitled "Swinging the Maelstrom," published as "Le caustique lunaire" in 1956. The two versions of the story differ in one important respect: "The Last Address" ends darkly with the protagonist withdrawn from life as in the published *Lunar Caustic,* whereas "Swinging the Maelstrom" closes with a touch of hope as the protagonist breaks through the isolating circle of self to accept a gesture of compassion. As the second title suggests, it may be possible to avoid the descent into a Poe-like maelstrom and instead to weather the storm.

Lowry's discussion of *Lunar Caustic* (36:5) makes it clear that he intended to follow the characterization in "Swinging the Maelstrom" more closely than that of "The Last Address," but he had reservations about using the "metaphysico-political-ironical posture" (36:5, 15) with which "Swinging the Maelstrom" concludes. Certainly he intended the book to be an example of true Lowry *grand guignol* in which the hero, William Plantagenet, promoted and renamed the Earl of Thurstaston, would be burdened with a murderous past and a loathsome present of latent homosexuality and probable syphilis. Lowry had toyed with the title, *Lunar Caustic,* for many years:

> Lunar Caustic as a sardonic and ambiguous title for a cauterizing work on madness has, I feel, a great deal of merit. But lunar caustic is also silver nitrate and used to be used unsuccessfully to cure syphilis. And indeed as such it might stand symbolically for any imperfect or abortive cure, for example of alcoholism. (36:5, 4)

Towards the end of this discussion, he emphasizes that *Lunar Caustic* should end with "a sort of hope," "even though we know the protagonist isn't being promoted to the Purgatorio, is not free from his own hell, but is heading for a worse one yet" (36:5, 16). In spite of his elaborate plans for integrating *Lunar Caustic* into the "Voyage," Lowry left only two endings for his novella. In choosing the final words of "The Last Address," his editors remained faithful both to the mood of *Lunar Caustic* and to the pattern of increasing failure and self-destruction called for at this point in the "Voyage."

Lunar Caustic traces the inner torment of its hero, an alcoholic and ex-jazz musician, from his drunken admission into a mental hospital to his release shortly afterwards as much of an alcoholic failure as before. As the historical implications of his name suggest, Plantagenet is a man at war with himself, and his struggles are played out within a distorted mindscape reminiscent of the settings in Melville and Poe. The hospital, a symbol of physical imprisonment and emotional constraint, is juxtaposed with the life of the busy river that flows past the barred windows. But the river, which represents movement and freedom, remains inaccessible to Plantagenet as well as to the boy Garry and the old man Kalowsky whom Plantagenet befriends in the hospital. Unable to help either of them, incapable finally of escaping from the circle of self, Plantagenet leaves the hospital and descends deeper into his private hell.

The novella falls into three distinct sections. The first and last portray Plantagenet before and after the hospital experience, and the last section repeats several details (for example, the bar, the old lady, the church) from the first. Together they frame the central action, setting off and emphasizing the world of the insane. At the same time this framing technique lends an ironic note to the entire story, for Plantagenet gains nothing from his pilgrimage and the world outside appears as threatening as the hospital. Within the central hospital section, five separate scenes are presented from Plantagenet's uncertain point of view. His first impressions of the ward, disturbed as they are by hallucination and fantasy, gradually give way to the puppet show, which is followed by the episode at the piano and the discussion with Claggart. The fifth scene occurs at the hospital window as Plantagenet watches the storm. His struggle to understand the experience reaches a climax with his vision of catastrophe and destruction.

The central metaphor of *Lunar Caustic* is that of the madhouse, and Lowry's use of the hospital to explore the boundary between sanity and madness bears striking resemblance to the theme and structure of one of his favorite German expressionist films, *The Cabinet of Dr. Caligari* (1919). In *Caligari,* the main story of the mad doctor and his somnambulist is set off (as in *Lunar Caustic*) by a framing device. The movie opens with two men talking. As one starts to tell the strange account of his life, the scene fades to a fair ground and the story of Caligari. At the end, these men appear again and turn out to be inmates of an asylum. Futhermore, the Director of the hospital, now in white coat, looks exactly like the madman Caligari. Is the man's story merely the result of a diseased mind? Or is it an accurate portrayal of the true nature of authority? The distinction between madness and sanity is disturbingly blurred in both film and novella. It is no coincidence that Plantagenet should say to Claggart: "There are always two sides, nicht wahr, Herr Doktor, to a show like this?" (47)

The horror of *Lunar Caustic* springs from its claustrophobic atmosphere in which temporal distinctions do not exist and there are no clear boundaries (apart from the oppressive bars and walls of the hospital itself) between reality and fantasy. In addition to its significance as a physical enclosure, the hospital also provides a frightening image of the protagonist's mind:

> Looking down at [the river] a delicious sense of freedom possessed him, a sense of being already outside, free to run with the wind if he wished, free to run as far away from the hospital as he liked. Yet the bars were still there, and they resembled the bars of his mind. . . . He had not escaped them yet, nor would he escape them merely by leaving. (65)

The hospital bars are only the outer manifestation of the more terrifying prison of his mind.

Lowry describes this mind—much as he does the minds of his other "Voyage" protagonists—in terms of stasis and enclosure. Thus, Plantagenet's circling of the hospital prior to his sudden entrance parallels the futile circling of the ward by the patients, and both patterns of meaningless movement underscore the possibility that, despite the furious whirling of his mind, he is in the doldrums. During the puppet show, Plantagenet glimpses the truth about this timeless mental world:

> He had the curious feeling that he had made a sort of descent into the maelstrom, a maelstrom terrifying for the last reason one might have expected: that there was about it sometimes just this loathsome, patient calm. (37)[12]

Plantagenet's realization that there is a "loathsome, patient calm" about the maelstrom is important. Later, in his interview with the doctor, he blames the hospital for encouraging a fatal acceptance and resignation in its patients; lack of activity, he maintains, leads to increased withdrawal from life and ultimately to physical and spiritual paralysis. However, the doctor, who is undeceived by Plantagenet's rhetoric, knows that he is talking, not about the hospital inmates, but about himself. By blaming external forces for his inability to play jazz, to love, or to act, Plantagenet (like Geoffrey Firmin) tries to ignore the fact that it is his own inertia that is destroying him.

Bill Plantagenet is a failure. His adopted name, "Lawhill," the name of "a windjammer that survived more disasters than any ship afloat" (50), is *not* his real name; he is not made of such sturdy stuff. Futhermore, his mission is a failure. He enters the hospital shouting,

> "I am sent to save my father, to find my son, to heal the eternal horror of three, to resolve the immedicable horror of opposites!" (11)

The slamming of the hospital door undercuts this messianic cry: "With the dithering crack of a ship going on the rocks the door shuts behind him" (11).

The danger of mental collapse, implied by the "dithering crack" of the hospital door, culminates in Plantagenet's nightmare vision of the storm prior to his hospital discharge:

> There was a furious crash of thunder and simultaneously Plantagenet felt the impact of the plane, the whale, upon his mind. While metamorphosis nudged metamorphosis, a kind of order, still preserved within his consciousness, and enclosing this catastrophe, exploded itself into the age of Kalowsky again, and into the youth of Garry, who both now seemed to be spiralling away from him until they were lost .... But while that part of him only a moment before in possession of the whole, the ship, was turning over with disunion of hull and masts uprooted falling across her decks, another faction of his soul ... knew him to be screaming against the renewed thunder and saw the attendants closing in on him. (72)

In this striking passage (reminiscent of the *Oxenstjerna* passage from *Ultramarine*), the rigid psychological defences behind which Plantagenet hides apparently shatter. Because this image of the "disunion of hull and masts" represents an aspect of the flux and chaos of life, it should prefigure a positive change in Plantagenet. But the hellish descent into the maelstrom can only lead to the renewed voyage of life if the ordeal leads to wisdom, if, like the "s.s. *Lawhill*," the ship of the soul struggles through to rebirth.

The moment for Plantagenet's rebirth has not come. He leaves the hospital after the storm "with no sense of release, only inquietude" (73) and makes his way into the sterile space of a bar "where, curled up like an embryo, he could not be seen at all" (76). Assumption of the fetal position dramatically symbolizes Plantagenet's rejection of reality and his withdrawal into a timeless, static, inner world. The embryo image, which recalls the description of Dana in *Ultramarine* (43) and recurs in *Under the Volcano* to portray Hugh's retreat from reality, is consistently negative and explicitly regressive. In *Lunar Caustic*, the hero is unable "to resolve the immedicable horror of opposites"; the lunar caustic does not work. Plantagenet moves deeper into the nightmare of self which Geoffrey Firmin must relive.

3

The Luminous Wheel: *Under the Volcano*

Under the Volcano is Malcolm Lowry's masterpiece and one of the great works of fiction of the twentieth century—despite Lowry's view that it "is a cub that can still stand a little further licking" ("WP," 6). When *Volcano* was published in 1947 it was immediately acclaimed, not in Canada, as Lowry ruefully noted, but in France and the United States. Three years after publication Lowry described *Volcano's* successes to Derek Pethick of the Canadian Broadcasting Corporation in his inimitably amusing fashion:

> Finally thank you for your interest in the book—it is rather discouraging very often being a writer in Canada. Somebody put the *Volcano* in the *Encyclopedia Britannica Year Book* 1948-49, ranking it as the work of a Canadian over and above anything then current in American literature, but not one word did I ever hear of that here. In fact, apart from a few kind words by Birney and Dorothy Livesay, all I have heard was from my royalty report, namely that the sales in Canada from the end of 1947-49 were precisely 2 copies. The *Sun* published only a few syndicated lines that called it a turgid novel of self-destruction, not for the discerning (or something) reader . . . though it went very well in the States, and was even miraculously a best seller for a while: one month, believe it or not, it even sold more than *Forever Amber*. . . . In England it failed but quite honourably; in France they have put it in a classic series. . . . As to the Swedish,

Norwegian and Danish translations, I understand they are out, but I have not seen them. Nor, I imagine, has any Swede, Norwegian or Dane.[1]

Since 1965 and the publication of *Selected Letters,* interest in Lowry has grown widely, and critics have devoted most of their attention to *Volcano.* The acclaim it has received is not hard to understand, for in spite of its density and technical virtuosity, it is more readable and accessible than, say, *Ulysses* or *Gravity's Rainbow. Volcano* is fascinating, as well, for the view it offers of our modern world, and it is increasingly cited by younger writers as an influence.[2] Perhaps like the film, *The Cabinet of Dr. Caligari,* which it resembles in striking ways, *Under the Volcano* will never exert wide influence, but it does stand as a unique work of genius.

Because Lowry's obsession with dipsomania is usually overemphasized, *Volcano* is too often described as a novel about drinking. As Lowry slyly remarked in "Work in Progress," "in the Volcano, you will be right to suspect that drinking is a symbol for something else, wrong to imagine that to the drinker, while drinking, a drink is symbolic of anything else but the next drink" ("WP," 16). But *Volcano* is not exclusively about alcohol any more than its author was *absolutamente borracho* while writing it, and the book's vision of hell is not limited to the mescal bottle any more than the collapse of human communication and the destruction of love and sanity are *caused* by drinking. Baffled by Geoffrey's seeming indifference, Jacques demands, "Have you gone mad?" and Yvonne mourns silently, "Oh Geoffrey, why do you do it!" Why indeed? Why is it that lovers become "two mute unspeaking forts"? Why do countries destroy each other in the name of peace? Why can a man abhor his corruption and yet, like John Bunyan's sinner, be unwilling to fight it? These are the large questions which Lowry raises, and his great theme, for which alcohol is a metaphor, is human isolation and the collapse of Western culture. *Under the Volcano* is, in Lowry's words, "passionate poetic writing about things that will always mean something" (*Selected Letters,* 80).

Most criticism on *Under the Volcano* has understandably approached questions of theme, allusion, symbol and metaphor, and influences separately. In his biography, however, Douglas Day begins his fine discussion of five levels in *Volcano* by calling for an "eventual *Gestalt* approach to the novel" (*Malcolm Lowry,* 326). In the discussion that follows, I have attempted to see the novel as an aesthetic whole with influences, allusions, style, symbols, and narrative strategies as functioning parts of its intricate system.[3] While such a discussion can never be exhaustive, it does illustrate that *Volcano,* unlike Dr. Vigil's "eclectic systemë," works very smoothly and with great beauty.

Under the Volcano, which took Lowry nearly ten years to complete, was finally accepted for publication in 1947. Before accepting it, the publisher wrote Lowry suggesting that he make substantial changes in his manuscript. Lowry, angry and stubborn, treated these remarks as a challenge and sent Cape, in one of the most fascinating letters of literary history, a chapter-by-chapter exegesis of the form and theme of his masterpiece (*Selected Letters,* 57-88). He asked for belief in the book based upon his painstaking efforts to make every detail integral to a work of art which "was so designed, counterdesigned and interwelded that it could be read an indefinite number of times and still not have yielded all its meanings or its drama or its poetry" (*Selected Letters,* 88). And while it is always wise to treat a writer's comments on his work with caution, *Under the Volcano* supports Lowry's claims.

Cape's reader, William Plomer, complained of tedium caused, in part, by long flashbacks, especially in chapters 1 and 6. While Lowry's handling of Geoffrey's *delirium tremens* was acknowledged to be superb, Plomer found the book to be overelaborate, long, and with "too much stream-of-consciousness stuff." Finally, the character drawing was considered weak. With astonishing patience and good humour, Lowry explained the crucial importance of chapter 1 and the subsequent flashbacks; the stream-of-conscious was only one of several techniques for handling certain problems and, together with the flashbacks, provided solid Jamesian exposition. The characters were another matter, for Lowry was neither drawing character in the traditional sense, nor writing a traditional novel.

Speaking of the temporal shift from chapter 1 to 2, Lowry explained that he was "in rebellion, both revolutionary and reactionary at once," against novels of "pure reporting." He was not writing a realistic novel, if that term is used to signify a mimetic work of art that sets out to represent an accepted external world. His subject was "the forces in man which cause him to be terrified of himself." Lowry had absorbed many different examples of the style of art loosely described as expressionist from the famous "UFa" (Universum Film-Aktiengesellschaft) films, from the Mexican muralists Oroxco and Rivera, and from O'Neill's plays *The Hairy Ape* and *The Emperor Jones.* Expressionism, portraying soul states and the violent emotions of the subconscious in images and forms that seek to engage and include the spectator or reader, is an important element in Lowry's fiction, especially in *Volcano* and is discussed further below as well as in chapter 5.[4]

Representational characters would have to wait for another book. Lowry's purpose was to tell us "something new about hell fire":

> I see the pitfalls—it can be an easy way out of hard work, an invitation to eccentric word-spinning, and laboured phantasmagorias, and subjective inferior masterpieces . . . but just the same in our Elizabethan days we used to have at least passionate poetic writing about things that will always mean something and not just silly ass style and semicolon technique. (*Selected Letters,* 80)

Although he hoped the four major characters would be superficially believable, Lowry intended them to be less individuals than "aspects of the same man, or of the human spirit." Hugh and Geoffry are *Doppelgängers* after Poe's "William Wilson" and Galeen's *The Student of Prague* in a book that "obeys not the laws of other books"; Hugh, furthermore, is "Everyman tightened up a screw . . . the youth of Everyman," and Yvonne is "the eternal woman," like Kundry in *Parsifal.*

An appreciation of the non-mimetic basis of *Volcano's* characters is important, for their development or etiology is not of first importance to the novel. Indeed, they are meant to function on several levels besides the immediate story level. *Volcano* is an allegory "of the Garden of Eden, the Garden representing the world" with the Consul's drunkenness "used on one plane to symbolize the universal drunkenness of mankind during the war" (*Selected Letters,* 66). On this level, Mexico is both "paradisal" and "unquestionably infernal," and within this dramatic setting an Adam and Eve suffer. The historical and political levels of the narrative, while based on "fact" and authentically portrayed (Lowry's understanding of Mexico's political realities and daily life was considerable), require the characters to represent ideological positions as well as concepts such as freedom and necessity. Thus, Geoffrey can be seen as a country constantly bothered by people with ideas, "and what profundity and final meaning there is in his fate should be seen also in its universal relationship to the ultimate fate of mankind" (*Selected Letters,* 66). On this level, *Under the Volcano* comprises a political fable.

Volcano also functions on the level of myth. In his letter to Cape, Lowry explains his poetical use of the Cabbala which "represents man's spiritual aspiration." He warns, however, that the Cabbala is deeply buried and need not trouble the reader. In terms of Cabbala, Geoffrey is a failed adept. He has abused his powers (*"No se puede vivir sin amar"*) and lost his way on the Tree of Life thus plummeting into the spiritual abyss of "Qliphoth, the world of shells and demons, represented by the Tree of Life upside down."[5] A second, and more fundamental, aspect of myth is the narrative "mythos" of the *Volcano* which situates the novel firmly within "The Voyage That Never Ends" and within Lowry's concept of withdrawal and return.

Under the Volcano, then, has four basic narrative levels—story, fable, allegory, and myth—and, as Lowry only half-jokingly suggests,

> The novel can be read simply as a story which you can skip if you want. It can be read as a story you will get more out of if you don't skip. It can be regarded as a kind of symphony, or in another way as a kind of opera—or even a horse opera. It is hot music, a poem, a song, a tragedy, a comedy, a farce, and so forth. It is superficial, profound, entertaining and boring, according to taste. It is a prophecy, a political warning, a cryptogram, a

preposterous movie, and a writing on the wall. It can even be regarded as a sort of machine. (*Selected Letters*, 66)

Humour and hope are also important elements in the novel. Too often *Volcano* is viewed as a depressing work with no allowance made for Lowry's sometimes subtle, more often grim, humour. He suggested reading passages aloud, and was convinced that much of chapter 6 was "hilarious." He also believed that his story and theme embodied suggestions of hope because, on the one hand, he intended the reader to feel a continually renewed hope for Geoffrey and Yvonne up to chapter 9, while, on the other, he tried to create a sense of hope which would transcend the characters and settle on the wonder of man suggested in the opening quotation from Sophocles.

The Cape letter shows that Lowry had thought out his text with consummate care. Aware of his weaknesses—he felt he had the subjective equipment of a poet rather than the usual abilities of a novelist—Lowry was perceptive and emphatic about *Volcano*'s achievement. The form of the novel was, he argued, of absolute importance. Each chapter was presented through one point of view, and the interrelationship and juxtaposition of chapters was crucial. In a fascinating appeal to Cape against wanton editing, Lowry compared his use of time to the sense of tempo in film; for the overall effect to be successful, the internal rhythm must be exact. Furthermore, the novel was "essentially trochal . . . the form of it as a wheel so that, when you get to the end . . . you should want to turn back to the beginning again" (*Selected Letters*, 88).

Under the Volcano, the story of the last twelve hours in the life of its tortured drunken hero, begins twelve months *after* Geoffrey's death, the number twelve being of great importance for mystical, astrological, and literary reasons. The twelve chapters of the novel, each a carefully constructed "block," create the essential "form of the book, which is to be considered like that of a wheel, with 12 spokes, the motion of which is something like that, conceivably, of time itself" (*Selected Letters,* 67). Lowry's concern with time, both in his theme and form, is clear; his concern with space emerges in the metaphors he uses to describe its structure—the text is a "wheel," or a circle, and at the same time, "like some Mexican churrigueresque cathedral." The early version of *Under the Volcano* was refused by no fewer than thirteen publishers in 1940-41, and the major changes that Lowry made in his manuscript directly affected the structure of the novel, which developed only slowly into the "designed, counterdesigned and interwelded" final product.[6]

Lowry's creative method was architectural. Beginning with a key block or episode in a chapter—for example, the peon in 8, the bullthrowing in 9, or Laruelle's conversation with Bustamente in 1—Lowry worked outward on either side of his foundation. The manuscript versions of the novel, as well as Lowry's notes, illustrate this process clearly. Frequently Lowry worked upon several versions of a sentence, paragraph, or episode concurrently. Once sections of a chapter were satisfactory, he would begin to shift them around within the chapter or even from chapter to chapter until they fitted properly. For everything he cut, he added something else, a word, an allusion, and so forth, gradually building up his "churrigueresque"—or overloaded—edifice.

With the exception of chapter 1, the early version of the *Volcano* is a temporally straightforward story of the Consul's last day. In chapter 1 Lowry attempted to make Jacques Laruelle actually *become* the Consul via an unconvincing dream mechanism in order to report on Geoffrey's last day:

> Laruelle was sinking down, ever more rapidly downward until the sensation of sheer falling was choking, and then, just when he felt that were it protracted a moment longer he must wake up and save himself, it was as if he entered, in some mysterious way, into the Consul's consciousness.... At the same time, as though he had waked from some strange sleep within sleep, Laruelle was instantly acquainted with all the events of that Day of the Dead long past which led up to this conscious moment. (8:1, 24)

Fortunately, Lowry altered the opening chapter and dropped the awkward dream technique entirely. But the idea of an implicit dream continued to attract him, for in "Work in Progress" he speaks of *Volcano* "as a dream or ideal movie made by M. Laruelle himself" ("WP," 3). The typescript is choked with naive social criticism, boring character analyses, and tedious exposition. The time scheme is vague; when the story opens the Consul has been dead two or three years. Little attempt is made to make the flashback clear at the beginning of chapter 2, which gets off to a very slow start with Yvonne (Geoffrey's daughter instead of his wife) still in her hotel in Acapulco.

The temporal and spatial links between the chapters are clear; chapter 3 follows on, assisted by a strong omniscient narrator, from chapter 2 and so forth. It was not until 1941 that Lowry divided up the chapters according to the strict point of view of one or other of the characters, telling chapter 1 from Jacques' point of view, chapters 4, 6, and 8 from Hugh's, chapters 2, 9, and 11 from Yvonne's, and leaving the five remaining chapters to be perceived through Geoffrey's liquor-fogged eyes. In shifting the narration away from an intrusively omniscient narrator to a subtle combination of cryptic narrative voice and character point of view, Lowry was well on his way to creating the self-enclosed tragic world of the *Volcano's* characters.

When Lowry rewrote his novel, he heightened the reader's sense of the characters' dislocation and isolation by cutting all the direct temporal and spatial links between chapters. For example, in the 1940 typescript, chapter 9 opens with Yvonne, Hugh, and Geoffrey arriving in Tomalín and attempting to phone for medical aid. The temporal and spatial sequence develops clearly out of the scene with the dying peon in 8. In the final version, of course, there is no such carefully delineated cause and effect. The reader is thrust abruptly into

"Arena Tomalín . . ." and Yvonne's mind.[7] The disjunction between chapters 9 and 10 of the novel is still more complete. The closing scene of 9, in which the three characters watch an aged Indian shuffle out of sight, is dramatically juxtaposed with the opening word of 10—"Mescal." In the 1940 version, however, chapter 10 opens with temporal and spatial explanation: "Finally they walked down toward the restaurant Salón Ofélia." "Finally" refers to the end of 9 when the three paused to watch the old Indian, and the rest of the sentence carries the action forward, specifying their movement through space and their destination.

The changes Lowry made in his novel—telescoping chapters 4 and 5, and 11 and 12, using character point of view rigorously, recasting chapter 1 within a tight temporal framework symbolized by the backwards revolving, luminous wheel, above all, creating breaks or gaps between chapters—illustrate the direction in which he was moving. All of these changes help to spatialize *Under the Volcano*, to break up traditional temporal narrative sequence, and to force the reader to consider the book reflexively with a view, in Lowry's words, to the "poetical conception of the whole" (*Selected Letters*, 59).

So far publishers' reasons for rejecting the 1940 version of *Under the Volcano* are unknown, and only one specific criticism appears to have survived. An unpublished letter to Lowry from his agent Harold Matson (dated 7 October 1940) records some of Martha Foley's remarks:

> It is a very unusual book but one that we feel does not quite emerge from under the burden of the author's preoccupation with what might be described as the Dunn [sic] theory of time. (1:40, n.p.)[8]

Lowry agreed, and in a reply to Matson remarked: "I think on rereading that Martha Foley's judgement is maybe a just one in part; there *is* too much preoccupation with time, and the pattern does not emerge properly" (*Selected Letters*, 39). During the late twenties and thirties, J. W. Dunne's *An Experiment with Time* was in great vogue and references to Dunne and the law of series occur repeatedly in Lowry's letters and manuscripts.

Dunne's book is an attempt to base an epistemology upon the theory that time is serial:

> Now, we have seen that if Time passes or grows or accumulates or expends itself or does anything whatsoever except stand rigid and changeless before a Time-fixed observer, there must be another Time which times that activity of, or along, the first Time, and another Time which times that second Time, and so on in an apparent series to infinity.[9]

This time series gives rise to a universe of Chinese boxes, one contained within the other *ad infinitum*, and the observer of this serial universe is also serial. Far from being a passive receptacle, Dunne's observer is capable of psychic penetration into other time levels or, what amounts to the same thing, of transforming himself from Observer A into Observer B and so on.

The implications of such a serial identity are vast. If an individual can move from the smallest time level to a greater encompassing one, then he can perceive the past *and* the future of the first observer as well as of other observers. In this way Dunne believes that he has "scientifically" accounted for the phenomenon of precognition in dreams and time travel. He goes on to suggest that by being able to penetrate other time levels and foresee, so to speak, the future, the observer can interfere in that future. Even death is overcome, for when a person dies he simply ceases to exist on one time level and passes on to another.

The entire question of Dunne's influence upon *Under the Volcano* is interesting but unanswered. Agreeing with Martha Foley that there was too much concern with serial time in the 1940 version of the novel, Lowry set about to bury this influence deeper in his narrative, but he certainly did not eradicate it. In the 1940 version of chapter 1, Jacques is a serial observer who *becomes* Geoffrey and is thus able to dream the events of the past Day of the Dead, which enables him to observe a larger slice of Geoffrey's time dimension; he can see Geoffrey's past and future with hopes of intervening in that future. However, the chapter is laboured and unconvincing. Although Lowry dropped his original vehicle for precognition in chapter 1, he did not rule out precognition altogether. Geoffrey's hallucination in chapter 3 of the final version is meant to be a glimpse into his own and the peon's future. The newspaper headline "Es inevitable la muerte del Papa" functions in a similar way. More importantly, Lowry deliberately casts the reader of *Under the Volcano* as a Dunnian serial observer because the reader who has carefully read chapter 1 is aware of the past and the future which chapters 2 to 12 create.

Dunne's concept of serial containment, which underlies his serial universe as well as the serial observer, is most important for the structure of *Under the Volcano*. For example, in chapter 12 of the *Volcano,* the Consul moves from the bar "into an inner room, one of the boxes in the Chinese puzzle" (361) of El Farolito. This principle of containment is fundamental to Lowry's book, which is itself a kind of Chinese puzzle enclosed finally in its "trochal," or wheel-like, form. The condition of containment, suggested by the Consul's destructive withdrawal inside his own circumference and by the images of containment (bars, rooms, gardens, toilets, and the bus) dominating the narrative, is created by all aspects of the text from its style to its chapter divisions.

At the beginning of this chapter, the importance of structure in *Under the Volcano* was emphasized, and Lowry's Cape letter and his manuscript changes help to clarify his purposes as well as to underline his own awareness of the formal problems before him. *Under the Volcano* is a book about failure and *acedia,* and each of the four main levels of the text contributes to this general theme. Basically, Lowry creates the story, or immediate level, as Dale Edmonds calls it, by using a traditional sequential narrative pattern.[10] The esoteric levels (fable, allegory, and myth), however, operate within another, opposing pattern.

In his discussion of *Under the Volcano* in the biography, Douglas Day maintains that nothing is static in the novel.[11] Certainly little appears "static" in *Volcano*; everything is wheeling, reeling, and rushing, but this hallucinatory movement is circular, repetitive, and infernal. The gigantic wheeling form of the book is only one symbol of the paralysis portrayed on all levels. Time most certainly moves within the fictional world of twelve consecutive hours in a single day, and the total time span includes the pasts of the main characters, as well as glimpses of the future, but the meaning of the text arises only in part from this sense of what Forster called the "and then, and then" of the narrative. Equally important is a reflexive pattern which, together with the circular form of the novel, parallels and at points threatens to subsume the sequential narrative of events. It is this pattern which creates what some critics describe as "spatial form," or what Tzvetan Todorov describes as a "vertical... narrative of substitutions."[12]

There are, then, two conflicting narrative patterns or rhythms in *Under the Volcano*, and to understand *Volcano* is, in large part, to understand how these two function together to constitute the narrative organization of the text. On the one hand, Lowry exploits a reader's expectation of sequential temporal flow. The cryptic narrator of the novel is present only as a voice that introduces the reader to Quauhnahuac, comments obliquely upon the story, tells of Geoffrey's burial in the *barranca*, and keeps the tale moving with the consequent illusion of time passing and of one event leading on into another. Geoffrey himself is constantly aware that time is passing. Throughout the hot, tragic day the reader hears a relentless ticking as the characters constantly check the time on ubiquitous Mexican clocks. Horological time, a relentless, mechanical time totally removed from the psychological time of human suffering, represents the civilized, technological world that repels and mocks the Consul. On the other hand, Lowry's handling of chapter, symbol, and scene, and the special techniques discussed below counteract this narrative and temporal flow by breaking it up and by drawing the reader's attention away from the sequential story to the symbolic importance of almost ritualistically repeated image, motif, and situation. The most significant characteristic of *Under the Volcano*, when compared with the 1940 manuscript, is its spatio-temporal transformation. Lowry went to great lengths to create a reflexive narrative rhythm which would counteract and eventually overwhelm the temporal narrative flow. It is this reflexive rhythm, counteracting the realistic progression of the story, that carries the three symbolic levels of the text. The following discussion is an examination of the ways in which Lowry creates and sustains the double narrative pattern of his novel and the results of these opposing rhythms for the meaning of the text as a whole.

Because the immediate level of story is straightforward and has been so well described by Edmonds, it is possible to begin an examination with the symbolism. But in a novel like *Under the Volcano*, which is so rich in symbol and evolving image, it is necessary to isolate key symbols or image patterns. The *barranca* runs through the book linking chapter 1 to 12, linking 1938 to 1939, Geoffrey's garden with the Farolito, Mexico of the Conquest with modern Mexico, even linking "opposite sides of the Atlantic" (22). Therefore, in addition to its role as a "gigantic jakes," the *barranca* represents that sense of inevitable and necessary connection, in time and space, which pervades Lowry's world. Popocatapetl and Ixtaccihautl also have various symbolic meanings, but Popocatapetl functions above all as a magnet at the centre of Geoffrey's circular journey drawing him ever closer. Of lesser importance are the Hellbunker, the lighthouse (*pharos*, El Farolito), the Samaritan, the horse, bull, and goat, the scorpions, the vultures, and the numbers. However, the narrative strategy of *Under the Volcano* is best approached through the symbol of the circle or wheel which whirls on forever in the same place. Thus, the great "luminous wheel" spinning backwards in the dark night of chapter I symbolizes Buddha's wheel of the law, a cinema wheel, and the wheel of time (*Selected Letters*, 70, 80). The chapters themselves are like wheels encircling a particular point of view and, as in *Ultramarine*, Lowry employs a protagonist's closed circle of perception, trapped in turn within a self-contained chapter, as an image of the "madly revolving world." In fact, not even the reader — or so Lowry hoped — would escape the wheels within wheels of his "trochal" text because he would be compelled, at the end of chapter 12, to turn back to the beginning.

From the beginning of his work on the novel, Lowry was determined to emphasize the wheel symbol and the related circle imagery. Several passages deleted from the early version of the novel because they were over-explanatory make this clear. For example, in notes for the 1940 typescript of chapter 1, Señor Bustamente explains the reappearance of *Las Manos de Orlac* at his cinema with the remark: "And neither do we revive them. They return. They redonde, and begin all over again. It is the redonde eternal" (10:2, n.p.). In chapter 8 of the early version, Lowry made the significance of his whirling wheels blatantly clear. Staring at the busy fairground, Geoffrey bitterly reflects:

> Round and round went the Mexican children on the improvised merry-go-rounds. . . . Round and round up in the square went the men and the women who tonight would be segregated, drifting round the bandstand when the gutter crawlers would creep in bottom gear around the outer pavements of the plaza, squaring the circle. . . . Round too would go the dancers . . . cavorting like devils or like Dante's trimmers under the wavering flags, skipping all night in the same limited circle, with no variation of tune or step, their homage to St. Vitus.
>
> Round and round swung the planets, the moons, the satellites, round and round reeled the drunken, bawdy earth, and round and round went the circumpolar conversations, which were always with oneself. (8:1, 219)

Apart from the most obvious wheels in the book, the great ferris wheel brooding over Quauhnahuac and the wheeling stars (in his notes for chapter 11 Lowry jotted down, "continue the procession of the constellations . . . as a GIGANTIC WHEEL" [11:18, 9], each chapter contains its own wheels and circles. The streets of Quauhnahuac, in chapter 1, describe "an eccentric orbit." In chapter 2 there is "the already spinning flywheel of the presses," and the Consul compares his drunken-mystical state "to the paths and spheres of the Holy Cabbala" in chapter 3. These paths, and with them gates and doors, are inextricably associated with Lowry's wheels and circles; they symbolize the way in or out of an enclosure, be it a garden, cantina, or even the Cabbala. For example, Geoffrey thinks of intercourse with Yvonne as "that jewelled gate the desperate neophyte, Yesod-bound, projects for the thousandth time on the heavens to permit passage of his astral body" (98), and the aim of the Cabbalist is to pass through the "jewelled gate" into *Yesod*, the first sphere (a circle in its beneficent guise) of the innermost sanctum of knowledge. (See the diagram of the Tree of Life from Frater Achad's *Q.B.L.* or *The Bride's Reception* on page 80 in chapter 5.)

Geoffrey's vision of the cantina Puerto del Sol during his abortive lovemaking with Yvonne illustrates Lowry's circuitous, deliberately convoluted, style. The stylistic effect is one of immobilization, what Brian O'Kill calls "simultaneity," as physical action gives way to the images in Geoffrey's mind and finally to his impotence.[13] It is a long passage, but selections suggest Lowry's intention:

> But now, now he wanted to go, passionately he wanted to go, aware that the peace of the cantina was changing to its first fevered preoccupation of the morning... now, now he wanted to go, aware that the place was filling with people not at any other time part of the cantina's community at all, people eructating, exploding, committing nuisances, lassoes over their shoulders, aware too of the debris from the night before, the dead matchboxes, lemon peel, cigarettes open like tortillas, the dead packages of them swarming in filth and sputum. Now that the clock over the mirror would say a little past nine ... now he wanted to go! Ah none but he knew how beautiful it all was, the sunlight, sunlight, sunlight flooding the bar of El Puerto del Sol, flooding the watercress and oranges, or falling in a single golden line as if in the act of conceiving a God, falling like a lance straight into a block of ice — (98-99)

Lowry extends and prolongs the moment of Geoffrey's evasion of reality through the repetition of "Now," while the accumulated phrases pile up to form small buttresses between the Consul's repeated wish for the cantina. The final line of the passage, "falling like a lance straight into a block of ice — " works in two directions simultaneously. The harsh consonants coupled with the punctuation move the passage towards an abrupt close which parallels the Consul's failure; the "block of ice" refers back paratactically to the preceding detail of "the iceblock dragged in by a brigand with an iron scorpion" (99). The entire cantina vision is an example of Geoffrey's mental habit of circling out and away from a physical encounter only to be struck by reality as the circle closes. By withdrawing into himself at this point, he becomes incapable of entering the one enclosing space which offers salvation — and a future in the form of a child — his wife's body. The tragic irony of this failure will be clear in chapter 12 during the last hour of his life.

Even in chapter 4, where the characters *appear* less trapped and enclosed, ominous images of wheels and circles abound. Yvonne's once beautiful flowerbed is "completely, grossly strangled by a coarse green vine" (107). Birds loop-the-loop "immelmaning at unbelievable speed" (118). A stream casts "mill-wheel-like reflections" on the wall of the brewery — an image which recurs in chapter 9 — and an innocent armadillo becomes a symbol of destruction on "tiny wheels." Any doubt about the power of the wheel and circle imagery to convey Lowry's vision of hell is dispelled by the whirling vortex of Geoffrey's mind in chapter 5. Enclosed within his garden, the ruined garden of Eden, surrounded by fences and the *barranca*, Geoffrey who feels "hemmed in" suggests to the Jehovah-like Quincey that God's curse on Adam may have been to leave him trapped in Eden "alone." Only in the Tlaxcala episode does the reader again enter so dramatically into the infernal world of Geoffrey's consciousness. In chapter 6, as "reflections of vultures a mile deep wheeled upside down" (162) in the pool, Hugh circles through his ever-present past until he hears Geoffrey's call for help. The Consul, it would seem, is suffering from "the wheels within wheels" (185) of *delirium tremens* (if not Ezekiel's wheels). As he shaves the Consul, Hugh recalls a caricature of himself at Cambridge "as an immense guitar, inside which an oddly familiar infant was hiding, curled up, as in a womb" (189) — yet another image of regression recalling the conclusion of *Lunar Caustic*.

Chapter 7, on "the side of the drunken madly revolving world" (207), is the focal point of the wheel and circle imagery because the whirling machinery of the fair is a dramatic counterpart to Geoffrey's "great wheeling thoughts." In his panic he boards the "Máquina Infernal"[14] where "alone, in a little confession box," he is flung around and around until

> All at once, terribly, *the confession boxes had begun to go in reverse*: Oh, the Consul said, oh; for the *sensation of falling* was now as if terribly behind him, unlike anything, beyond experience; certainly this *recessive unwinding* was not like looping-the-loop in a plane, where the movement was quickly over. . . . Everything was falling out of his pockets, was being wrested from him, torn away, a fresh article at each whirling, sickening, plunging, retreating, *unspeakable circuit*, his notecase, pipe, keys, his dark glasses. . . his small change . . . *he was being emptied out, returned* empty, his stick, his passport. . . . What did it matter? Let it go! There was a kind of fierce delight in this final acceptance. Let everything go! *Everything particularly that provided means of ingress or egress*, went bond for, gave meaning or character, or

purpose or identity to that frightful bloody nightmare he was forced to carry around with him everywhere upon his back, that went by the name of Geoffrey Firmin. (236 [italics added])

References to the Tarot, the Karmic Wheel, and eternal recurrence cohere to reinforce the horror of this image of the Consul trapped in the steel cage of a "confession box" and stripped of identity by the recessive whirling. The passage contains echoes from preceding chapters (the looping-the-loop birds of 4, the recessive unwinding of the luminous wheel in 1) and prefigures Geoffrey's "sensation of falling" in 12. It is at this point that he loses his passport, symbol of his identity, "means of ingress and egress," and vital document in Mexico. The entire scene recalls the fair grounds in some of Lowry's favourite German films — *Caligari, Sunrise, Waxworks*, even Robison's *Looping the Loop*. The purpose of these scenes, in *Volcano* as in the films, is to create a sense of an inhuman force overwhelming helpless mortals because on entering the whirling realm of the fairground, man enters another world and surrenders his autonomy if not, indeed, his soul and sanity.

It is not a coincidence that Geoffrey is enclosed in a steel "confession box" taking "fierce delight in his destruction," for he has given in to powers of evil, and his prime sin is his *acedia*. His destiny is to be so encircled and contained within the whirling machine of fate that he will be destroyed. Although there is a type of motion here, the Consul himself is unmoving inside the blindly whirling box, and time and space have lost all meaning as the Consul hangs suspended, "motionless," over the world. The only further movement he makes during the day is to substitute (in Todorov's sense) one enclosure for another: the confession box gives way to the bus, the bus to the circular arena, the arena to the toilet, and the toilet to the series of cell-like rooms inside El Farolito. In essence, his situation does not change.

With the bus ride of chapter 8, Lowry employs his favourite device for creating movement through time and space which is simultaneously, for the characters, a psychological and moral paralysis. Inside the bus the characters sit "lulled into a state from which it would be pain to waken" (254), while for Hugh "the naked realities of the situation, like the spokes of a wheel, were blurred in motion toward unreal high events" (250). As Yvonne, Hugh, and Geoffrey wait for the bull throwing in chapter 9, the reader is reminded of the containing shape of the arena by the poor bull's futile circling of the ring. In a retrospect paralleling Hugh's in chapter 6, Yvonne reviews her past, envisioning it as a film unwinding mercilessly from the middle on with the reason for her destiny buried in the past, perhaps to "repeat itself in the future" (281). Even the bull (symbol of them all, possibly of life itself) resembles "some fantastic insect trapped at the centre of a huge vibrating web" (282). Chapter 10, the most intensely claustrophobic of all the chapters, represents one enclosure containing yet another and another with Geoffrey enthroned in the centre amidst his "whirling cerebral chaos" (325).

But circles do not always or necessarily symbolize a negative state for Lowry's protagonists; therefore, at strategic points in each of the "Voyage" novels Lowry uses the circle in its beneficent form. This is the case in chapter 11 of *Volcano* when, shortly before her death, Yvonne describes the stars as a "luminous wheel" rivalling and opposing the "luminous wheel" of chapter 1:

> And to-night as five thousand years ago they would rise and set. . . . To-night, as ages hence, people would . . . turn in bereaved agony from them, or toward them with love. . . . And the earth itself still turning on its axis and revolving around that sun, the sun revolving around the luminous wheel of this galaxy, the countless unmeasured jewelled wheels of countless unmeasured galaxies turning, turning, majestically, into infinity, into eternity, through all of which all life ran on — (338-39)

Here the wheel appears in its positive form representing the possibility of hope and salvation through the beauty of nature. For Yvonne, time and space are a continuum: tonight is connected to "five thousand years ago" and "ages hence"; life runs on "into infinity, into eternity." At her death Yvonne is drawn up, like Faust's Marguerite, towards the "beneficent Pleiades" through "eddies of stars scattering aloft with ever wider circlings like rings on water" (354). The eddies of stars recall the "Eddies of green and orange birds scattered aloft with ever wider circlings like rings on water" (333) from the opening of the chapter, and these "ever wider circlings," like Geoffrey's vision of "infinite evolving and extension of boundaries" (380), express Lowry's concept of the creative aspect of wheels and of containing circles. They are not closed, whirling meaninglessly, but open, forming and reforming, above all expanding in dramatic contrast to Geoffrey, who is at this very moment contracting finally in upon himself. As Lowry told Cape, "the very end of the chapter [11] has practically stepped outside the bounds of the book altogether" (*Selected Letters*, 84). He is referring to the "ever wider circlings" (a central image in "Forest Path" and *October Ferry*) through time and space of the voyage that never ends.

The Farolito of chapter 12 is the perfect serial image of the Consul's withdrawal and paralysis, and here Goeffrey waits while "the clock on the Comisaria de Policia, annular, imperfectly luminous" (371), strikes the note of his approaching doom. The images and symbols of the text fuse here to reinforce the Consul's perception of everything as alive, menacing, and a disjunct projection of himself. Ironically, tragically, for it is now too late, Geoffrey reads Yvonne's lost letter for the first time:

> "Oh Geoffrey, how bitterly I regret it now. Why did we postpone it? Is it too late? I want your children, soon, at once, I want them. I want your life filling and stirring me." (364)

Yvonne is the one encircling space that offered Geoffrey salvation in a future. This is the space, empty now forever, which he was unable to enter in chapter 3.

The images of paths and gates from earlier chapters which relate the mythical (Cabbala) and allegorical (Garden of Eden) levels of the narrative to the immediate level of Quauhnahuac and Geoffrey's actual forest path to the Farolito reverberate throughout chapter 12 and contribute to the sense of familiarity and inevitability about this place. In other words, the incremental and reflexive force of the circle imagery, with these related images of paths and gates, complements the final moments in the sequential unfolding of events on Geoffrey's last day by emphasizing the reader's awareness that this is where he has been from the start. Having lost his passport, his means of ingress and egress, Geoffrey is enclosed on all levels within the infernal cantina. He has lost the Cabbalist's path, he has lost Christ's way of love, he has lost his wife, his future, his life. Doors stand open, but Geoffrey remains immobile.

There are many brilliant scenes throughout the novel in which Lowry pauses in the narration of events in order to suggest the cessation of temporal process through a heightened awareness of space. The description of the burning of Geoffrey's letter in chapter 1, for example, captures the effect of space collapsing enclosed upon itself because the time required for the letter to burn is conveyed in metaphors of space:

> The flare lit up the whole cantina with a burst of brilliance in which the figures at the bar . . . appeared, for an instant, frozen, a mural. . . . M. Laruelle set the writhing mass in an ashtray, where beautifully conforming it folded upon itself, a burning castle, collapsed, subsided to a ticking hive through which sparks like tiny red worms crawled and flew, while above a few grey wisps of ashes floated in the thin smoke, a dead husk now, faintly crepitant. (49)

The dramatic visual quality of this passage — "burst of brilliance," "sparks like tiny red worms," "grey wisps of ashes" — reinforces the emphatically *a*temporal nature of the scene and draws the reader's attention to Lowry's transformation of an evanescent moment into the space of "a mural" with the "burning castle" of the letter foregrounded against the *chiaroscuro* of the bar. Of course, the irony of this spatialization of time is acute because this is the letter Geoffrey never sent, and it parallels those letters in chapter 12 which he had not read — in time. All these letters are objects which never acquired a temporal existence and, therefore, could neither be responded to nor acted upon.

The most graphic example of spatialization in the *Volcano*, however, is the Tlaxcala scene in chapter 10. This episode, which Lowry intended as a play or a poster, is a paradigm of the text. The toilet, the "Cave of the Winds" contained within the Salon Ofélia, surrounds the Consul, who in his desperation wonders why he is "always more or less, here":

The Consul sat, fully dressed however, not moving a muscle. Why was he here? Why was he always more or less, here? He would have been glad of a mirror to ask himself that question. But there was no mirror. Nothing but stone. Perhaps there was no time either, in this stone retreat. Perhaps this was the eternity that he'd been making so much fuss about, eternity already, of the Svidrigailov variety, only instead of a bath-house in the country full of spiders, here it turned out to be a stone monastic cell wherein sat — strange! — who but himself? (309-10)

Significantly, this is the Consul's eternity, and as the scene develops, the sensation of timelessness, created through spatial form, reveals its truly infernal nature: Lowry knew from Bergson that time is needed to keep everything from happening at once.

The scene begins abruptly with Geoffrey's realization that he is not eating with the others. The toilet of cold grey stone suggests the sacrificial blocks of the Aztecs (mentioned in the Tlaxcala tourist folder).[15] To make matters worse, Cervantes answers the Consul's call for help with offers of a stone, "A stone, hombre, I bring you a stone" — whether the philosopher's or Sisyphus' stone is not clear. Then Geoffrey, his perception increasingly distorted by mescal, begins to read snatches from the Tlaxcala tourist folder proclaiming the historic importance of this state, home of Mexico's betrayers, with its "density of 53 inhabitants to the square kilometre" (311). Key phrases stand out for Geoffrey. Tlaxcala city is *"said to be like Granada, said to be like Granada, Granada"* (the place where Geoffrey and Yvonne first met), and "in the inside" of the San Francisco Convent "there is a secret passage, *secret* passage" (a passage which Geoffrey will now never find). The Consul's mutterings about Parían, "In the Farolito —," are ironically juxtaposed with another paragraph from the folder entitled: "SANTUARIO OCOTLÁN IN TLAXCALA" (315).

From the dining room the voices of Hugh and Yvonne, who are discussing the peon, penetrate Geoffrey's consciousness. Together with disjointed snatches of this overheard conversation and disembodied passages from the tourist folder, the Consul hears a babel of voices from earlier in the day — his own, Vigil's, Yvonne's, his familiars', even Weber's:

'Have another bottle of beer . . . Carta Blanca?'
'Moctezuma . . . Dos Equis.'
'Or is it Montezuma?'
'Moctezuma on the bottle.'
'That's all he is now —'

TIZATLÁN

In this town, very near to the Tlaxcala City, are still erected the ruins of the Palace, residence of Senator Xicohtencatl, father of the warrior by the same name. In said ruins could be still appreciated the stone blocks where were offered the sacrifices to their Gods . . . In the same town, a long time ago, were the headquarters of the Tlaxcaltecan warriors . . .

'I'm watching you . . . You can't escape me.'
'— this is not just escaping. I mean, let's start again, really and cleanly.'
'I think I know the place.'
'I can see you.'
' — where are the letters, Geoffrey Firmin, the letters she wrote till her heart broke — '
'But in Newcastle, Delaware, now that's another thing again!'
' — the letters you not only have never answered you didn't you did you didn't you did then where is your reply — '
'— but oh my God, this city — the noise! the chaos! If I could only get out! If I only knew where you could get to!'

OCOTELULCO
In this town near Tlaxcala existed, long back, the Maxixcatzin Palace. In that place, according to tradition took place the baptism of the first Christian Indian.

'It will be like a rebirth.'
'I'm thinking of becoming a Mexican subject, of going to live among the Indians, like William Blackstone.'
'Napoleon's leg twitched.'
' — might have run over you, there must be something wrong, what? No, going to — '
'Guanajuato — the streets — how can you resist the names of the streets — the Street of Kisses — ' (316-17)

Earlier versions of this scene illustrate Lowry's painstaking efforts to balance the sequence of conversation, folder material, and remembered voices as the Consul sinks deeper into his private maelstrom. The disjointed cry, " — but oh my God, this city — the noise! the chaos! If I could only get out! If I only knew where you could get to!" first appears in chapter 3 (92) as the Consul prepares for the impending sexual encounter with his wife — an encounter from which he wishes to escape. Ironically, the act of love represents an escape from his abyss of self; it could be his way out of himself. But here in the toilet, as there in Yvonne's room, Geoffrey is trapped. The two enclosures, bedroom and toilet, fuse to emphasize the closed circle of Geoffrey's consciousness. Furthermore, the city of Tlaxcala and the city of New York are like Geoffrey's mind, traitorous and noisy. In this one brief passage, space is condensed and stripped of demarcation or boundary. All places, his house, Yvonne's bedroom, Tlaxcala, New York, exist here in Tomalín, in the stone toilet of the Salón Ofélia, and in the Consul's mind.

Time is similarly compacted in this scene. No distinctions exist between past, present, and future — everything is happening now. The history of the ancient

Tlaxcaltecans and the history of the conquest co-exist with November 1938. Yvonne's plea from chapter 9 that "It will be like a rebirth" melts into Vigil's description of Guanajuato from chapter 5. The present moment — "Have another bottle of beer . . . " — loses all distinction as it disappears behind the voices of Geoffrey's familiars and the inquiring voice of the English tourist from chapter 3: "might have run over you, there must be something wrong, what?" The spatial form of this scene with its intense sensation of simultaneity is the perfect dramatic projection of the state of Geoffrey's mind and soul. He has become a self-enclosed destructive circle, unable to distinguish past from present or even to perceive physical and spiritual boundaries. He is in Hell.

Lowry uses some striking metaphors, motifs, descriptions of plastic art, and what are loosely labelled as "cinematic" devices to contribute further to the spatial form of the text. Of the many rich metaphors in *Volcano*, the metaphor of the town or city stands out. Images of towns, usually with roads and communications "decompuesto," form a crucial metaphoric network within the narrative and complement descriptions of real towns such as Cuernavaca, Tlaxcala, Granada, lost cities such as Atlantis, the biblical city of Babylon, where Belshazzar beheld (like the Consul) a "Mene-Tekel-Peres," and Bunyan's City of Destruction. Most important, Geoffrey compares his soul to a town:

> a picture of his soul as a town appeared once more before him, but this time a town ravaged and stricken in the black path of his excess . . . then at last to know the whole town plunged into darkness, where communication is lost, motion mere obstruction, bombs threaten, ideas stampede—(155)

The novel closes with the image of "black spouts of villages catapulted into space, with himself falling through it all" (395). This central metaphor, then, functions in two important ways. On the one hand, it provides an important image of Geoffrey's soul which foreshadows his approaching disintegration and death. The fate of Geoffrey's "ravaged and stricken soul," in turn, suggests the fate of all towns, for as Lowry maintained in his letter to Cape, Geoffrey's fate parallels "the ultimate fate of mankind." In this way, the metaphor links the reader's perception of the fictional character with his knowledge of experiential reality and fuses the immediate story level with the political and religious levels of the narrative. On the other hand, the metaphor functions incrementally within the text by echoing and recalling earlier references to towns. Each time the metaphor recurs, new associations develop around those already present; thus, the town metaphor connects otherwise disparate scenes and episodes, forcing the reader to read reflexively and thereby to see the state in which Geoffrey's soul *is*.

Before moving on to examine other techniques in the novel, this is an appropriate point at which to pause briefly and consider the wider importance of rhetorical figure in *Under the Volcano*. O'Kill draws a useful distinction between metaphor and simile and points out that Lowry uses simile, more often than metaphor, to suggest analogous relationship instead of identity, but an equally important distinction should be made between Lowry's use of metaphor or simile and metonymy.[16] Despite the presence of such striking similes as that of Geoffrey's "soul as a town" or even the controlling analogy of the book, that to live in the modern world is like living "under the volcano," metonymy is of equal importance to the syntax and structure of the text. In the passage quoted above from chapter 3, for example, the narrator presents Geoffrey's thoughts of the cantina metonymically: people "eructating," lassoes over shoulders, dead matchboxes, lemon peel, filth and sputum, the clock, mirror, and sunlight are all parts of the Puerto del Sol, parts of that special place where Geoffrey would rather be. Often the sense that the prose style is weighted down with details results from Lowry's metonymically organized sentences—Yvonne's memory of the Acapulco harbour while she scans the Quauhnahuac *zócalo* is another example.

But the concepts of metaphoric and metonymic association also provide useful ways to consider the larger units of a narrative. Commenting upon Roman Jakobson's pioneering study of metaphor and metonymy, Robert Scholes remarks:

> Jakobson finds this distinction between metaphoric and metonymic processes in language discernible not only at the level of individual expressions in language but at the level of larger patterns of discourse as well. Thus in any work of literature the discourse may move from topic to topic according to relationships of similarity or of contiguity, which is to say according to metaphorical or metonymic thought processes.[17]

The entire Tlaxcala scene from chapter 10 discussed above is a fine example of *Volcano's* narrator working metonymically. The many voices, snatches of conversation, and passages from the tourist folder are related to each other in terms of contiguity and are apparently perceived as parts of a larger whole by Geoffrey, whose point of view, of course, the reader shares. One might, in fact, argue that the twelve chapters of the novel are related to each other according to the principle of contiguity, in which case, the rich metaphors of *Volcano* would be seen as operating *within* a larger metonymy. A consequence of this syntactic and structural strategy (whether entirely conscious on Lowry's part or not) is the creation of a text in which the characters, and narrative levels, are contiguous with each other as parts of a larger whole. While such a perspective on *Volcano* by no means reduces the power of its specific metaphors, it does highlight Lowry's ability to create a text which reflects his belief that events, people, or aspects of an individual psyche (even texts themselves) are not only analogous to each other, but are also parts of one and the same thing.

Lowry's use of motif is, to continue the rhetorical terminology, synechdochal; the Strauss *Allerseelen* stands for Yvonne, the phrase, "losing the Battle of the Ebro" represents Hugh, while many Promethean, Faustian, and other allusions evoke the Consul. Each time a motif appears, it carries associations, regardless of context or chapter. *No se puede vivir sin amar* and *Le gusta este jardín* become more like semantic codes than motifs, however, for they encapsulate and contain the message of the text.

Two motifs which bear upon the temporal scheme of the narrative are the traditional Spanish toast *Salud y pesetas y amor y tiempo para gastarlas* and the Spanish greetings *buenos días - buenas tardes - buenas noches*. In chapter 1, Laruelle and Vigil use part of the toast, "Salud y pesetas. Y tiempo para gastarlas" (12), but neglect to mention *y amor*. Later, in chapter 11, Yvonne and Hugh repeat "Salud y pesetas" three times (345). The omission of "Y tiempo para gastarlas" here becomes significant; there is no longer time for health or wealth— time has run out. The irony of dropping the *y amor* from the toast each time it is used seems clear; the story is about the loss and crippling of love. Important for the narrative structure of the text, however, is the fragmentation and positioning of the toast because its full meaning can only be appreciated in a reflexive reading of the text.

Buenos días and *buenas tardes* or *noches* refer, of course, to the three main divisions of the day—morning, afternoon, and evening. At seven in the morning (chapter 2) the Consul greets a Mexican in dark glasses with "Buenas tardes, señor." Much to Yvonne's embarrassment, the Consul addresses another ragged man in the same way. Then, lest the joke be overlooked, the two Mexicans nudge each other "as if to say: 'He said "Buenas tardes," what a card he is!' " (59) Later in the morning, in chapter 4, Yvonne correctly greets the little girl with the armadillo: "Buenos días, muchacha" (122). Finally, in chapter 12, the Consul greets the fascist police with a polite "Buenas tardes, señores" (388). The implication is obvious; for the Consul it is always "tardes" (*tard,* tardy)—it is always too late. The *buenas tardes* motif comments ironically, sadly, upon the Consul's obsession with time and suggests in retrospect that time as movement or change does not exist for him. After his encounter with María, he asks the pimp "Qué hora?" only to be assured by the filthy little man who is "fliend Englisman all tine, all tine" that it is "half past sick by the cock" (370). Time for Geoffrey is a state, not a process.

In three important instances Lowry uses paintings (murals and the poster "Los Borrachones") to suggest a stasis that reflects and comments upon the events of his story. In chapter 7, Geoffrey and Jacques Laruelle look at the Rivera frescoes depicting scenes from Mexican history. Time, here the historical time of the Conquest, is spatialized, laid out in the space created by plastic art. At the end of the same chapter, as Geoffrey gulps tequila in the "Cantina El Bosque," he suddenly perceives the unfinished murals running around the cantina walls:

> They were precisely the same in every detail. All showed the same sleigh being pursuded by the same pack of wolves. The wolves hunted the occu-

pants of the sleigh the entire length of the bar and at intervals right round the room, though neither sleigh nor wolves budged an inch in the process. (243)

The pictures of movement that do not move, repeated again and again around the room, comment obliquely upon the paralysis in the Consul's life.

"Los Borrachones" adumbrates still more emphatically the unchanging image of Geoffrey's damnation. In chapter 12, as he recalls the picture from Laruelle's bedroom, the Consul realizes that it depicts his damnation, with the now forfeited alternative of salvation in tragic juxtaposition. Like the drunkards in the painting, his identity is dispersed, lost, indistinct. The people around him, even "the ash and sputum on the filthy floor . . . correspond . . . to some fraction of his being" (380). For Geoffrey, what might be called psychological space, that rudimentary and essential ability to distinguish self from not-self, does not exist. He realizes, furthermore, that had he continued to struggle, to act, to break out of the circle of self, he could have become free, separate and distinct like the righteous spirits in the picture. The Consul sees this salvation in terms crucial to an understanding of *Volcano* and to Lowry's concept of the voyage that never ends:

> Here would have been no devolving through failing unreal voices and forms of dissolution that became more and more like one voice to a death more dead than death itself, but an infinite widening, an infinite evolving and extension of boundaries, in which the spirit was an entity, perfect and whole. (380)

Here is the secret passage, the lost passport, the philosopher's stone in Lowry's *magnum mysterium*. By consciously striving the Consul might have achieved a life of infinitely "widening," "evolving," and extending boundaries. The very words, echoing Frater Achad and Ouspensky, reveal the importance of positive temporal and spatial movement in Lowry's cosmology.

Lowry's debt to film is difficult to assess because a rigorous but at the same time familiar language in which to discuss formal influences and stylistic parallels is lacking, and an examination of semiotic theory is beyond the purpose of this discussion. He always claimed that *Under the Volcano* was a kind of movie, and certainly references to various films occur frequently, both in *Volcano* and *October Ferry to Gabriola*. However, it is important to remember that Lowry was trying to capture certain technical effects of cinema—subtitles, double exposures, perhaps a metaphoric sense of *chiaroscuro—in prose,* so that any statements made about the "cinematic" quality of *Volcano* are finally metaphoric. More relevant than generalization about the cinema-like nature of the book are the questions, why did Lowry want to use "cinematic" effects in the first place, and which films captured his imagination?[18]

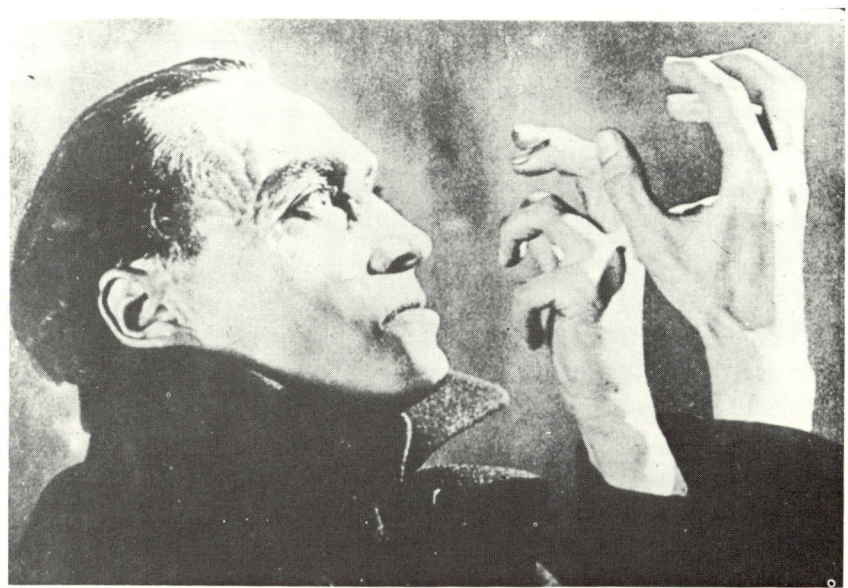

Conrad Veidt in Weine's *The Hands of Orlac* (1924), reproduced from Lotte Eisner, *The Haunted Screen: Expressionism in the German Cinema.*

The films of obvious importance to *Under the Volcano* are examples of German Expressionism: *The Cabinet of Dr. Caligari* (1919), *The Hands of Orlac* (1924, with *Mad Love,* 1935, the weak Hollywood remake starring Peter Lorre, central to *Volcano*), *The Student of Prague* (1926, with Conrad Veidt the famous expressionist actor), and *Sunrise* (1927).[19] Their influence on the *Volcano* is both thematic and stylistic. Each of these films portrays the essentially expressionist subject of a cataclysmic struggle within man's soul or mind. The stories are invariably macabre—a mad mountebank doctor unleashes a murderous somnambulist, a musician with the grafted hands of a murderer goes mad, a young student sells his soul to the devil and commits suicide. The characters operate less as individuals, despite the projection of subjective states of dream, hallucination, and madness, than as symbols of universal problems, of social ills, or disturbed psychic states. The acting, especially of Conrad Veidt and Werner Krauss, is exaggerated and stylized. The settings are often non-realistic studio sets of geometric shapes. Mirrors, whirling fairgrounds, double and multiple exposures, and *chiaroscuro* create the sensation of a landscape come alive with menacing power; the landscape, in effect, mirrors the turmoil of the soul at the same time as it *appears* to embody evil and hostile forces.

Fascinated by the subjects and the style of these films, Lowry employed comparable techniques to present his tragedy of the human soul. Thus, his characters are less novel characters than aspects of "the human spirit" and dramatizations of human malaise and social collapse. Lowry brings the chthonic elements of his text alive through his teeming imagery so that the landscape mirrors Geoffrey's confusion as well as seeming to participate in his destruction. Popocatapetl, for example, becomes a Moby Dick, and a sunflower stares at Geoffrey "like God." In chapter 12 he realizes that the filth and sputum on the floor correspond to his being, and his surroundings appear to come to life in order to taunt him:

> Why am I here, says the silence, what have I done, echoes the emptiness, why have I ruined myself in this wilful manner, chuckles the money in the till, why have I been brought so low, wheedles the thoroughfare, to which the only answer was—The square gave him no answer.(359)

In addition to this parallel between Lowry's vision and German expressionist film, Lowry wanted to adapt specific "cinematic" techniques to prose. Two of the most successful "cinematic" effects in *Volcano* are the use of signs and the suggestion of double exposure, both of which contribute to the emphatically spatial and visual quality of the text. Lowry uses signs and advertisements to interrupt the reader's sense of physical orientation and temporal continuity. For example, in chapter 2 as Geoffrey and Yvonne pass through the *zócalo*, perspective collapses suddenly when the sign for boxing or *"Las Manos de Orlac"* leaps before the eye. The reader is catapulted from the midst of dialogue or reflection into an unexplained confrontation with a disjunct object rising from the landscape. The recurrence of these signs creates an uneasy aura because, wherever the characters turn, the signs appear to meet them until gradually the signs assume the status of sinister and menacing warnings. In addition to creating a dramatic sense of entrapment for the characters, Lowry's handling of signs forces the reader to piece the story together around these visual interruptions. The signs themselves, especially the advertisement for *"Las Manos de Orlac"* and the mysterious *"Le gusta este jardin,"* reflect backwards and forwards on the events and situations of the story to create a mosaic of symbolic and ironic comment.

In 1928 Lowry saw Fred Murnau's *Sonnenaufgang* about which he said in 1951: "70 minutes of this wonderful movie—though it falls to pieces later, doubtless due to the exigencies of Hollywood—have influenced me almost as much as any book I ever read, even though I've never seen it since" (*Selected Letters*, 239). In chapter 11 of the 1940 version of the *Volcano* there are several references to the movie. Although the overt references are cut in the final version, in chapter 7 the Consul pictures "El Farolito" in his mind's eye and remembers a sunrise he had watched from there as "a slow bomb bursting over the Sierra Madre—*Sonnenaufgang!*" (214). Although Murnau's *Sunrise* was not the only film to make its way into the *Volcano* (Laruelle's house looks like something from *The Cabinet of Dr. Caligari*, and *The Hands of Orlac* is omnipresent), it is probably a more profound influence. Murnau's subject is an adulterous marriage in which "The Man"—none of the characters has a name, which universalizes the theme—attempts to kill his unwanted "Wife." The first part of the film uses interesting double exposures to produce the effect of good and evil battling for possession of the man's soul. The man's tortured form takes on symbolic proportions, and the landscape comes to life via menacing lighting effects. The couple are reconciled after near disaster, and while they gaze at wedding photographs in a window, there is a sequence of shots which resembles Lowry's handling of double exposure in the chapter 2 scene with Yvonne.

The reader first sees Yvonne standing outside the Bella Vista bar at seven in the morning on the Day of the Dead, but superimposed upon this description is another one of Yvonne sailing into Acapulco the evening before. Two different times and places are fused, not simply juxtaposed, through the double exposure effect. Later, as she and Geoffrey pause outside the printer's shop, Lowry elaborates still further on the double exposure device:

> They stood, as once, looking in.... From the mirror within the window an ocean creature so drenched and coppered by sun and winnowed by sea-wind and spray looked back at her she seemed, even while making the fugitive motions of Yvonne's vanity, somewhere beyond human grief charioting the surf. But the sun turned grief to poison and a glowing body only mocked the sick heart, Yvonne knew, if the sun-darkened creature of waves and sea margins and windows did not! In the window itself, on either side of this abstracted gaze of her mirrored face, the same brave wedding invitations she remembered were ranged.... but this time there was something she hadn't seen before, which the Consul now pointed out with a murmur of 'Strange.' (61)

The image of Yvonne in the present moment and in the near and more distant past is superimposed upon the photographs and invitations within the window. These, in turn, are seen against the enlargement of "La Despedida"—"set behind and above the already spinning flywheel of the presses" (61). Gazing at the multiple images reflected and framed by the window, Yvonne sees Geoffrey and herself as they once were: "They stood, as once, looking in." She sees herself as she has recently been, "coppered by sun and winnowed by sea-wind." There is even the suggestion that a completely different Yvonne appears in the window, a Venus-like Yvonne "somewhere beyond human grief charioting the surf." But apparent through these fragmented images of Yvonne's personality are further levels of present and past reality—the photographs and invitations linking past to present, the spinning flywheel which temporally precedes the invitations, and finally the ancient glacial rock, at one time whole, now split by fire. The passage is a fine example of the way Lowry uses visual effects to support his overall design of containment. The window serves as a mirror to frame and reflect a series of temporal and spatial dimensions; it is a miniature serial universe.

Under the Volcano is a story about the hell man inflicts upon himself through his emotional sterility and *acedia*. The immediate level of this story depends upon a traditional, linear narrative, a sequence of events which carries the reader forward through the last tragic day in a man's life as each chapter (with the exception of 1, 5, and 12) moves on relentlessly from 7 A.M. to 7 P.M. However, this relatively simple tale of a woman's futile attempt to rebuild her marriage conveys only one dimension of Lowry's subject. The allegory of the Garden of Eden, the political fable complete with writing on the wall, and the Cabbalistic parallels gather force and consistence from the incremental, reflexive image patterns and highly visual, static scenes which create what I have been calling spatial form in the text. Much of the dramatic power and success of *Under the Volcano* as a work of art is attributable to the juxtaposition (which in chapter 12 becomes fusion) of the two narrative patterns. However, the power of the novel only begins there because each reader, in turn, participates in the Lowry "mythos" of never-ending voyage while reading the book. As in an expressionist film of madness and death, the Consul comes to life again for one day, and the reader is obliged to watch a repetition of the predetermined events of the fateful Day of the Dead. This repetition, of course, is an image of Geoffrey's (and Sigbjørn Wilderness') suffering and punishment, as well as a warning to the reader: by refusing to love, mankind will also bind itself to a mechanical, irreversible wheel of destruction.

Wheels and containing circles, however, are not always negative for Lowry. Like most of Lowry's symbols they are profoundly ambivalent—all depends upon the individual's perception and effort. As long as the wheel whirls eternally in the same place, there can be no meaningful movement forward; the wheel of consciousness must expand through "ever wider circlings" in order for life to become dynamic and regenerative. Even in *Under the Volcano,* where Lowry stresses the negative side of his vision through the trochal form of the text, the wheel and circle imagery, and the wonderful-horrible Tlaxcala scene with its hell of simultaneity, there are glimpses of the regenerative wheel of life. Although the *Volcano* was to be a hell, if not the worst, in Lowry's "The Voyage that Never Ends," the novel embodies glimpses of hope, prefigurings of "ever wider circlings," because the voyage *never* ends.

To the degree that *Under the Volcano* can be seen as one of many low points in Lowry's never-ending voyage, it is clearly not final; despair and negation are unavoidable stages in a journey. To the degree, however, that *Under the Voclano* stands alone as Lowry's masterpiece, it offers a tragic vision of destruction and loss; it is a story of hellfire, and hellfire, for Lowry, means paralysis of the will. Without the will to "unceasingly strive upwards," the human spirit, like the "obscene circular movement" of Señor Zuzugoitea's hips, deteriorates in a "progresíon al culo."[20]

4

Withdrawal and Return:
"La Mordida" and *Dark as the Grave*

In "Work in Progress" and *Selected Letters* (307), Lowry speaks of *Dark as the Grave Wherein My Friend Is Laid*, "Eridanus," and "La Mordida" as a trilogy. However, little, if any, of this trilogy ever reached completion. The "Eridanus" material survives in "The Forest Path to the Spring" and *October Ferry to Gabriola*. "La Mordida" was to continue the story of *Dark as the Grave*, and at one point Lowry placed it last in the "Voyage" cycle because it "throws the whole thing into reverse and issues in triumph" (*Selected Letters*, 267). (The position of "La Mordida" within the "Voyage" is discussed in chapter 1). If the typescript is ever to be published, it will require editing, for it is a rough combination of prose passages, journal notes, and Lowry's debates with himself about art. However, because of "La Mordida's" close ties with *Dark as the Grave*, it is worthwhile to examine aspects of the typescript before turning to the novel.

In "Mordida" Lowry explains the significance of his concept of return. "La Mordida" (the bite or bribe) grew out of the Lowrys' 1945-46 trip from Cuernavaca to Acapulco, their trouble with the Mexican authorities over an allegedly unpaid fine, and their final release at the United States border after nightmarish harassment. The typescript is adorned with Lowry's pencilled references to Ouspensky and Bergson, as well as to Yeats, Swedenborg, and others. As in each of his novels, Lowry planned to explore the perception of time and space through the constant movement of the hero and his wife between their hotel and the Immigration Office and through the symbol of the border, which plays a key role in *Dark as the Grave* as well. Once again the hero's problem arises from his withdrawal behind the borders of self, his obsession with the past, and the danger of a total inability to act.

It quickly becomes apparent, as Sigbjørn and Primrose travel by bus towards Acapulco, that they are heading into trouble because of the guilt and fear which plague him. In a fascinating "Note" to the "La Mordida" typescript Lowry remarks:

> (Note: the antimonsoon of the past. the Bergson motif again. the antimonsoon—the upper, contrary moving current of the atmosphere over a monsoon;—in this regard, while they are travelling toward Acapulco they are going in the same direction as the monsoon, toward the future; while static in Acapulco, because Sigbjørn instead of going ahead futilely worries about the past, in an attempt to discover its meaning in relation to the present, the monsoon reverses itself, Cuernavaca and Mexico City is now the direction of the monsoon, while Sigbjørn and willy-nilly Primrose are caught in the continually contrary moving current of its upper air in the lofty Hotel Quinta Eugenia. (12:9, 35-36)

While the future blows by them in the opposite direction, Sigbjørn and Primrose are trapped in the past as if to parallel and complement their physical incarceration in the Quinta Eugenia. Lowry's monsoon, moving two ways simultaneously, appears in *Dark as the Grave* in an allusion to Chaucer's *Troilus and Cressida:* "*Al stereless and in a boot am I, amid the sea, between windes two, that in contrarie standen evermo*" (11). Both the monsoon and the "contrarie windes" convey Lowry's idea of a spatio-temporal stasis in which the characters are trapped, unable to move with the wind, and locked into a past that has not been sufficiently understood or expiated. Someone must continue to pay *la mordida*, the full toll to hell.

Later in the "La Mordida" typescript, at a particularly horrible point in Sigbjørn's incarceration in the hotel, Lowry incorporates notes on the FU Hexagram from the *I Ching* treating the subject of return:[1]

> "Fu indicates that there will be free course and progress (in what it denotes) (the subject of it) finds no one to distress him in his exits and entrances, friends come to him, and no error is committed. He will return and repeat his (proper) course. In seven days comes his return. There will be advantage in whatever direction movement is made." . . . But the I Ching then goes on to show the meaning of each line making up the Hexagram, from bottom up, and the last section contains a warning. It may have been bad to repeat (or revisit) the scene of your book. (12:19, 319)

Victories are never easily won with Lowry; the Fu Hexagram contains a threat in its sixth line:

> The topmost line, divided, shows its subject *all astray on the subject of returning.* There will be evil. There will be calamities and errors. If with *his views he puts the hosts in motion,* the end will be a great defeat, *whose issues will extend to the ruler of the state.* Even in ten years he will not be able to repair the disaster. (12:19, 320)

Lowry apparently planned to introduce the *I Ching* Hexagram to suggest further levels of meaning for Sigbjørn's return to Mexico and the past. The FU Hexagram indicates that return will be propitious, and a propitious return to the past is consistent with Lowry's aim to have "La Mordida" reverse the fortunes of his protagonist. Whether Lowry would have developed the *I Ching* references in "La Mordida" or in *Dark as the Grave,* which is also about return, is impossible to say. Certainly he was impressed by the *I Ching,* for in the typescript he goes on to say:

> This reminds them [Sigbjørn and Primrose] of happy days, it should be pointed out that, while this may seem hocus pocus to the ordinary person, it bears in part upon the most remarkable book in all the world's literature. (12:19, 320)

"La Mordida" remains a raw transcript of Lowry's Mexican trip, but passages such as those of the Bergsonian monsoon and the FU Hexagram clarify his concept of a necessary, though profoundly dangerous, return to the past. Although the past must be fully understood and incorporated in the flow of time into the future, entrapment in the past can destroy both present and future. Thus, the voyage into the past is a necessary descent into the hell of self in which one risks all in the quest for regeneration.

Dark as the Grave received extensive editorial treatment from Douglas Day and Margerie Bonner.[2] Although the book inevitably represents a splicing job, it holds considerable interest, not so much for information about *Volcano,* as for Lowry's treatment of withdrawal and return and of the writer entrapped in his work. As late as 1951 Lowry still had considerable work to do on *Dark as the Grave:* "I calculate it would take me a year's intensive work to produce a real working copy, perhaps 15 months altogether to finish" ("WP," 22). The published version and typescripts barely suggest some of the elaborate configurations outlined in the "Work in Progress," and several other aspects of the book also remain undeveloped. Nevertheless, the "quest for faith or toward faith" ("WP," 209), emphasized as important to *Dark as the Grave* and central to the "Voyage," is obvious, and Oaxaca is a convincing "symbol of the *scene before the renuncia-*

tion" ("WP," 20). Sigbjørn must return to this scene of failure and excess, to a past he thought he had already outgrown, but the danger of this return threatens to overwhelm him. Lowry hoped the novel would be an "Under Under the Volcano," a still worse hell.

Dark as the Grave is best seen as a type of crossroads, or better still, a window between the earlier works, *Ultramarine, Lunar Caustic,* and *Under the Volcano,* and the later works, *October Ferry* and *Hear Us O Lord.* In terms of the "Voyage" cycle, it looks both ways, reflecting back upon the *Volcano* and opening on to *October Ferry.* The idea of moving in two directions simultaneously is as important to *Dark as the Grave* as to the monsoon of "La Mordida," and it is explicit in the symbol of the border. *Dark as the Grave* also holds a key position in Lowry's theory of the writer being written, of life being a novel and man the novelist. In one sense "The Voyage That Never Ends" explores the relation of life to art, and in this respect *Dark as the Grave* is particularly important, for it is a fiction about fiction whose hero is the author of *Under the Volcano,* renamed *The Valley of the Shadow of Death. Dark as the Grave,* then, like an aspect of the larger dimension in Dunne's serial universe, is part of the outer frame of the "Voyage." Finally, as William New has remarked, *Dark as the Grave* holds a mediating position between a fully projected work of art like the *Volcano* and an autobiography of Malcolm Lowry, the man.[3]

The manuscript of the 172-page draft of the novel explains the relation of *Dark as the Grave* to his work. The analysis, marked "Material from the Ledger," reads in part as follows:

> Note: In order to relieve the reader of a certain aversion of embarrassment at sight of what is apparently naked autobiography pretending to be surprised to be functioning as a sort of novel, I feel it better to state at the outset that this book was planned before Under the Volcano (The Valley of the Shadow of Death) was accepted by any publisher, with the notion that the protagonist—or a protagonist—or Hugh or the Consul—of the former should be the author of the latter, the intention being a sort of imaginary descent of the creator into the world of his creation.... [W]hile it has become useless to conceal that some of these happenings in question are autobiographical, the author requests humbly of the reader that he bear the original plan in mind, and to regard Sigbjørn Wilderness as he was originally conceived, namely, a separate entity conceived of as the author of U.T.V., which was a work of imagination within a larger reality, and not simply as the author himself, or as a whipping boy for the same.... What I had wanted to do at one point was to write, as E. M. Forster had suggested someone should, the history of someone's imagination. Sheer panic at where I was arriving at, combined with a philosophical deficiency, have made me decide to push this quest no further and at that I think it has gone quite far enough. (14:24, 377-78)

Dark as the Grave was intended as a fictional frame for *Under the Volcano*. Thus, in one way, it contains that novel while simultaneously exploring the dangers of entrapment for an artist who enters his own fictional world. With *Dark as the Grave* Lowry tried to push the idea of withdrawal into a closed circle one step further than in *Ultramarine* or the *Volcano*. Hence, the circle becomes both a structural device and an image of the serial relationship of life and art (as Lowry saw it) in which it is difficult to say whether life or art is the larger containing dimension. Lowry's remarks make it absolutely clear that Wilderness is intended as the major character in "The Voyage That Never Ends." He contains the many other Lowry heroes who represent isolated aspects of his imagination or particular troubled levels of his psyche. (The function and significance of Wilderness is discussed in greater detail in chapters 1 and 6.) Fascinating as Lowry's intentions may have been, *Dark as the Grave* remains the least successful of his posthumously published works. His attempt to portray the artist within his own fiction, unlike Gide's *Les Faux-Monnayeurs* or his own much more successful "Through the Panama," remains raw and awkward. It is not enough that "the author requests humbly of the reader that he bear the original plan in mind."

Dark as the Grave Wherein My Friend Is Laid explores the abyss — a "setting out into the future . . . by setting out smack into the past" (39). The book deals with the Wildernesses' flight from Vancouver to Mexico, where in the Quinta Dolores (five sorrows), none other than Jacques' tower in the *Volcano*, they await news from the would-be publishers of Sigbjørn's book. Depressed by the Quinta Dolores, depressed further by partial rejection of his book, Sigbjørn sinks into a by now familiar Lowry hell:

> In bed Sigbjørn tried to move, to stretch out toward his wife lying beside him, but he could not: he could not even move a little finger. Though bits of the ceiling crumbled, sifted down ceaselessly on his face, still he did not, or could not move. (117)

He attempts to reverse this destructive pattern by setting out further into his past. He travels to Oaxaca in order to find an old friend, Juan Fernando Martinez, and as a result of this effort, he is able to meet and overcome the past, then to move forward into the future.

Although not a literary palimpsest like *Under the Volcano*, *Dark as the Grave* draws upon a wide spectrum of literary reference. In addition to scattered allusions to Julian Green, Yeats, Nietzsche, Chaucer, Poe, Thomas Mann, Swedenborg and Grieg, Lowry uses Pirandello and Keats to emphasize his concept of "life flowing into art." For example, as Sigbjørn stands in the airport queue dressed in second-hand clothes, he reflects on the flow of his identity into his characters as well as into the identity of other authors and their characters. He decides that this shared identity comprises a "more-than-Pirandellian theme."[4] All Sigbjørn's possessions — his clothes, his watch, even his copy of Julian

Green's *The Dark Journey* (which Lowry also owned) — are second-hand, suggesting, somewhat sardonically, his multifaceted identity. As with the Consul in *Under the Volcano*, Sigbjørn's great danger is that he will lose the sharp outlines of personal identity and gradually disintegrate into a confused reflection of external reality.

The balance, however, between a clear personal identity and the acceptance of a Heraclitean reality is supremely difficult to achieve. While waiting for the El Paso flight, Sigbjørn has a vision of this flowing reality:

> [H]e had suddenly a glimpse of a flowing like an eternal river; he seemed to see how life flowed into art: how art gives life a form and meaning and flows on into life, yet life has not stood still; that was what was always forgotten: how life transformed by art sought further meaning through art transformed by life; and now it was as if this flowing, this river, changed, without appearing to change, became a flowing of consciousness, of mind, so that it seemed that for them too, Primrose and he, just beyond that barrier, lay some meaning, or the key to a mystery that would give some meaning to their ways on earth. (43)

Significantly, it is over the barrier or the border, on another level of consciousness, that this reality moves. But Sigbjørn loses contact with this vision of life when he withdraws behind the borders of his own tormented psyche. Flow and movement cease, leaving him frozen in a kind of life-in-death.

As Sigbjørn points out in a long conversation in chapter 7, this balance between preserving a core of personal identity and accepting the flowing vitality of art and reality is particularly acute for the artist because, like the universe, which according to the Rosicrucians "is in the process of creation," the "organic work of art . . . must grow in the creator's mind, or proceed to perish" (154). While Eddie snores, Sigbjørn laments this Rosicrucian universe and suggests that a short poem "thrown up in an instant of inspiration" may "manage to outwit the process" (155). Better still, a play by its very nature is not always the same because actors recreate it: "For that matter a reader is likewise an actor" (156). Ideally life continues to flow through a narrative work of art, making it new for each reader. However, the idea that the reader's recreation of a novel may save it from destruction seems slight consolation for a writer who believes that art like life must flow perpetually. Lowry set himself a Promethean task indeed.

Although *Dark as the Grave* lacks the complicated form of *Under the Volcano*, it does not have what George Woodcock calls a "depressingly linear structure."[5] Lowry strove for a structure that would incarnate his vision of a Rosicrucian universe where "life flowed into art [and] . . . life transformed by art sought further meaning through art transformed by life" (43). Although he did not live to tighten the structure of the novel, there are many indications in the published text and manuscripts that Lowry saw the first eight chapters taking place on a single night, the moonlit night in Cuernavaca prior to the crucial Oaxaca trip.

As early as the extant pencil draft of *Dark as the Grave*, Lowry was working out the dream mechanism for the first five chapters. In a marginal note to himself he wondered when it would "prove advisable... that it should be divulged ... that Martin is already in Cuernavaca..." (14:17, 1). (It was not until a later stage in the novel's genesis that Lowry changed the hero's name to Sigbjørn Wilderness.) In the 172-page typed draft, this "Note" appears:

> Yet another, and probably the best alternative, is to have Sigbjørn aware that he is in Cuernavaca itself, when the rhythm of this section breaks and they are in Cuernavaca actually! One should come to earth by gradations. (1) transition from plane to bus (2) transition from bus to realization he is in Cuernavaca (3) transition from the realization he is in the tower. (14:21, 165)

In another typed copy, the following note appears at the beginning of what was to become chapter 6 in the published text:

> It is at this point that Sigbjørn either wakes up or you realize he is in bed all this time at the tower thinking these things.... Sigbjørn lies there half awake, perhaps the full moonlight in the room, the moonlight of precisely one month later, recalls him to his sense. (15:3, 569-70)

Chapters 1 to 5 are a dream containing a retrospect of Sigbjørn's life, including his return trip to Mexico. The dream constitutes a powerful opening for a book concerned with return to the past and the "regressive unwinding" of the self in an effort to be reborn. As Sigbjørn puts it, paraphrasing Dunne, this is a book about "re-experiencing the past [and] prefeeling — horrible word — the future." Sigbjørn's dream ends in chapter 5 with the culminating vision of the lunar eclipse — "little by little the shadow of the old earth drew across the moon" (111). Chapter 6 opens with a brief bridging passage, reminiscent of the beginning of chapter 5 in the *Volcano*, which portrays Sigbjørn's confused thoughts as his sleeping consciousness, bathed in the light of the now "brilliant full moon," surfaces to present reality:

> Sigbjørn lay there with the moonlight of a month later streaming in upon him. Gradually he became aware that he was half dreaming, and at the same time that he actually was in Cuernavaca itself. Quauhnahuac! (113)

The significance of the lunar eclipse becomes clear through reference to Keats' *Endymion* in the dream bridge:

> *The moon sleeps with Endymion.... Thus, whilst Endymion is given an opportunity of rising out of his own fatal self-absorption to help*

another, the fate of Glaucus throws additional light upon the problem, which is before Keats's mind all through the poem, the relation of love in its different forms to higher ambitions of the soul. . . . La Luna ilumina la noche. Enfolded by her light he slid swiftly with her once more into total eclipse. Then the horrible shadow of the earth fell over her. (113)

Endymion, the leader of his people, falls into lassitude and undertakes a journey through heaven and the underworld in search of the ideal. His mystical voyage begins as he falls asleep, and it develops through a "dream within dream" technique until the quest ends with Endymion realizing that only through the real can mankind approach the ideal. The moon (Cynthia), symbol of ideal beauty in nature, art, and life in Keats' poem, has also been Endymion's first love, and for Keats, "the horrible shadow of the earth" blotting out the moon's light would suggest the destruction of the ideal by gross reality.[6] In Lowry's terms, the eclipse symbolizes annihilation of the future, of creativity, of life itself, by the dark ominous shadow of the past. Significantly, however, for Sigbjørn and his Cynthia, "the moonlight streaming in upon him" heralds the return to waking reality. The eclipse is over, the past finished — at least in terms of the five dream chapters.

A further temporal and spatial convolution in the structure of *Dark as the Grave* occurs in chapter 3. In a dream within a dream paralleling *Endymion*, Sigbjørn imagines himself to be a wife-slayer being flown over the border to face punishment in Vancouver (53-55). Although its relevance remains vague, the dream is a deliberate Dunnian attempt to create different time levels in serial containment: "It was as if, and this was to happen with the experience itself, he had opened his eyes upon another reality" (53). The dream in chapter 3 is contained within the larger dream of chapters 1 to 5 which in turn is contained within one night in Cuernavaca. That night itself is contained within the fiction/ life of Sigbjørn Wilderness.

The dream within a dream mechanism supports the overall circling structure of chapters 1 to 5; from one point in time and space Sigbjørn circles through his past and returns to the present.[7] Lowry conveys necessary exposition through the dream and also captures the present force of the past which is so crucial to *Dark as the Grave*. Furthermore, the serial containment of the first five chapters creates a sensation of paralysis which parallels that of the plane trip to Mexico when Sigbjørn is motionless, enclosed within the moving plane. Clearly, chapters 1 to 5, far from being linear, suggest the convoluted nature of Sigbjørn's mind and the plane trip to Mexico is a *mental* voyage where "the sense at once of descent, tremendous regression, and of moving, not moving" (1) suggests the stasis of an inner, surreal landscape.

Chapters 7 and 8 are the least artistically transformed and the weakest chapters in the book. Sigbjørn's lumbering monologues in 7 require prior knowledge of *Under the Volcano* to be fully comprehensible, and two characters, Eddie and

Dr. Hippolyte, remain undeveloped and irrelevant. The important point about both chapters, however, is that Sigbjørn is now awake in the present and in a specific place. It becomes possible to move either into the future or deeper into the past; he does both, of course, the trip to Oaxaca signifiying simultaneous movement into past and future. Chapter 7 ends on a symbolic note: cathedral bells ring for matins — "it was the madrugada, the hour of dawn, the last hours of the condemned" (159) — while Sigbjørn stands at a threshold or border, on the other side of which lies his future and his past.

Chapter 8 is Sigbjørn's "madrugada." Standing motionless beside his sleeping wife, he recalls their weeks in Mexico during which he "had found it more and more difficult to move at all" (162). He thinks of his withdrawal into self as a kind of stasis:

> Even as the garbage would, Sigbjørn found himself sinking more and more into fear, into a barranca, his own, a barranca of fear of he knew not what! Ah, the strangeness of Mexico, and this fear that possesses one like a paralysis — (164)

> And yet, while Primrose was being renewed again, Sigbjørn seemed to see nothing, to love nothing, to sway away from her into some anguish of the past, into some agony of self, chained by fear, wrapped in the tentacles of the past, like some gloomy Laocoön. (165)

Because he is not yet ready to break lose from his spiritual and physical bonds with a trip to Oaxaca, Sigbjørn's memories of their New Year's Eve trip to Yautepec flood over him (167-86), creating another loop in the narrative. That trip had been a disaster culminating in the arrival of the publisher's letter questioning the value of his novel, and consequently, his effort to be reborn on the last day of the old year, like all previous attempts to rebuild, had resulted in yet another backward swing of the pendulum.

Looking back on the Yautepec trip, Sigbjørn discovers the reason for his failure:

> Actually this was the first trip they had made north, back in the direction of Mexico City, by extension, of Canada. All their other trips were still south, still *toward* their destination, whether Oaxaca or Acapulco. . . . [I]t was curious how this little trip had seemed to illustrate how dangerous or even impossible this turning back was, until at least whatever strange discords had been set playing by the original error, inherent in his return to Mexico at all, had been somehow resolved. . . . But come what might there was no return yet, and this is what this little day seemed to have to tell them. (185-86)

"No return yet." As in "La Mordida," Sigbjørn's return must be further into the past if it is to be propitious.

Chapters 9 to 12 describe the journey into the past-future of Oaxaca. This trip represents the beginning of movement for Sigbjørn, who finally breaks out of the enclosing mental world of chapters 1 to 8: "His getting up, as it were, symbolized the struggle between life and death to him" (191). Another Lowry bus ride brings the couple to Oaxaca where they stay in the hotel "La Luna." (Evil associations of this hotel from Sigbjørn's past are balanced by its name, for the moon has already been established as a good omen.) Here Sigbjørn meets Stanford, a representative of "the past and the difficulty of transcending it" (219), and he learns that Fernando, the friend whom he had ostensibly returned to Mexico to find, has been dead for six years: "MURIÓ IN VILLAHERMOSA"—dead in the beautiful city. Stanford's role is undeveloped, but the discovery of Fernando's death clearly releases Sigbjørn from his fatal attachment to the past. It is now possible for him to believe in a future.

Despite his absence, Fernando is an important force in the novel. Like Stanford, he represents the past, but for very different reasons. Sigbjørn, who suffers from such paralysing fear of the present and future, has been encouraged by happy memories to withdraw into the past he had once shared with his Mexican friend. The relationship between the two men, however, had been still more complex because Fernando became an integral part of Sigbjørn through their shared experiences and through Sigbjørn's book. He has therefore represented both Sigbjørn's past and a character in the book about the past. Furthermore, his murder uncannily parallels the murder of the hero in Sigbjørn's book. Given Sigbjørn's belief in the contiguity of life and art and his feeling that he is a character in his own book, it is not difficult to appreciate the magnetic power that Fernando has held over him, but the discovery and acceptance of Fernando's death allows Sigbjørn to bury his obsession with the past and enables the goodness that Fernando represented to be released in the present. As a rider for the Banco Ejidal, he had been devoted to enriching the land in Mexico,[8] and at the end of his Oaxaca journey Sigbjørn understands that Fernando lives on in the renewed fruitfulness of the valley of Etla: "The Banco Ejidal had become a garden" (255). The implication is that Sigbjørn's life will flower like Oaxaca; the past will sustain, instead of engulfing, the present. The journey to Mexico has become a last rite for the past, and the visit to the Milta tombs completes Sigbjørn's symbolic death.

Chapter 12 which follows the discovery of Fernando's death, is poorly controlled. Sigbjørn and Primrose visit the tombs of Mitla, walk through the early morning streets of Oaxaca, visit the Church of the Soledad, and begin the trip back to Cuernavaca. This time they travel on the first northward stage of their voyage home. For the moment, at least, Sigbjørn is released from the need to "traverse this route many, many times again, backward and forward" (96). Now he can cross the state borders of Mexico with hope; the journey into the past has become a journey into the future. Despite its meanderings, the general direction of chapter 12 in relation to the book is clear. *Dark as the Grave* does not have a circular structure like *Under the Volcano*. Instead its open-ended structure suggests movement into the future.

Because of the emphasis on themes of pilgrimage and return, Lowry's characters again bear slight resemblance to realistic novel characters, but, unfortunately, they are much less interesting than the characters in *Volcano* and *October Ferry*. Sigbjørn represents the artist or, more generally, the imagination, and Lowry wanted to present Sigbjørn's perceptions of life "*without* the novelist's touch, as a human being ... really sees them" ("WP," 8). Sigbjørn, however, lacks the powers of observation and curiosity associated with an artist. Instead he depends increasingly on alcohol and on Primrose, whom Lowry envisioned as an Yvonne without the sense of guilt: "she is an extremely important and attractive character, and a more creative one ... than her husband" ("WP," 9). Throughout her "unconscious quest for a faith," she was to reveal "gaiety, intelligence, courage, and innocence." Despite Lowry's good intentions, his women are never deeply interesting, and Primrose appears the silliest and slightest of them all.

Lowry's use of symbol is much more successful, particularly in the case of the border, circle, and cross. The border is a versatile symbol representing a barrier, if one is stopped, or a point of passage into another level of time, space, or consciousness. Facing, Janus-like, in two directions at once, the border is both obstacle and entrance, the way up or the way down, all in one. Of course, border towns such as El Paso (the pass), a point of ingress or egress, are precisely what the Consul lacked.

Lowry develops the border symbol through associated images of thresholds, crossings, movement, and stasis. Throughout the book the characters constantly cross national and state borders thereby triggering Sigbjørn's memories of his deportation over the Mexican border and of his refusal of entry into the United States. The movement of the narrative parallels his crossing of the borders of time, from the present into the past and finally into the future, and he frequently crosses borders or "thresholds" from one level of consciousness to another, hovering in chapter 6 on the borderline between dream and waking. This achievement of a waking state is perhaps the most important border-crossing in the novel because he then crosses from a state of withdrawal into a present where a future also becomes possible.

The most interesting use of the border image occurs in chapter 1 when Sigbjørn broods upon his refusal of entry, years before, at the border town of Blaine.[9] As the plane approaches Los Angeles, the scene of his meeting with Primrose and his destination when he had been turned back at the American border, he recalls his poem commemorating the mishap:

Sigbjørn remembered that he had wanted to give the impression of the bus going one way, toward the border and the future, and, at the same time, of the shopwindows and streets flashing by into the past: he had wished to do that, but something more: since the poem was to be about his being turned *back* at the border, these shop windows and streets that he was so glibly imagining in the past were in the future too, for tonight and at the end of the poem he would have to return *from* the border by a similar bus along exactly the same route, that is, in both an opposite direction, and an opposite mood. (17).

Only part of the first stanza of "The Canadian Turned Back at the Border" appears in *Dark as the Grave* (16), but the significance of the eight-stanza poem lies in the way it reflects the voyage of Sigbjørn's mind into the past-as-future, which is the theme of both the poem and the novel. The unpublished seventh stanza of the poem emphasizes the dual nature of this voyage:

The packed bus that brought me back glared and stunk
Of beer, chiefly mine, in vaporous quarts.
But chaos caught me in the suction
Of a roaring parallel darkness, now
Stabbed with landmarks in the wet night, none quite
Verified, all of a heartbreak flowing
Past lovers united on bill boards, through
The crash—sigh—of juggernauts borderward,
And the grinding of hypocrites voices,
And the mind jammed in reverse forever. (14:19, 23-24)

"The mind jammed in reverse" aptly summarizes the first five chapters of *Dark as the Grave*. Indeed, the entire Mexican journey is a regression, a journey into the past, a descent into self, and unless Sigbjørn can overcome the "forever" in his poem and somehow cross a border into a new world, he will be trapped within "the suction of a roaring parallel darkness." The most difficult border to cross, in the poem as in the novel, is the border of the mind isolating Sigbjørn from communication with others. As in *Under the Volcano*, the protagonist becomes trapped within the circle of self.

In all Lowry's fiction, the circle with its threat of containment plays an important symbolic role, but in *Dark as the Grave* the circle is an entirely negative symbol, especially in the first five chapters which constitute a miniature serial universe of enclosures. During the stay in Mexico City, Sigbjørn finds himself enclosed in a hotel room whose windows will not open (77), and later, when he enters the underground Bach café

it was much as if by so entering the past, he had stumbled into a labyrinth, with no thread to guide him, where the minotaur threatened at every step, and which was moreover a labyrinth that now at each turn led infallibly to a precipice. (80)

Futhermore, in *Dark as the Grave,* as in *Under the Volcano* and *October Ferry,* the reader finds himself on another Lowry bus ride with "weary circling" to signify Sigbjørn's passivity: "for there was something in his nature that loathed to break the rhythm; only more than stopping at all did he hate to move on, lulled into a certain mood" (98). And as this passage suggests, it is his state of mind which determines whether the Lowry protagonist will respond with joy or hatred to the repetitive circling and the serial order of the universe.

The sidetrip from Mexico City to the Guadalupe Basilica prefigures Sigbjørn's later dilemma in Cuernavaca. The square in front of the Basilica contains merry-go-rounds and sideshows in preparation for a carnival, and amidst this "tumultuous scene," Sigbjørn has "the feeling of definite pilgrimage toward the Basilica, and yet the virtual impossibility of moving a step, or one found that one was only going round and round the square" (101)—squaring the circle. The Bishop, attempting to speak over the noise, reminds Sigbjørn of Mann's Mynheer Peeperkorn pronouncing an "encyclical to a closed order" (101). That Sigbjørn is re-living these past events in a dream constitutes a further involution.

In chapter 12, Mitla, the site of prehistoric tombs, powerfully symbolizes the dangers of encircling space. Mysterious Mitla, place of sorrow, burial ground, image of death, represents the very depths of the past and the finality of containment. While exploring subterranean vaults, Sigbjørn suddenly realizes "that this was what he was doing in Mexico: was it not for him too a sort of withdrawal into the tomb?" (249) At the entrance to one tomb stands the "Column of Death" which captures his attention because, according to legend, "if one embraced the Column of Death, the number of fingers that could be placed in the space between the hands denoted the number of years the person embracing the stone would live" (247). The oracular column, itself a cylinder, announces death when encircled, and Sigbjørn fears that despite his refusal to consult the column, his death is nevertheless within it.

As Sigbjørn meditates on the significance of Mitla, he realizes that he has "withdrawn into a daydream," a daydream "framed as it were in yet another withdrawal, by the cinema" (248). Interestingly, the film Sigbjørn remembers is Epstein's brilliant *Fall of the House of Usher* (1928) in which Usher is a possessed artist mysteriously destroying his wife by painting her portrait. In *Dark as the Grave* and the film, life and art bear a terrifying intimate interrelationship. The most important aspect of the film to Sigbjørn's mind, however, is the hopeful ending imposed on Poe's gruesome material.[10] At the end of the film, a brilliant cross-shaped tree of stars sprouts from the crumbling house to suggest that horror and evil have given way to faith, beauty, and peace: apparent disaster becomes triumph. Sigbjørn wonders if he is the director of the film of his own life and if he can, like Epstein, impose a happy ending.

The Mitla tombs are cruciform, and the cross is another major symbol in *Dark in the Grave*. Like the circle, the ancient symbol of the cross expresses a mystical and metaphysical truth in spatial terms. Although less well developed than the circle, the cross imagery is important, not only because it recalls Dana's cross in *Ultramarine* and foreshadows the crossroads in Ethan Llewelyn's life, but also because it evokes the Christian cross with its associations of death and resurrection, it suggests the Southern Cross of the heavens, and it is the only thing upon which Sigbjørn can focus during the flight from Vancouver to El Paso—"the moving shadow of the plane below them, the eternal moving cross" (1). The irony at this stage is that Sigbjørn, as yet unable to understand the meaning of the "eternal moving cross," finds solace in his condition of physical and spiritual stasis. However, in a more positive sense this vision of the cross during his dream prefigures the later resolution of chapter 12.

Finally, the cross represents a turning point or crossroads in Sigbjørn's life, and for this association Lowry drew upon his knowledge of Voodoo in which the crossroads is a central metaphor. Although the extent of Lowry's understanding is debatable, he certainly had some acquaintance with it.[11] The manuscripts indicate that Lowry planned to expand the character of Dr. Hippolyte, who describes Sigbjørn's problem in terms of Voodoo:

> In Voodoo, there is a great lesson. There is discipline. The dancers do not leave the blazing circle. If you like to call it neuroses that they get rid of then that is what they do. And even if the priest becomes possessed, the ceremony goes on. A bell is rung when it has reached a certain point beyond which it might become dangerous. You have to be your own priest and ring your own bell. . . . You are possessed too, you are possessed by Sigbjørn Wilderness. (151-52)

Within the "blazing circle" the celebrants become possessed by the "loas" or Gods, and the cross, representing the intersection of the physical and metaphysical orders, is symbolically located within the circle.

In *Divine Horseman: The Living Gods of Haiti,* Maya Deren describes the importance of the cross in Voodoo cosmography:

> The metaphor for the mirror's depth is the cross-roads; the symbol is the cross. For the Haitian this figure is not only symbolic of the totality of the earth's surface as comprehended in the extension of the cardinal points on a horizontal plane. It is, above all, a figure for the intersection of the horizontal plane, which is this mortal world, by the vertical plane, the metaphysical axis, which plunges into the mirror. The cross-roads . . . is the point of access to the world of les Invisibles.[12]

The crossroads as a point of intersection between physical and metaphysical worlds is, of necessity, the point of access, of ingress and egress, the juncture for communication between mortal and spiritual realms. The cross is the way out of the circle; it is, as Lowry says, "the eternal moving cross." Sigbjørn's inertia can be overcome through the Voodoo ritual of the cross because this cross is a dynamic symbol of time and space, including on its vertical axis all time, on its horizontal, all space.[13]

As he explores the tombs of Mitla, Sigbjørn wonders: "Cruciform tombs. Cruciform tombs—Christ—what was this strange persistence of this symbol? What was the real significance of the cross?" (248) The cross symbolizes hope and the rich multiplicity of the world, a world that unites Christian death and resurrection with the dynamic vitalism of Voodoo. Furthermore, the positive cross imagery balances the negative circle imagery: both are necessary, but the cross represents a way out of the infernal, closed circle into renewed voyaging.

In *Dark as the Grave Wherein My Friend Is Laid*, the obstacle of the border and the closed world of the circle give way to the power of the "moving cross," symbol of intersection and communication. To an extent, Lowry did succeed in shaping the narrative of *Dark as the Grave* because the structure of the novel (like its position within the "Voyage") can be compared with that of the cross-roads: the dream chapters 1 to 5 provide the dimension of space in which all constructive movement ceases, and chapters 6 to 12 provide the dimension of time, for in chapter 6 time and Sigbjørn's life at last begin to move.

Dark as the Grave signals a spiritual advance on *Under the Volcano* because it marks a point of return within the withdrawal-return rhythm of "The Voyage That Never Ends." In a moment of illumination recalling similar images in *Volcano*, Sigbjørn envisions the human mind and soul as the city of Oaxaca:

> Ah, these walled closed streets of Oaxaca that did not give out their life at all, these blank thick-walled cantinas behind which lurked such deepness, such complexity, such beauty of patios and sawdust rooms when you entered them, depth beyond depth, those barred prison windows, and huge worn wooden doors through which how occasionally you would see some enchanting vista of stone courtyards, arches, and gardens—what was all this an image of? It was not enough to ask. Did not men too have such walled closed streets, such hidden gallantries, such concealed gardens and cloisters and misericordes, and rooms wherein took place such invisible debauches? What soul, moreover, did not have its invisible Farolito, where it drank itself to awareness in the dead watches of the night? And here was the Church of the Soledad, of the Virgin for those who have nobody them with. (253)

Sigbjørn has visited the depths of his own mind; he has wandered through the labyrinthine rooms, with "barred prison windows," of his own soul. He has withdrawn into the circle of the past, understood and accepted it, and returned, crossing the borders of "the state of Oaxaca"—the state of the soul—into the future.

5

Beginning Yet Again:
October Ferry to Gabriola

October Ferry to Gabriola represents Margerie Lowry's editing of a work-in-progress, but although the text is unfinished and there are undeveloped aspects of the writing, *October Ferry* is by no means a raw effort. The novel functions very well and is a rich, often moving work which, together with "The Forest Path to the Spring," presents Lowry's most sustained vision of paradise.[1]

Lowry began work on the *October Ferry* theme shortly after a 1946 trip to the British Columbia gulf island of Gabriola when he and Margerie joined forces to write a short story (20:1) based on the trip. Dissatisfied, Lowry put the story aside, but interestingly enough, the twenty-eight-page story contains the narrative scaffolding of the novel to come. The bus, the level-crossing, the bastion hiding the Gabriola ferry, the beer parlour, Mrs. Neiman, and the return to the dock— each element is present in miniature. Most notably, the twilight approach to the island, with its hopeful swinging lantern and welcoming voice, persists from this first attempt through later reworking of the material.

Lowry began working in earnest on the Gabriola theme in 1950 (*Selected Letters*, 216), and by late 1951 he believed the novella to be "a hell of a fine thing." By 1953 he was obsessed and delighted by *October Ferry*, which was threatening to become a novel, though still closely related to companion stories in *Hear Us O Lord*. As the novel grew it severed its close relationship with the stories in *Hear Us O Lord*; however, both books deal with the return from withdrawal to a state of balance. Along with "The Bravest Boat," "Present Estate of Pompeii," "Gin and Goldenrod," and "The Forest Path to the Spring," *October Ferry* grows out of Lowry's profound, almost symbiotic, relationship with the British Columbia coast. In December, 1956, Lowry wrote to David Markson that he was "working like absolute sin on *Gabriola* with which I have completely fallen in love" (*Selected Letters,* 394). Lowry's destructive love-affair with the novel arose perhaps, as he himself suggested, from some "fanatical narcissism or other that makes me set the touchstone impossibly high, as a result of which I am now writing a huge and sad novel about Burrard Inlet called *October Ferry to Gabriola*" (*Selected Letters,* 409).

October Ferry to Gabriola is the superficially simple story of the search of a husband and wife for a new house because they face eviction from a much beloved fore-shore cabin on Eridanus Inlet; however, what Lowry means by eviction, secular and divine, not to mention the significance of the new house (their fourth), is not simple. The theme of eviction and the search for a new house, combined with the protagonist's problems of guilt, fear, and hatred, become increasingly important as the book proceeds. The story covers approximately twelve hours of the day on which Ethan Llewelyn (a semi-retired lawyer whose name means "of strength unknown") and Jacqueline travel from Victoria to Nanaimo by bus, wait in Nanaimo for the Gabriola ferry, and then leave on the ferry for the gulf island. This simple immediate level, however, acquires increasing complexity and significance through the consciousness of Ethan, who spends the first part of the day reliving his past, including his boyhood in England, his courtship and marriage in Ontario, the burning of a second house in Niagara-on-the-Lake, and the finding of a third home in British Columbia. Using Ethan's memory, Lowry condenses considerable time and space into the present three or four hours spent on the bus and thereby incorporates the necessary background exposition and, more important, dramatizes the presentness of the past.

Two insufficiently developed subjects counterpoint the main theme of eviction and search. Throughout, Ethan suffers paralysing guilt over the suicide of a university friend, Peter Cordwainer—a subject which had long haunted Lowry himself, as is clear from his plans for the "Ordeal" and *Lunar Caustic* (both discussed in chapter 1). Lowry has Cordwainer follow Ethan from England to British Columbia in the guise of billboards advertising the Cordwainer Industries' product: "Mother Gettle's Kettle Simmered Soups." In addition, Ethan is tormented by the case of a fifteen-year-old Vancouver boy sentenced to hang for murder. Despite his horror at society's condemnation, Ethan finds that he is unable to defend the Chapman boy.

October Ferry portrays the ordeal of life in terms of the usual Lowry predicament. Ethan, who has withdrawn from civilization, is in danger lest his "retreat" become totally atavistic. During the long bus ride, which occupies two-thirds of the book, he withdraws simultaneously into his own guilt-ridden consciousness and into his past. His perception of reality, like the Consul's, grows increasingly distorted; the landscape bristles with symbols, signs threaten, snatches of overheard conversation are strange messages for him, and films appear to mirror and comment upon his life. Ethan has been a sailor and a musician, and like similar Lowry heroes, he is also divided against himself. Thus, Lowry refers to Poe and to the film *The Student of Prague* in order to suggest the disturbing presence of a *Doppelgänger* in Ethan's life, and even the opening quote from George Eliot reminds the reader that when men sell their souls to the devil, "there is a dark shadow beside them for evermore." Again, as in the previous novels, the Lowry protagonist is outward bound: "beginning: beginning: beginning again; beginning yet again" (5), and *October Ferry* can best be understood, thematically and technically, in terms of Lowry's obsession with movement and growth. Eridanus represents the past and the necessity to move on, to begin again; Gabriola symbolizes the future.

Although there is no magnificent "Apologia" for *October Ferry* as there is for *Under the Volcano,* Lowry did write Albert Erskine about his plans. This unpublished letter from December 1953 (3:6, 1-4) contains his most detailed extant analysis of the book. He wrote the letter to Erskine shortly before departing on a visit to his friends, the Neilsons, on Bowen Island—"a December Ferry to Bowen Island"—and his comments are typically wayward and amusing. At this point, he was nearing completion of a final draft, but if Day's interpretation of the following months is accurate (see Day, 431-37), Erskine was far from reassured by his claims. Lowry, however, was optimistic:

> As for where the story's going there is an excellent and sinister reason for its apparent inability to move into the future: it turns out that both characters are potential suicides. Each has also become afraid that in a fit of hysteria or drunkenness one may murder the other. Thus the difficulty of the future taking any shape at all, as of the present having any meaning for the protagonists, is really the whole plot. They have more trouble getting to Gabriola than K to the castle though Gabriola is not a castellan symbol; it *is,* finally, the future. (3:6, 1)

Lowry found writing *October Ferry* especially difficult: "[I]t has cost me more pains than all the *Volcano* put together" (*Selected Letters,* 334), and toward the end of his life he felt that it had become a "challenge" to his personal salvation. The published letters, especially from 1953, contain many references to his plans for the book. For example, in another letter to Erskine, he compares the form of the novel to a triangle:

> You will be wondering at the length of this first chapter too . . . so I will expound thus far the magic of Dr. Lowry's dialectical-Hegelian-spiritualism-Cabbalistic-Swedenborgian-conservative-Christian-anarchism for ailing

paranoiacs: the first chapter . . . is as the base to a triangle or a triad (and/or a radical having a valence of three): viz

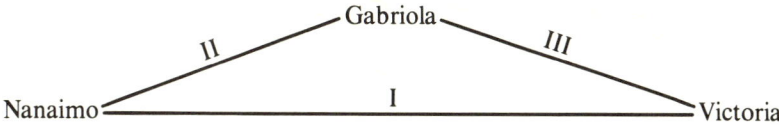

Which is meant to illustrate no more than that Chapter I might be 180 pages long, Chapters II and III each half that length, without its form being overbalanced—to the contrary. (*Selected Letters,* 346)

This concept of a "triangle or a triad" is crucial to an understanding of the novel's structure as well as to an appreciation of the Cabbalistic ordeal of the protagonist, which is discussed further below. Lowry goes on to assure Erskine that the repetitions of the first part of the narrative are meant "to give the effect of the man *caught,* washed to and fro in the tides of his mind, unable to escape."

In the unpublished letter to Erskine, Lowry again explains the structure of this book. The three chapters of *October Ferry* have now become three "parts":

> However I'm only equipped to write all this: not to describe it. I believe it to be bloody good and that it gets better. But it's not intended to fall into any particular category or obey any of the normal rules of a novel. The second part of the book concerns their difficulty in finding the ferry and takes place in Nanaimo, mostly in a pub, where Ethan gets pretty tight; there are powerful dramatic scenes (though I sez it) in Nanaimo both in the present and the past: a scene of lyrical beauty is balanced against a Grand Guignol horror that takes place on the scaffold. (A waiter turns out to be a man Ethan's saved.) The third part is on board the ferry itself. (3:6, 1)

The triangle or triad represents the structure of *October Ferry* to the same extent that the circle denotes the *Volcano.* The number three appears throughout the text: the Llewelyns have had three houses, and with Tommy they form a family of three. The three parts of the book correspond to the three temporal dimensions (past, present, and future) as well as to the elements of fire, earth, and water. During the bus ride Ethan broods about fire, in Nanaimo he is on *terra firma,* and on the ferry he is surrounded by water. The fourth element, air, is present throughout—rushing past the bus and ferry, through Ethan's soul, and through his own personal "Cave of Winds." The protagonist sits, talks, and thinks within three specific spaces—the bus, the Ocean Spray Bar, and the ferry. There are three bars in the book, and in the third Ethan reflects upon the way the partitions can be moved in order to expand the men's side:

> These partitions were usually movable, for at crowded hours the Men's side was much fuller than the Ladies and Escorts: the partition would thus often be found slowly moving in on the territory of the latter, producing, sometimes, if you were obliged to leave your lady for several minutes, on your return a certain eerie feeling of perichoresis. An isolation that was, at the same time, begotten by an interpenetration. (251)

"Perichoresis" literally means the act of going around, rotation, and there is a great deal of literal perichoresis in *October Ferry*. However, it is also a theological term for the unity of the divine trinity through interpenetration,[2] a point Ethan notes when, catching sight of the astrological magazines by the Nanaimo dock, he contemplates "the duplication of the cube, or the trisection of the right angle, not to say the Symbol of the Divine Trinity in Unity" (233). Lowry delighted in unusual words like this which hold such different meanings and belong in such different contexts but at the same time can be forced, as in this passage, to *mean* both things at the same time. Here Ethan's immediate context of "movable" partitions and an "isolation" which is paradoxically "interpenetration" contribute to Lowry's particular sense of "perichoresis" as a spiritual unity somehow discoverable in circular movement.

Lowry found the triangle a useful structural paradigm for *October Ferry* because of its versatility and all-inclusiveness. Geographically, it represents the Llewelyn's voyage:

> For they had been travelling as it were along the upended base of a triangle of which Eridanus itself on the mainland could roughly be considered the apex. (153)

Spiritually, it indicates the result of their voyage; not only may they find the Divine Trinity in Unity, but they may also anneal their little secular family of three and achieve the social unity which William Plantagenet and Geoffrey Firmin lack. Most important, the triangle or triad is, together with the circle, the main structural element of Achad's Tree of Life. According to Achad, the Tree of Life is composed of a "Trinity of Triads," with the second and third triads derived from the first by reflection to form a balance.

The Cabbala is far from the only influence upon Lowry's novel, but it is significant that Achad's *Q.B.L.* was one of the few books that Lowry asked specially to have sent to him in 1956 (*Selected Letters,* 387).[3] The Cabbala with its "method of thought" is important to the epistemology of the book, and in addition to the figure of the McCandless, who is a Cabbalist, the text contains many images drawn from Achad's studies. The noteworthy point about the "Trinity of Triads" in the *Q.B.L.* is that it represents a path or a way, a method, in fact, for the adept to achieve balance. By progressing from one triad or level to the next, the adept gradually attains inner balance, wisdom, harmony, or, if you will, God. The three triads are contained in the fourth level of the Tree, the tenth *Sephira* called "Malkuth," or "The Kingdom":

> Finally, this TRINITY OF TRIADS being in itself a UNITY is Symbolized by the TENTH SEPHIRA called MALKUTH, THE KINGDOM, a SINGLE SPHERE pendant to the above and summing up in itself all the foregoing qualities which it MANIFESTS according to the Creative Plan. All these qualities may be said to be Potentially inherent in KETHER The Crown—with which MALKUTH is, in a certain Mystical sense, ONE, as it is written: "Kether is in Malkuth and Malkuth is in Kether but after another manner." (*Q.B.L.*, 8-9. For Achad's diagram, see Figure 4, from *Q.B.L.*)

As Lowry himself emphasizes, there are three parts to *October Ferry*, and the Llewelyns are searching for their fourth home on Gabriola, which represents their salvation. Without forcing the novel into a constraining mould, it is possible to see the three parts of *October Ferry* as parallel with the "Trinity of Triads" in Achad's Tree of Life. The fourth house on Gabriola, which they have such difficulty in reaching, parallels "Malkuth," "The Kingdom"—the Divine Trinity in Unity. Each of the three stages of the journey on bus, land, and ferry represents a stage in the ordeal, and the arrival at Gabriola symbolizes Ethan's attainment of balance, his self-unification.

Certainly, Achad's system offers rich metaphoric possibilities. His Tree of Life embodies constant movement and expansion and is thus an image of time as flowing and creative and of space as never enclosing or stopping this flow of life. In *The Anatomy of the Body of God*, for example, Achad explains that the Tree of Life is

> not a fixed design but capable of indefinite progression towards the Infinitely Small or the Infinitely Great. For it can be so drawn that it appears with all its details and properties, repeating themselves in every direction of Space to Infinity. (12)

Similarly, the three parts of *October Ferry* flow and expand, each mirroring and reflecting the other through Lowry's brilliant use of image, motif, and allusion, and equally important, Ethan perceives the nature of reality in precisely Achad's terms:

> All at once, without knowing why, he felt as if he were seated at the center of the infinite itself, then, that this was indeed true, that the center of the infinite was everywhere, just as its circumference must be nowhere. Everything seemed part of a miraculous plan, in which nothing stood still, everything good was capable of infinite development, everything evil must inevitably deteriorate. (224)

Q. B. L. OR THE BRIDE'S RECEPTION

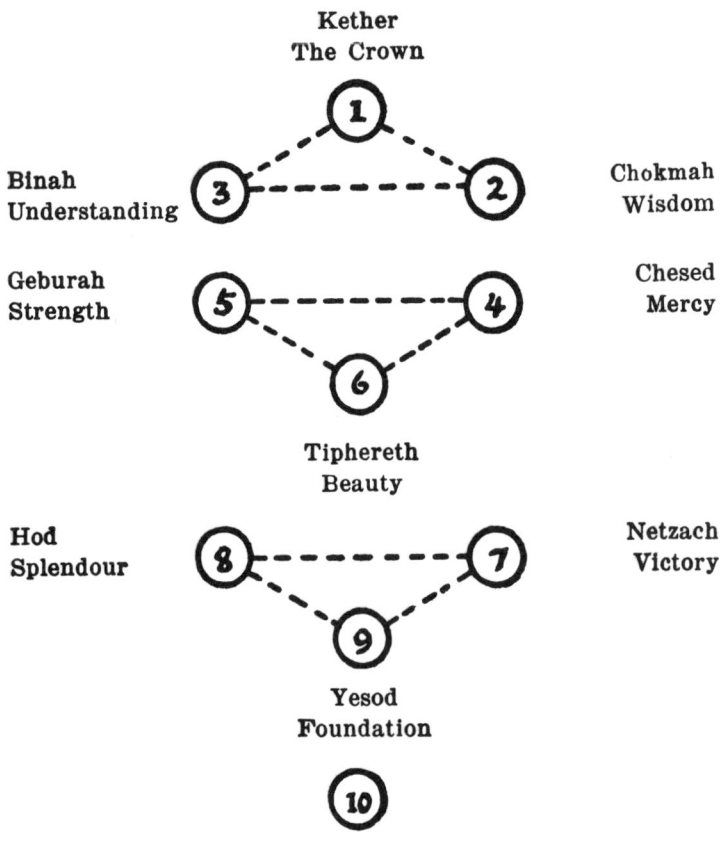

Fig. 4

This shows clearly the TRINITY of TRIADS with MALKUTH pendant to them, manifesting their Influence in the Material Universe.

Although the entire time span of *October Ferry*'s tripartite structure is approximately twelve hours, Lowry expands the few hours on the bus to include the thirty-nine years of Ethan's life through a further structural division of the first part of the text into another triad. Thus, part one of *October Ferry* presents three distinct time loops within Ethan's mind: the first loop includes chapters 1 to 10, the second chapters 11 to 21, and the third chapters 22 to 27.

Each of these loops develops a period from the past which Ethan is, in fact, reliving. The first loop consists of Jacqueline's and Ethan's earlier years, as well as their courtship and marriage. Here Lowry introduces details of Jacqueline's birth, her mother's suicide, her father's beliefs, and important information from Ethan's past. The Cordwainer theme is also initiated and the significance of the films, especially *Outward Bound,* is dramatically established.

In the second time loop, Ethan's mind travels over the early years of his marriage, the birth of his son Tommy, and, most important, the burning of his second home. As Ethan moves closer to the surface of the present, he plunges deeper into despair and fear. Fire and loss, which threaten the sanity of both characters as well as their marriage, dominate the Niagara-on-the-Lake period. In this time loop, Lowry counterpoints a film of Temple Thurston's, *The Wandering Jew,* with an account of Thurston's death by fire in order to explore the interpenetration of reality and illusion, life and art. Horrified by the intuition that life and art are contained in each other or that both are contained in some larger dimension of a serial universe, Ethan experiences a hellish "St. Paul's vision upside down" arising from "an almost complete and mysterious identification of subject with object" (146):

> Yet this [vision] seemed the home also of more conscious mental abortions and aberrations; of disastrous yet unfinished thoughts, half hopes and half intentions, and where precepts, long abandoned, stumbled on. Or the home of a half-burned man, himself an imperfect visualization, at the stake; this place where neither death nor suicide could ever be a solution, since nothing here had been sufficiently realized ever to possess life. (146)

Ethan's predicament parallels the Consul's. As he sits in this bar, he gradually loses all sense of separate identity or even reality.

The third time loop of the first part of *October Ferry* brings Ethan's consciousness to the most recent past, his life at Eridanus and the threat of eviction. Peter Cordwainer continues to haunt him as he becomes more and more certain that his life has been one long penance for Peter's death. Ethan, "bound to these thoughts like Ixion to his wheel" (192), sinks deeper and deeper into despair. To make matters worse, the apartment house where he and Jacqueline have stayed while searching for their fourth house turns out to have been an abortionist's clinic. As Ethan points out, they seem to be living in the world of Sartre's *No Exit* (198). The descent into the abyss of self reaches its climax as Ethan, his mind surfacing to a present in which he feels "strapped into his seat" (208), confronts his image, or perhaps his *Doppelgänger,* in the rear-view mirror of the bus:

> The face in the mirror, a half face, a mask, looked at him approvingly, smiling, but with a kind of half terror. Its lips silently formed the one word: Murderer! (216)

This expressionistic touch recalls Ethan's earlier memory of "the face of a sort of devil" that had confronted him in the mirror of a Niagara-on-the-Lake bar (47).

In each of his works Lowry employs complicated temporal involutions, and in *October Ferry,* as in *Dark as the Grave,* they intensify the protagonists' struggle to break free from the tentacles of the past. A sense of psychological time is suggested by these narrative loops, which contrast ironically with the relentless unilinear movement of the bus and of clock time. In this way, Lowry establishes the crucial rhythm of "the man *caught,* washed to and fro in the tides of his mind, unable to escape" (*Selected Letters,* 347). In each time loop Ethan's consciousness flows back and forth between present reality on the bus and the greater reality of his past. Lowry's intention was to suggest the flux and reflux of the tides, so that in chapter 13, "The Tides of Eridanus," Ethan would become aware of a "slow, stealthy, despairing *deepening* of the medium of his thoughts [which is] like a tide of Eridanus coming in" (76). With the steady advance of the second loop into the past, Ethan faces greater and more dangerous "snags":

> Now there was only this tide of his mind still rising, and deepening, reaching out toward those other grislier, more menacing timbers that were fears, anxieties, obsessions, horrors, it had not yet set afloat. (81)

In addition to establishing this tidal rhythm of the mind and introducing terrifying "snags" from the past, the temporal loops of this part of the narrative create the rhythm of withdrawal and return within *October Ferry,* as well as contributing to the larger pattern of the "Voyage" cycle. With each loop Ethan's thoughts are swept from brightness to a state of darkness, from communication with others to utter isolation, and with each, Ethan must begin again to confront the meaning of his past by moving deeper into an inner hell.

The second phase of *October Ferry* takes place in the present, beginning with the arrival of Jacqueline and Ethan in Nanaimo in chapter 28, "Wheel of Fire." The bus follows a hearse into the town, and this chapter, enclosed within the fiery wheel of Ethan's consciousness, prefigures his symbolic death and descent into hell in the Ocean Spray Bar. The bar in chapter 31, "Twilight of the Raven," with its "columns of mirrors, carefully designed to look broken, under a ceiling of dried blood," its light that turns the "denizens of the place into corpses," and its view-destroying glass of "a thick corrugated verdigris green" (25) portrays a closed, static hell:

> Though its boundaries seemed yet to be determined, if the purpose were not to leave them flexible as now, this newly renovated Men's section proper of the beer parlour appeared to be finished to the satisfaction of whatever inverted genius had created it. Finished. It was the end. (258)

The reality of present time and the sense of temporal flow fade as Ethan, trapped within the bar and his own tormented mind, presents his statement for the defence—the defence of Chapman and his self-defence. Chapter 31, in many ways the most powerful and extraordinary chapter in the novel, is reminiscent in its complicated richness and temporal stasis of chapter 10 in *Under the Volcano* and is discussed in greater detail below.

The third and final phase of the narrative begins with chapter 33 as Ethan and Jacqueline board the little ferry outward bound for Gabriola. At last, time regains reality as the ferry, not without a final setback, approaches the island amidst "a *boundless sense of space,* cleanliness, speed, light, and rocketing white gulls" (329 [italics added]). The boundlessness of space is crucial because, in Lowry's view, space with rigid bounds constricts and destroys. Only when boundaries are flexible and open to the flow of time are life and creativity possible. Although the return to Nanaimo threatens to cancel their hopes of reaching Gabriola, it proves to be a good omen. Someone throws the evening newspaper on board, and they learn of the reprieve from eviction which is essential to their victory in the future because it frees them from restrictions and entanglements in the past.

The novel closes with Ethan's vision of the approaching evening when he will walk along the shore of Gabriola with Jacqueline in "the moonlit, meteor-bright night" (331). This vision of the stars and moon, consistent Lowry symbols of life and hope, gives way to the present reality of Gabriola with its "sheltered valley that sloped down to a silent, calm harbour" (33). For the moment, Lowry's protagonist has achieved wisdom, balance, and a temporary point of rest.

Lowry establishes the conflict between motion and stasis, or time and space, in the opening paragraphs of the book where the prose reflects the poles of Ethan's experience: on the one hand, Ethan moves swiftly with the bus; on the other, he is immobilized, bound by his ticket. Lowry first accentuates the flow of his narrative before sharply disrupting this rhythm—but a long passage is necessary to illustrate his method:

> The October morning sunlight filled the swift bus, the Greyhound, sailing through the forest branches, singing straight out to sea, roaring toward the mountains, circling sudden precipices.

They followed the coastline. To the left was the forest; to the right, the sea, the Gulf.

And the light corruscated brilliantly from the windows in which the travelers saw themselves now on the right hand en-islanded in azure amid the scarlet and gold of mirrored maples, by these now strangely embowered upon the left hand among the islands of the Gulf of Georgia.

At times, when the Greyhound overtook and passed another car, where the road was narrow, the branches of the trees brushed the left-hand windows, and behind, or in the rearview mirror ahead reflecting the road endlessly enfilading in reverse, the foliage could be seen tossing for a while in a troubled gale at their passage. Again, in the distance, he would seem to see dogwood rocketing through the trees in a shower of white stars. And when they slowed down, the fallen leaves in the forest seemed to make even the ground glow and burn with light.

Downhill: and to the right hand beyond the blue sea, beneath the blue sky, the mountains on the British Columbian mainland traversed the horizon, and on that right side too, luminous, majestic, a snowy volcano of another country (it was Mount Baker over in America and ancient Ararat of the Squamish Indians) accompanied them, with a white distant persistence, and at a different speed, like a remote, unanchored Popocatepetl.

Name: Mr. and Mrs. Ethan Llewelyn   Seat No.   17
Address: c/o Mrs. Angela d'Arrivee   Northbound   X
           Gabriola Island, B.C.   Southbound
           Date: October 7, 1949

Important: to insure your return space on the Vancouver Island Limited register your ticket upon arrival at your destination.
Victoria   Duncan   Nanaimo

"Well, damn it," he said, "I don't think I'm going to."

"Not going to what, Ethan sweetheart?"

Ethan and Jacqueline sat, arm in arm, in the two back left-hand seats of the Greyhound and once when he saw their reflections in the window it struck him these were the reflections of some lucky strangers who looked too full of hope and excitement to talk.

"Register our tickets at the depot to insure return space. It seems to be tempting fate either way you look at it."

Jacqueline smiled at him with affection, absently, patting him on the knee, while Ethan regarded their ticket again.

Victoria . . . Duncan . . . *Nanaimo hath murdered sleep.*
And in Duncan too, the poor old English pensioners, bewhiskered, gaitered, standing motionless on street corners, dreaming of Mafeking or the fore-topgallant studding sail, or sitting motionless in the bankrupt rowing club, each one a Canute; golfing on the edge of the Gulf, riding to the fall of the pound; bereaved of their backwaters by rumors of boom. Evicted . . . But to be evicted out of exile: where then?
The bus changed gear, going up a hill: beginning: beginning: beginning again: beginning yet again: here we go, into the blue morning. (3-5)

The sentences describing the movement of the bus through the trees and morning light gradually become longer, then slightly shorter as the bus slows. Participial phrases and temporal clauses accumulate, frequently joined with conjunctions or adverbs and separated by commas. In this way, the sense of flow is established. Finally, with "downhill:" and the increased speed of the bus, the sentence opens out into a sweeping six-line description of sea, sky, and distant mountains.

Abruptly, this rhythm breaks. Time stops on the space of the printed page as the reader (and Ethan) confronts the bus ticket. The preceding sentences read beautifully aloud, but it is impossible to capture in spoken words the visual impact of the ticket with its oblong angular shape, categories, and spacing. The Llewelyns are objectified, distanced, isolated within the visual bounds of the ticket; their reduction to names and numbers robs them of individual identity. A major theme of *October Ferry* is the search for identity, and here Lowry skilfully introduces the quest through his style. Who are these people anyway? The black and white fact of the ticket offers no answer.

After the interruption of the ticket, dialogue begins and the focus narrows to the present of two passengers on the back seat within the bus. The sense of speed and movement has vanished, although the full irony of Ethan's refusal to tempt fate by insuring "return space" on the bus awaits future reversals for its full impact. Even the old pensioners, left behind in Duncan, stand or sit "motionless," their limbo projected in the cumulative adjectives and right-branching phrases which throw the sentence into reverse by drawing the reader back to the subject of this long sentence fragment. The disjunct verb "Evicted," the ellipsis, and the final question bring the sentence and the reader's attention to an abrupt halt, and not until the bus changes gear does the sensation of movement, at first jerky and tentative then more decisive, recommence.

Chapter 31, "Twilight of the Raven," like chapter 10 in *Under the Volcano,* marks the climax of horror in Ethan's struggle for balance as Lowry intensifies themes of eviction, guilt, and social responsibility through the fusion of external and internal reality within Ethan's troubled mind. While he sits in the bar, physical immobility paralleling spiritual paralysis, time seems to stretch and blur until he loses his grip on the present. A close examination of chapter 31 reveals how well Lowry uses narrative techniques to achieve his effects.

"Twilight of the Raven" (the title recalling Poe's nightmare poem "The Raven" and Wagner's *Gotterdämmerung*) takes place in the third bar. The fact that Ethan's visions occur in bars is important, for the bar is a place of secular and divine law, a place of judgment and prosecution, a place where the soul sits in judgment upon the excesses of the flesh. Furthermore, to Ethan's eyes, "life was like this bar, from which you could not see out" (263). Ethan's plight is intensified by the fact that he is breaking Canadian law as soon as Jacqueline leaves him sitting unaccompanied in the Ladies and Escorts. The waiter, who has just seen "the goddam inspector" (257), asks him to leave, so that Ethan, evicted from the room with a view, from communion with his wife, must sit in the infernal Men's bar where

> [t]he windows were either boarded up, like those of prisoners, he thought, in the citadel of Parma, against the view, or the glass was a thick corrugated verdigris green. (259)

Once in the Men's, Ethan is trapped "in a deliberately uncomfortable attitude he could not, for some reason, change" (260). Like Geoffrey, like all Lowry's heroes, Ethan the "misoneist" (199), or hater of change, becomes paralysed. Moreover, the lack of a view in this repulsive bar mirrors his own distorted, self-enclosed, destructive perception, and Ethan, in fact, describes the bar in expressionist terms:

> Considered as a painting, as a work of imagination . . . a modern master could scarcely have improved on it, for the room seemed to be the perfect outward expression of its own inner soul. (258)

Slowly, as Ethan becomes more and more enclosed by his distorted perception, external reality gives way to inner nightmare. "Sunrise! Twilight of the Dove" (255): the repetition of the phrase (263 and 264) enfolds the opening of the chapter into the inferno of Ethan's thoughts because "Sunrise," as well as signifying beauty and rebirth, is the time for hanging. At this point, rebirth merges with death as the negative associations of sunrise reflect back to cancel Ethan's earlier vision of an Eridanus sunrise. As is typical with Lowry, the interpretation of a sunrise depends upon point of view and ability to act; therefore, as Ethan's thoughts shift from "the delight of swimming at sunrise" (255) to "a thick morning mist . . . creeping out of the hollows into the prison cabbage patch" (264), he seems less and less able to transcend his abyss of self.

The sunrise of the condemned man ushers in one of the most gruesome passages in any of Lowry's works, as Ethan presents, "by prolepsis" (266), his arguments for the defence of young Chapman. Lowry's use of the term "prolepsis" is interesting. In rhetoric it refers to the anticipation of arguments or the setting forth in brief the details of what is to follow. The word also signifies, in a more literal sense, the taking of a future event as already existing. In this sense, "prolepsis" sums up aptly the temporal stasis of this chapter by suggesting the impossiblity of the flow of time into a future that already exists.

With the long quotation from *Demian,* it becomes evident that Ethan is defending himself as much as the Chapman boy. It is Ethan who is the murderer, and it is Ethan who is afraid to leave his "own lost Paradise, his own irrevocable past, in short that of Eridanus itself" (269). At this point accusatory voices take over, embodying simultaneously the most acute distortion of Ethan's consciousness and the truth itself. The chapter concludes with a chorus of past and present voices screaming at Ethan—voices from the bar, voices from the newspaper (Lowry collected newspaper clippings concerning the actual trial of a Vancouver boy), voices from his own divided consciousness:

"Save him!"
"Oh, shut up!"
"It's no good, this kind of life."
"But you, Ethan Llewelyn, what did you say? What did your able pen do, your pen more able than mine, or your still small voice, the one voice, the one pen still able to save him?"
"Hang him!"
"Hang him!"
"The appeal for clemency of Richard Chapman, the fifteen-year-old rapist has been refused by the Cabinet today. Richard must keep his date with the hangman next December thirteenth."
"Hang him!"
"Hang Ethan Llewelyn!" (271)

It is impossible in a short space to recapture the entire chapter with its many echoes from the rest of book, its refrains of reprieve, sunrise, scaffold, Dweller on the Threshold, and so on.[4] The chapter reflects, contains, and develops the two previous nightmare moments in bars. The essential function of the chapter, however, is to serve as a temporary stasis within the flux and reflux of the narrative. It is at this point, in the present, that Ethan experiences his most intense hell, for he is immobilized, trapped and surrounded by his own mind until he loses touch with physical reality. Here the rhythm established in part 1—the rhythm symbolized by the rising of the tides—breaks, in preparation for the gradual ebbing and creation of a new rhythm in part 3.

Lowry's use of specific techniques in *October Ferry,* if not as refined as in *Under the Volcano,* is nevertheless interesting. In addition to allusions, Lowry uses motifs, filmic devices, signs, newspapers, dialogue, visions, hymns, and several languages to support his expanding edifice. Even chapter headings serve specific purposes, counterpointing or balancing other chapters, commenting ironically upon chapter contents, stating and repeating themes, always forcing the reader to read reflexively.

Lowry's notes for *October Ferry* contain references to "visual Murnau-like" techniques, and he appears to have considered writing in terms of shots and cuts. In fact, films are of considerable significance in the text. Jacqueline and Ethan attend, or see signs for, more than a dozen old films, among them *The Student of Prague* (1926), *Looping the Loop* (1928), and *From Morn till Midnight* (1920). Griffith's *Isn't Life Wonderful* (1924) along with *Outward Bound* (1930) and *The Wandering Jew* (1933) provide three important allusions, and to Ethan, who sees life as "a sort of movie, or series of movies" (42), films are more "realistic" than novels because they create an illusion of motion (61). Lowry goes so far as to have Ethan search for faith in "the Faith Thriller at the Reel Pulpit" (273).

More than once, Ethan reflects on the interpenetration of life and art encountered in film:

> (and ah, the eerie significance of cinemas in our life, Ethan thought, as if they related to the afterlife, as if we knew, after we are dead, we would be conducted to a movie house where, only half to our surprise, is playing a film named: *The Ordeal of Ethan Llewelyn*, with Jacqueline Llewelyn). (26)

This is very much what happened in *Volcano,* chapters 2 to 12 of which can be seen as Jacques' film, "The Ordeal of Geoffrey Firmin." In a draft for a section of *October Ferry* entitled "Plato's cave," Lowry reflects on the "reality" of films. At first he thinks of cinemas as caves of illusion with the life at Eridanus as real. After leaving his cabin he is not as sure:

> Now it was the other way around. They lived in the cave, they were travelling toward the grave, and yet, if poetry was life, life was art too, what they saw in the film was life. . . . It was all very odd: two kinds of life perhaps, a life of life and a life of death. It was a continuous performance. (17:13, 4-5)

Road signs and advertisements appear constantly, and in keeping with the camera's ability to endow inanimate objects with meaning, these signs acquire an exaggerated, almost supernatural significance. "Safeside-Suicide," "Mother Gettle's Soup," even the billboards in chapter 28 (221-25), provide external glosses on the action of Ethan's mind.

One of the more complicated instances of a film allusion in *October Ferry* is that of Temple Thurston's *The Wandering Jew*.[5] In chapter 20, entitled "The Wandering Jew," Ethan sees the film and experiences the terrifying sensation that he *is* the accused Jew (132). Here, as in *Volcano,* the Lowry hero under stress loses all sense of psychological space; he is unable to distinguish the boundaries between self and not-self. Of course, the parallels between Ethan and the Jew are not just fanciful; Ethan *is* chased from one home to another in his journey through life, and, like Thurston's Jew, he does finally receive grace.

Lowry, however, attempts to make more of the film than simply a thematic parallel for his story, and here the allusion becomes confusing. When Ethan learns of the death-by-fire of Temple Thurston, he perceives a precise parallel between the writer's death and that of the Jew in the film. This coincidence provides him with "a glimpse into the very workings of creation itself" (147). It is as if Thurston "created" his own death on one plane only to re-enact it on another. The film apparently functions as a kind of gate or secret passage into the realm of connection and coincidence that, for Lowry, constitutes reality. Consequently, the film reassures Ethan of the significance of the universe: "Gone was his fright. In its stead was awe" (148). Nevertheless, the meaning of the elaborate Wandering Jew-Temple Thurston complex is less clear than this summary would suggest, and in an amusing marginal note on the manuscript, Lowry spoke for the reader too when he wrote that "its purpose in the book baffles me."

Lowry's use of Griffith's *Isn't Life Wonderful* is also a puzzle in some respects. Ethan's version of the film bears small resemblance to the actual film except for the presence of two lovers in a forest who comment, after being robbed, "Isn't Life Wonderful." In Griffith's film there is no fire and no looting soldiers, and the film ends with the marriage of the lovers as they begin life in a tiny cottage. According to Mrs. Lowry, Lowry would frequently be carried away by an idea, shot, or scene, in a film and proceed to create his own version.[6] In subsequent discussions he believed his "creation" to be the actual film. If this is what happened to the Griffith picture, it is not difficult to understand his invention of the fire (especially for chapter 15), but it is strange that Lowry overlooked the symbolic parallel of the happy ending. Perhaps the reader is meant to infer that the Llewelyns will have a similar happy ending, for *Isn't Life Wonderful* provides a clear thematic parallel to their story. Like Griffith's lovers, Ethan and Jacqueline are homeless and beleaguered, but they too maintain their love and faith.

October Ferry is as rich in reference, quotation, and literary and filmic parallels as *Under the Volcano*. The most important allusion is to Sutton Vane's play *Outward Bound,* but Lowry also gleaned many references from Eino Railo's *The Haunted Castle,* a study of gothic and romantic literature, and from Charles Fort's books.[7] He uses Blake and Shakespeare to develop themes and refers to such diverse writers as Chaucer, Berkeley, Defoe, Bunyan, Carlyle, Bulwer-Lytton, Coleridge, Clare, Wordsworth, Keats, Emily Brontë, George Eliot, Hardy, Poe, Melville, Dostoevsky, Flaubert, Stendhal, Sartre, and Hesse.

Outward Bound, from which a film was made in 1930, casts the greatest light upon Lowry's intentions. Written in a disarmingly simple style, Vane's play portrays the postmortem voyage of a small group of passengers outward bound for heaven or hell: "It's the same place, you see."[8] The three acts of the play take place in the ship's bar, where the bartender, Scrubby, a kind of Charon, gradually reveals the nature of the voyage. Two of the passengers, Ann and Henry, have committed suicide and are, therefore, "half-ways" who must "go on like this ... backwards and forwards—backwards and forwards." In the unpublished letter to Erskine (discussed on page 76 above), Lowry describes his plan of making Peter Cordwainer appear to Ethan on the ferry as Scrubby:

> [Ethan] has to face the fact also that he actually is—or has been—next door to a murderer and a criminal himself in the case of Cordwainer: though it's time he stopped punishing himself—he's had 20 years of penal servitude already—and others for it, including Cordwainer himself, who appears in a dream to him on the ferry boat (Scrubby the barman in Outward Bound—you might expect to find him on a ferry boat) to inform him that in so far as Ethan had murdered him, he had saved him from the lot of a suicide in the next world. (3:6, 2)

In Act 3 of *Outward Bound*, the passengers hold a meeting in the bar—"in view of the shortness of time ... and the nature of the harbour we are approaching" (112)—to look over their pasts and to be examined by a clergyman. Each of the passengers receives his sentence except the suicides who remain suspended in limbo. Scrubby reminds Ann that time does not exist in limbo: "A week! A century! A moment! There's no time here" (170).

This lack of time and space—heaven and hell are the same place and time does not exist—is clearly paralleled in parts of *October Ferry*. Lowry has also incorporated the bar as place of judgment and the theme of suicide in his novel. The title *Outward Bound* is important, not only in *October Ferry*, where it provides two chapter headings, but throughout Lowry's "Voyage" cycle. From *Ultramarine* on, the "outward bound" motif recurs as a reminder that the voyage must always begin anew. In fact, Vane's play provides an interesting insight into Lowry's entire concept of the voyage: anyone who commits suicide (as Ethan nearly does in chapter 34) literally or metaphorically, remains trapped, like Ann and Henry, in a limbo where time does not exist and where the voyage cannot go on.

Motifs are important structural techniques in *October Ferry*, and like allusions, they are largely unexplored. Signs—"Safeside-Suicide," notices—"Vous qui passez/ayez pitié," seemingly casual puns such as "called to the bar," phrases like "beginning again," and Luther's hymn "*Ein Festerburg ist unser Gott*" recur throughout the book. The repetition, as Lowry pointed out to Erskine, is purposely "beyond that which you can believe" (*Selected Letters*, 339) because Lowry saw his use of motifs as something new to fiction. In a note to Margerie on the manuscripts, he remarks:

> Leit-motifs go backwards & forwards here as they don't in Wagner, & the whole technique & meaning is revolutionary & new to art, I believe, certainly

to fiction. And it has to be *simple,* unaffected naturalism 'au meme temp' (19:24, A).

The motifs serve many functions: they introduce and develop themes, comment ironically upon an event or thought, and generally enrich the meaning of the text. Most important, of course, they disrupt the cause and effect progression of the story by their "backwards & forwards" movement. Just as the closely interwoven texture of the narrative represents the consciousness of the protagonist, so the leit-motifs suggest the density of a mind that remembers and interprets everything it perceives.

The words "time" and "life," for example, occur repeatedly in the first part of the novel, but it is not until chapter 24 that their significance is sharply focused:

> And down down it was anyhow, what with *Time* and *Life* on the table with their bouncing advertisements of a bouncing life with Big Cousin that never was on land or sea, or if it was, in his opinion shouldn't be.... Christ Jesus how he hated it all. Where had *their* life, *their* time gone. (181)

"Time" and "life" reflect back upon the preceding chapters. Up to this point Ethan has only been remembering (not living) *"their* life, *their* time."

As the narrative moves into the present, the "time" and "life" motif recurs more frequently. The Llewelyns pass a magazine stand in their search for the Gabriola ferry ticket office, and on the stand appears: "Your weight and your destiny. *Time* and *Life*..." (234). With each repetition of the words, associations multiply. At this point the motif serves as a subtle reminder of the continuity between past and present, but the interpretation of this link is left uncertain; time and life will either continue to be only a memory *or* the present will become a lived reality. Later that afternoon, as they again make their way down to the ferry, the motif carries some help: "Libra's year ahead. Difficulties of the Fourth House... *Time and Life*" (284). The sign of Libra, with the balance or scales, symbolizes the supposed justice in Ethan's legal profession and suggests that in the year ahead Ethan will achieve balance. "Difficulties of the Fourth House," yet another leit-motif, refers to the Llewelyn's trouble in finding their fourth home (Achad's fourth world): until now the stars have been against them, not to mention Ethan's misanthropism; however, with "Libra's year ahead," they will surely have "time" to build a new "life" in the "fourth house."

In the last chapter, "Uberimae Fides" (bountiful faith), Ethan has discovered the faith necessary to go on into the future and relinquish the past. The reprieve from eviction reinforces the need for a new life: "No, it was time to leave, however much it hurts. Time to — " (325). Finally, as the ferry approaches Gabriola, the Llewelyns know that now they are moving in time once again: "Well, time and heart enough to find out about everything now..." (329).

Although *October Ferry* is as rich in symbolism as it is in motif and allusion, there are three symbols which are of particular importance: symbols of place (both Gabriola and Eridanus), the mirror, and once again the circle or wheel with its ambivalent associations of containment and movement. Gabriola and Eridanus symbolize the poles of human experience. Being an island, Gabriola calls to mind the references to Atlantis scattered through Lowry's work as well as the reference to Prospero's island in *October Ferry* (157). Situated in the Gulf of Georgia, the island is in a sense afloat on the gulf ("Golf-gouffre-gulf") that consumed Geoffrey Firmin in *Under the Volcano*. Angela d'Arrivee (the angel of arrival if not of the Annunciation), who lives on Gabriola, is waiting to welcome the Llewelyns, and, as Lowry told Erskine, the island "*is*, finally, the future." Despite its inaccessibility and mystery, Gabriola is a positive force, but Eridanus is a more ambiguous symbol. It is the name of their inlet and of a ship that ran aground there. It is also the name of a constellation — the river of life and death. More ominous still, the Eridanus is the river that, in the *Aeneid*, "watered the Elysian Fields of the Earthly Paradise" (164). Eridanus is a type of the earthly paradise, "a gift of grace, finally a damnation" (79), and as long as they are able to live there without wanting to possess it, physically or spiritually, the Llewelyns are safe. Ethan, however, has come to wear the cabin "like a shell"; he wants to secure it for himself forever. But in the Cabbala shells signify the *Qliphoth* or world of demons which in turn suggests that Ethan's desire to withdraw into the safety of Eridanus has transformed his paradise into a trap. So obsessed has he become with past happiness there, so terrified is he of losing it, that he is unable to face either the present trip or the future.

In an important sense, *October Ferry* is like a mirror in that many of the chapters are reflections of each other, and the constant repetition of motifs increases the mirror-like quality of the text. Mirror images, of course, are both positive and negative. Broken mirrors occur in each of the bars in which Ethan experiences his hellish visions, and twice he confronts his own face in a mirror (46, 216) only to perceive that he is a "murderer!" These mirrors inevitably recall the distorting and mysterious mirrors in expressionist films. In *The Student of Prague*, for example, young Baldwin sells his soul to the devil by giving him his mirror image, but when he finally frees himself from this satanic mirror image by shooting at it, he kills himself. More positively, the mirror is essential to Achad's theory of the Tree of Life, wherein the reflections will be clear as long as the glass is whole or undistorted. Certainly, for Ethan, who needs the help of Coleridge's *Aids to Reflection*, as well as the Cabbala, in order to achieve balance, the search for a clarity of mind and soul that will perfectly mirror the universe is just another set of parameters for his spiritual and metaphysical quest.

The text itself approximates, in Lowry's eyes, a magic mirror, for it reflects the creative process of God, and Lowry was forever searching for the art form that would be in constant motion and thereby incarnate his belief in change at the same time as it reflected the perpetual motion of the universe. In one of the novel's more striking passages, Ethan, who is sitting in the Ladies and Escorts side of the Ocean Spray (the bar *with* a view), describes the activity of the bartender:

> The bartender, glancing from time to time out of the window at the scene outside, began to pile *the glasses one within another* in a stack on the counter, a dull-seeming occupation, about which, Ethan now understood from the bartender's glances of satisfaction at the stack, the position of which he altered now and then, evidently to suit some aesthetic whim, there was, on the contrary, something almost godlike: *it was a creative process, an act of magic:* for within each glass lay trapped the reflection of the window, within each window the reflected scene outside, extended vertically by the glasses themselves, *the reflected windows flowing upward* in a single *attenuated but unbroken* line in which could be seen a multiplicity of lighthouses, seabirds, suns, fishing crafts, passenger boats, Australia-bound colliers, the minuscule coal rushing audibly down the minute chute. (250 [italics added])[9]

The stack of glasses is "a creative process, an act of magic" because it reflects "flowing," "unbroken," "multiplicity." Like Achad's Tree of Life or Dunne's serial universe (viewed positively), the stacked glasses reflect yet control the continuous movement of life. This passage expresses the heart of Lowry's philosophy and aesthetics while, at the same time, reflecting all his novels; glasses, bars, windows, ships, lighthouses, and seabirds echo and reverberate through *Ultramarine, Lunar Caustic, Volcano,* and *Dark as the Grave.* The very word "reflection" appears on practically every page of *October Ferry* to remind the reader of the "Voyage" and to heighten the reflexive nature of the individual text.

The symbol of the wheel or circle functions as dramatically in *October Ferry* as in *Under the Volcano.* Indeed, the narrative creates a kind of "perichoresis" of Ethan, Jacqueline, and Tommy, or, even more accurately, of the trinity of past, present, and future. But wheels and circles are as ambivalent in *October Ferry* as they are in the rest of Lowry's fiction. For example, Ethan is continually enclosed within the circle of his own consciousness, whether he is in a shell-like house, on a bus, in a bar, or on a ferry. (At one point Lowry toyed with the idea of bringing the bus on the ferry.) References to Ixion (St. Catharine's College, Cambridge), where Peter died, appear frequently, but the wheel in its negative guise appears most powerfully in chapter 28, "Wheel of Fire." The phrase, "wheel of fire" comes from *King Lear*, where it evokes an Ixion-like torture:

> You do wrong to take me out o' th' grave
> Thou art a soul in bliss; but I am bound
> Upon a wheel of fire, that mine own tears
> Do scald like molten lead.[10]

Ethan, like Lear, must continue to suffer.

Wheels and circles exist on every side — Nanaimo is laid out "like the spokes of a wheel," and as the bus follows a hearse leaving a Catholic church a Latin phrase (perhaps from a tombstone) catches Ethan's attention: *"Circum ipsam autem libamina omnibus mortuis"* (230). The wheel symbolism reaches its climax at the end of the chapter as Ethan overhears a conversation between two old men, a conversation "addressed mysteriously to Ethan himself; and ... almost every phrase had another meaning, perhaps many meanings, intended for his ears alone" (231). One of the men describes how a blacksmith makes huge coach wheels:

" — well, they shrink them on. Now the wheelwright has delivered the wheel to the blacksmith, and the blacksmith builds a ring of fire ... now they have the iron welded together and they put it in the fire. .... Then, when it's ready the blacksmith with his two helpers, they take it out of the fire with tongs, and they force it over the edge of the wooden wheel, and then it smokes *something awful*, it damn nearly sets fire to the wheel. So then they run like mad pouring water on it. Now you understand it has swelled in the fire, and now it shrinks quickly, and now it has clasped the wheel forever — " (231-32)

"Clasped the wheel forever" develops into a refrain that haunts Ethan through the second part of the book (236, 282) because the iron wheel is a terrifying image of Ethan's mind which has been relentlessly clasped by the past. The burning wheel, reminiscent of Blake's tiger, also suggests the plunging of the spirit into the moulding fires of experience, and significantly, the blacksmith builds a "ring of fire" in order to temper the iron. Ethan himself has been plagued by a "ring of fire" at several points in his past life; advertisements for Mother Gettle's soup seem "ringed with hellfire" (47), and the fires in Niagara-on-the-Lake spring up around the Llewelyns so that they are surrounded by an actual "ring of fire" (118). Ethan Llewelyn is being tempered in the fires of his ordeal, which, if they do not destroy him first, will shape him into a better man.

As Ethan moves into the future in part three, the circle changes from a searing static enclosure to a symbol of movement and life. The gliding, "free-wheeling" ferry with the seagulls circling overhead and "great whirlpools and whorls like seashells" (299) in the water beneath, the ferry with its circular lounge and wheelhouse in which the skipper twirls the wheel (297), transcribes one last complete circle before finally heading out to Gabriola. This last circle, superficially so full of despair, brings the ferry back to Nanaimo where Ethan learns of the Eridanus reprieve. He realizes then that the day's "multiplicity of signs," indeed the disasters, events, coincidences of his entire life, were full of an interrelated significance that contained this moment. Ethan has overcome the "extremity of motion that was no motion, where past and future were held suspended, and one began thinking of treadmills" (53). He has overcome his fear of change by obeying the Cabbalist command to "fear not CHANGE, but embrace it with open arms for all change is of the nature of love" (*Q.B.L.*, 100). The "free-wheeling" ferry is once again outward bound: "Beginning: beginning again: beginning yet again" (322).

October Ferry, like *Under the Volcano*, is a deeply religious novel, and Ethan Llewelyn's voyage is a multi-levelled quest: a search for "life" in every sense of the word. On the social level, the voyage represents Ethan's need to be reunited with mankind. During his three-and-one-half-year retreat at Eridanus, throughout his entire life in fact, he has become more and more withdrawn. Here, the Lowry dilemma of withdrawal and return is re-enacted with Ethan ultimately "received by mankind." In the unpublished letter to Erskine, Lowry clarifies this aspect of the quest:

> The ferry reaches Gabriola at dusk, where those meeting the boat are swinging lanterns along the wharf but you have the feeling that Ethan is now being received by mankind, that arms are stretched out to help him, help he now has to and is prepared to accept, as he is prepared to give help to man, whom he had formerly grown to hate so much: thus the characters journey toward their own recovery. (3:6, 2-3)

This social acceptance by mankind includes renewal of Ethan's marriage, which had been under considerable strain, and the finding of a new home for his wife and son.

The psychological level of the quest is perhaps more important, for it is on this level that Ethan must come to terms with his past in order to discover the future. Again, in his letter to Erskine, Lowry goes on to explain that,

> on this plane the whole thing can be read slightly differently and in a sense more hopefully, as a kind of abreaction of his past: I like the word cathexis, too. In some psycho-genetic sense also — if that's the word? — the news of their own reprieve (on this plane) would seem to precipitate Ethan's recovery, in the way that shell-shocked soldiers may recover at the news of the armistice. (3:6, 3)

Lowry's use of the term "abreaction," a psychoanalytic term for the release of psychic tension through verbalizing repressed traumatic experience, is important because the highly ratiocinative narrative may well be seen as therapeutic verbalization of the past.

Possessed by past traumas, Ethan is unwilling to relinquish his own youth, hence his guilt over Cordwainer's suicide merges with his reluctance to defend the Vancouver boy and intensifies his torment: not only was he Peter's murderer, but now, through professional inertia, he is also killing Chapman. The significance of both Cordwainer and Chapman crystallizes in his imaginary defence (self-defence) of Chapman when Ethan quotes a long passage from Hesse's *Demian*. According to Hesse, the time of puberty is a profoundly traumatic "sequence of death and rebirth." Loss and loneliness terrify the adolescent, making him long to stay within the comforting world of childhood: "They cling their whole life long painfully to the irrevocable past, to the dream of a lost paradise, the worst and most deadly of all dreams" (268). Because Ethan is unwilling to leave the paradise at Eridanus, which he has polluted with his repressed guilt over Cordwainer and Chapman, reliving the past trauma is the necessary therapy that finally frees him from the past and from his youth (from Eridanus, Cordwainer, and Chapman) and allows him to mature in the future.

Closely connected with the concept of Eridanus as a childhood paradise is the image of the cabin and the physical and spiritual Eden it represents for the Llewelyns. They are Adam and Eve, evicted from paradise, exiled from God, and beginning the soul's long voyage back to God, their harbour and home. William New, in "Gabriola: Malcolm Lowry's Floating Island," suggests that Ethan's voyage might be seen as the neo-Platonic journey of the soul in exile on its way back to God,[11] but the religious quest cannot be reduced to one myth. Ethan is searching for faith and this search continues through the book until, in the last chapter, "Uberimae Fides," he appears to have found it.

The metaphysical quest unites the social, psychological, and religious levels of the narrative. The Llewelyns, Ethan in particular, must come to understand the nature of reality. Significantly, Ethan recognizes that he has been a "misoneist" because the focal point of his voyage, the message of *October Ferry*, is that he must learn to accept the protean nature of reality. He has come to want to possess Eridanus, despite the profound truth

> [t]hat impermanence, indeed, the ramshackle tenuity of the life, were part of its beauty. The scene, too, that confronted them through their casement windows was ever-changing; the mountains, the sea never looked the same two minutes on end: why then be afraid of change? (171)

By refusing change, Ethan has attempted to stop time, to enclose and thereby spatialize experience. Through his fear and guilt he has become static, a piece of death. In a fascinating marginal note to a manuscript version of the ferry's approach to Gabriola, Lowry scribbled: "outside time, an ocean of suffering, just as he had seemed outside time in that three years on the beach" (16:11, 77). Only by placing himself within the flow of time, only by crossing the borders of self and escaping from the closed circle of consciousness, can Ethan be "received by mankind," transcend the past, or find the faith to carry him forward into the future.

Finally, the voyage in *October Ferry* is an epistemological quest, and it is on this level, more than on either the metaphysical or the religious, that Achad's interpretation of the Cabbala operates. Not only does it provide an interesting structural model, many images, and at least two important symbols (the numbers three and four), but it is also an epistemological tool for the achievement of harmony or balance. Ethan finds that a book on the Cabbala given him by the McCandless is

> not only extraordinarily interesting but, as a method of thought, profoundly helpful. In fact he could sum up no better their life on the beach than to say it had been, in a manner, *his* cabbala, in the sense that, if he was not mistaken, that system might be regarded on one plane as a means less of accumulating than of divesting oneself — by arrangement, balancing them against their opposites — of unbalanced ideas: the mind, finally transcending both aspects, regains its lost equilibrium. (169)

Achieving equilibrium through balanced opposites has been Lowry's and Ethan's goal throughout, and the reader shares in this epistemological quest by experiencing with Ethan the tortuous exploration of the past which is necessary for the growth of human consciousness.

October Ferry is not as successful as *Under the Volcano*. It is not as polished and interwelded and some minor inconsistencies persist: for example, the name of the boy accused of murder changes, and the wine becomes gin once Ethan is on the ferry. The son, Tommy, is dismissed from the story so quickly that the reader wonders why, apart from completing the trinity symbolism, he exists at all. These slips are unimportant, however, in comparison to the incomplete portrait of Ethan himself. Lowry had planned to develop Ethan, especially with regard to the reasons for his professional retreat, and the more recently discovered working notes for the novel contain many attempts to expand upon Ethan's drinking problem and his disillusionment with the law.[12] More thorough exposition of Ethan's despair would have lent him greater credibility, but as the novel stands it is hard to believe that Ethan's agony is like Lear's, whereas Geoffrey Firmin's tragic disintegration is totally convincing. The working notes also include long passages on the Cabbala, and Lowry, who was planning to expand the character of the McCandless, may have intended to incorporate more of the Cabbala into the portrait of Jacqueline's magician father.

As Lowry pointed out in the unpublished letter to Erskine, *October Ferry* does not "fall into any particular category or obey any of the normal rules of a novel." But *October Ferry* can be described as a "lyrical novel," at least insofar as it shares the qualities of formal design and a passive, solipsistic protagonist that Ralph Freedman identifies as characteristic of the mode.[13] Furthermore, because the narrative charts the growth of perception in a highly sensitive individual through the intensely personal reliving of past experience, it conforms rather closely to Aiken's definition of the novel as "the novelist's inordinate and copious lyric,"[14] and although there is little lyric tranquillity in *October Ferry*, Ethan does achieve a point of temporary rest and insight. As in "The Forest Path to the Spring," which *October Ferry* anticipates, "the characters journey toward their own recovery."

Despite weaknesses, *October Ferry* is successful in its own right. The intricate tripartite structure with its temporal involutions and complex motifs sustains the powerful rhythm of withdrawal and return, and Lowry succeeds wonderfully in his portrayal of eviction and quest with Ethan learning that he must accept change and leave his past in order to embrace the future. As the McCandless points out in his telegram to the Llewelyns after the burning of the Barkerville Arms:

> GREATEST COMMISERATION ON YOUR LOSS BUT CONSIDER SO-CALLED DISASTER CAN BE BEST POSSIBLE THING FOR YOU BOTH STOP I TOLD YOU LONG AGO WHAT PERILS CAN LURK AT THAT GATE OF UNCHANGE.(95)

And in a fascinating marginal note to himself on a draft of Ethan's final vision of the meteors, Lowry underlined the importance of the Llewelyns' search:

> "it must . . . be firmly implanted in the drang of the situation and the reader's mind *far more than ever* THEIR NEED for a house they can really call their own, for even if you feel they're not going to get one perhaps, it is on this continued search . . . that the pathos and drama of the situation depends." (19:15, 52)

Not a very comforting proviso, perhaps, but for Lowry it is not the finding but the *searching* that is important, and *October Ferry* ends with a sense of movement and expectation. Ethan, balance restored, is now ready to resume his multi-levelled voyage into the future.

October Ferry to Gabriola is a triumphant and integral continuation of the "Voyage" theme. In the unpublished letter to Erskine, Lowry leaves no doubt as to *October Ferry's* role: "The end is thus a kind of Volcano in reverse and the final theme Faustian, with everything from flights of angels, balls of fire, and Madonnas, to the intervention of grace and the Himmelphart" (3:6, 2).[15] With *October Ferry to Gabriola* the Lowry voyager escapes (for the moment) the negative circle of self and distorted perception, and the trap of the past. The luminous wheel moves bringing faith, life, and balance:

> Voyage, the homeward-outward-bound voyage; everybody was on such a voyage, the Ocean Spray, Gabriola, themselves, the barman, the sun, the reflections, the stacked glasses, even the light, the sea outside, now due to an accident of sun and dislimning cloud looking like a luminosity between two darknesses, a space between two immensities, was on such a voyage, to the junction of the two infinities, where it would set out on its way again, had already set out, toward the infinitely small, itself already expanding before you had thought of it, to replenish the limitless light of Chaos — (252)

6

Symbols of Tenuous Order:
Hear Us O Lord

Schoolbells toll from the invisible coast wise railway across the bay;
And other sounds, diatonic, of fog; a muffled cosmopolitan hum.
Other bells and explosions strike on the rail:
Gone too: circles of water spread; spider's web, like frosted
Symbols of tenuous order, the same order as the circles of water:
The fog comes rolling in before the sun that will drive it away again.
And behind, the huge green trees, guard the little house with friendly arms
    of benediction.
And in this paradise, one loves, swims, eats & works
And pays nothing, save in tribute to God, ordering past suffering.[1]

Hear Us O Lord from Heaven Thy Dwelling Place is a miniature "Voyage That Never Ends," a paradigm or reflection of Lowry's great masterwork. For this reason, and because individual stories bear important relations to the "Voyage" novels, *Hear Us O Lord* provides an excellent summary of Lowry's work. This chapter, therefore, discusses the stories in terms of Lowry's constant concerns — the protagonist's search for identity, the voyage of withdrawal and return, and Lowry's "symbols of tenuous order." The order envisioned in the book is "tenuous" in two senses: Lowry's life ended in miserable disorder just as he was finishing *Hear Us O Lord*, and more important for his art, Lowry believed that moments of order and balance must be followed by collapse and despair. To conclude this study of Lowry's art with *Hear Us O Lord* is not to imply that he has reached a final order, that the voyage is over. Even "The Forest Path to the Spring," written in the past tense, invokes a continuing voyage.

Margerie Lowry published *Hear Us O Lord*, with "Lowry's final revisions," in 1961, when it won the Canadian Governor General's Award for fiction, but Lowry had begun work on the stories sometime during 1950.[2] By November he had plans for seven stories, including one called, "October Ferry to Gabriola." Some were dropped, however, as he developed his idea of closely inter-related stories (*Selected Letters,* 216). By 1951 the book had taken clearer shape and, according to his "Work in Progress" statement, *Hear Us O Lord* was nearly ready for publication. Although he does not specify its relation to the "Voyage," he does explain that "in its resolution it relates to Eridanus" ("WP,"1).[3] In other words, the stories were to end on a note of harmony and rebirth paralleling the concluding vision of the "Voyage."

Lowry had not decided which of his stories should go in the final volume by 1951, but the general pattern was clear:

HEAR US O LORD FROM HEAVEN THY DWELLING PLACE

CONTENTS
THE BRAVEST BOAT
THROUGH THE PANAMA
ELEPHANT AND COLOSSEUM
STRANGE COMFORT AFFORDED BY THE PROFESSION
IN THE BLACK HILLS
THE FOREST PATH TO THE SPRING
("WP," Notes for *Hear Us O Lord,*1)

In "Work in Progress" he also discussed a number of other stories including "Gin and Goldenrod," and he mentions "Present Estate of Pompeii." "In the Black Hills" was dropped, to be published at a later date.[4] Three of the stories in the published collection are set in Canada, and all deal with Lowry's theme of "the basic human tragedy of today" ("WP," Notes, 5) which involves man's desecration of the world and consequent eviction brought about by civilization itself — a restatement of "Le gusta esta jardín?" Contrary to the *Volcano*, however, the stories were meant to be positive:

> Most of these stories deal, either humorously or seriously, but it is to be hoped not sentimentally, with those occasions in life when, whether consciously or unconsciously, some act of charity or faith or understanding, or perhaps only a coincidence, or even a mistake, has unwittingly testified to

the existence of something divine, or miraculous in human destiny. ("WP," Notes, 7)

Hear Us O Lord has been sharply criticized for lack of "vitality."[5] There is very little sense of plot in the stories, and the chief protagonist, while bearing the same name in three of the stories, differs from story to story. Judging by his letters, however, Lowry did not aim to write a conventional collection of short stories:

> *Hear Us O Lord* — with its 12 chapters — would be, if done aright, less a book of short stories than — God help us — yet *another* kind of novel: a kind of — often far less serious, often much more so — *Volcano* in reverse, with a triumphant ending, but ending (after "The Forest Path") in the same way, with the words Le Gusta Este Jardin, etc. (*Selected Letters*, 338)

As early as 1940 Lowry had been considering the possibilities of the short story, and he wrote to Jimmy Stern that,

> It is possible to compose a satisfactory work of art by the simple process of writing a series of good short stories, complete in themselves, with the same characters, interrelated, correlated, . . . full of effects and dissonances that are impossible in a short story. (*Selected Letters*, 28)

Hear Us O Lord is his "*another* kind of novel," for it is interrelated and correlated, as Rosemary Creswell says, through its "episodic, permutational and non-linear development of themes," while the characters, as William New suggests, can be seen as masks for Lowry.[6]

Hear Us O Lord from Heaven Thy Dwelling Place (the title coming from the Manx fisherman's hymn which runs through the book) consists of seven stories that comprise a voyage of the narrator from British Columbia to Europe and back again. The identity of the narrator and the significance of the voyage are the interrelated subjects of the book. Three of the stories are set in British Columbia, three in Italy, and one, "Through the Panama," carries the protagonist from Canada to Europe. Each story connects with its companions via motifs repeated throughout the book in "an assembly of apparently incongruous parts, slipping past one another — " (97), and many of the motifs, such as "outward bound," echo and recall Lowry's major novels.

The stories portray the evolution of the protagonist from a position of isolation, spiritual paralysis, and self-destruction to a position of wisdom and balance by a process "less of accumulating than of divesting oneself — by arrangement, balancing them against their opposites — of unbalanced ideas" (*October Ferry*, 169). Each of the stories explores, in turn, an aspect of the voyage. "Through the Panama," which embodies frequent references to *Under the Volcano*, is the abyss. "Forest Path," repeating once more the entire circle through hell and purgatory is the vision of paradise or moment of achieved balance. The stories are one cycle of the never-ending voyage complete with false starts, repeated explorations of the past, and recapitulation of the entire process, and they are, finally, an epistemological exercise in which Lowry arrives at a knowledge of reality and himself.

The protean protagonist is crucial to an understanding of Lowry's purpose in *Hear Us O Lord*, and together with *Dark as the Grave*, the stories offer the clearest insight into Lowry's concept of the narrator/protagonist of the entire "Voyage" cycle. There are five different protagonists in *Hear Us O Lord*: Sigurd Storlesen in "The Bravest Boat," Kennish Drumgold Cosnahan in "Elephant and Colosseum," Roderick MacGregor Fairhaven in "Present Estate of Pompeii," the nameless first person narrator of "Forest Path," and Sigbjørn Wilderness. In Norwegian, Sigbjørn means "victorious bear," and through the name Lowry may have wished to associate his wandering hero with Wagner's Siegfried (roughly, "guardian of victory"), but more importantly, the positive associations of the name contrast with the "*Ursus Horribilis*" (or grizzly) of "The Bravest Boat" (20) and recall the two constellations, Ursa Minor and Ursa Major.[7] In addition, the name sounds like "sea-borne," and together with stars and constellations, the sea provides perhaps the most affirmative imagery in the collection and throughout Lowry's work. His last name, Wilderness, evokes the wilderness-paradise of Eridanus or the possibilities of becoming lost in the wilderness. In "Gin and Goldenrod," Wilderness knows that the "conquering of wilderness, whether in fact or in his mind, was part of his own process of self-determination" (204).

Wilderness is the key protagonist of *Hear Us O Lord* where he appears as a writer being written in "Through the Panama," an "American writer in Rome on a Guggenheim Fellowship" (99) in "Strange Comfort," and a drunk in "Gin and Goldenrod," as well as Lowry's controlling persona and hero of the "Voyage," where he is the author of *Under the Volcano* and the other novels, the voyager in *Dark as the Grave*, and a character in someone else's fiction. He serves Lowry's purposes so well because in many ways he does not know who or what he is; in "Through the Panama" he asks, "—Who am I?—" (47). Lowry hoped that, for the reader, Wilderness would also represent mankind in the Jungian journey over the sea of the unconscious. Either way, as confused individual or universal archetype, in *Hear Us O Lord* and the "Voyage," he is Ortega's man in the process of creating (as opposed to finding) his identity through the creation of masks. Thus, even the "I" of "Forest Path" can be seen as Sigbjørn Wilderness, who contains or reflects all the other protagonists in the collection.[8] Lowry found support for this concept of the multiple "I" in the process of self-creation not only in Ortega, whom he discovered late in his life, but also in Ouspensky's theory of repeated incarnations, in the serial theories of Dunne, and in the poetry and fiction of Aiken.

The various protagonists in *Hear Us O Lord*, as in "The Voyage That Never

Ends," represent aspects of the chief protagonist Sigbjørn Wilderness or, perhaps more accurately, levels of his consciousness. In themselves, the subsidiary protagonists are not well-rounded, for Lowry was not interested in creating such characters; therefore, they usually represent projections of obsessions, weaknesses, fears, experiences, and sins which must be understood before the main protagonist is free to journey on. As Dana says toward the end of *Ultramarine*:

> I have identification with Andy: I am Andy. I regard it all now with sanity and detachment. But I have outgrown Andy. Mentally, I have surrounded Andy's position. (185)

Because Andy symbolizes the fearful world of experience, surrounding Andy's position enables Dana to evolve, to move on.

The most important feature of Lowry's concept of self-creation is the idea of constant change. By creating masks, the individual consciousness expands, or to use Ouspensky's term, evolves. These masks—for Lowry, the various protagonists in his novels — are not simply discarded, but understood and transcended in the constantly evolving identity of their creator. In a sense, the writer (or man) must repeatedly withdraw into a newly created protagonist and then return to a self which, if the voyage has succeeded, has evolved in the process. The ambiguity and danger of this aspect of withdrawal and return fascinated Lowry, for the writer runs the risk of becoming trapped in his own invention. In Geoffrey Firmin's crippling failure to distinguish subject from object, in *Dark as the Grave*, and in "Through the Panama," Lowry elaborates the horror of such entrapment. As he jokingly suggested in "Work in Progress," it is this "manuscript of one's life," carefully ordered and edited, that one submits to God: the life equals the work and the equation is more profound if the manuscript is rejected.

In *Hear Us O Lord*, as in the "Voyage," the subject is Lowry's great theme of withdrawal and return. During the voyage from west to south to north-east and, completing a geographical circle, west again, the characters explore the horrors of hell, wrestle with the past, sink into despair, and finally surface to a position of happiness and balance. As the last line of "The Bravest Boat" suggests, these are "the storms they had come through" (27). Lowry's emphatic use of the past perfect tense here serves two functions. First, it indicates that the stories following "The Bravest Boat" are from a fictional past. Second, it suggests a fictional present picked up again in "Forest Path," indicating that the Lowry protagonist has moved on into a future from which he is looking back upon the cycle of experience portrayed in the stories. He is creating another circle into the future through the writing of these stories.

"The Bravest Boat" functions as an overture to *Hear Us O Lord*, introducing and reflecting themes, motifs, and images that are to follow. The story describes the sea-shore walk of a couple, Sigurd Storlesen (uproarious laughter) and his wife Astrid (star), on their seventh wedding anniversary. They were originally brought together when Astrid discovered a toy balsa wood boat that young Sigurd had set afloat with his name and a message sealed inside it. In this modern world, where the rituals of Tammuz have degenerated to hypnotism (18), man must create his own sacred rites, and for Lowry, who believed in the magic power of language, numbers, and the significance of coincidence, the occasion for celebration in "The Bravest Boat" is the anniversary of this couple so mysteriously brought together by a small boat which had wandered for twelve years. Their ritual is the re-telling, "almost like an incantation" (25), of the events leading up to their meeting, and this "incantation" provides a model for the creative ordering and use of the past which the rest of *Hear Us O Lord* employs.

The musical analogy implicit in calling "The Bravest Boat" an overture is deliberate. Although the point should not be pressed too far, Lowry's love of jazz (Lang, Venuti, Beiderbecke, Reinhardt, Grappelli, and others), as well as his own musical ability, encouraged him to use musical analogies. The sequence of stories in *Hear Us O Lord* can be likened to jazz improvisations in that each story following "The Bravest Boat" picks up a thread of the central theme and plays it through with variations. "Forest Path" functions as a recapitulation with each theme restated in harmony with the others. Furthermore, the protagonist in "The Forest Path to the Spring" is a jazz musician who is writing an opera entitled "Forest Path to the Spring." By the end of the story sequence, the "demonic orchestras" of *Under the Volcano* have been transformed, and Poe's "Descent into the Maelstrom" (recalling *Lunar Caustic* and *October Ferry*) has become a jazz composition called "Swinging the Maelstrom" (250).

The most significant of the many songs repeated throughout Lowry's work is "Frère Jacques," which recalls Jacques Laruelle and imitates the sound of a ship's engines.[9] On an intermediate draft of "Through the Panama," Lowry explains in a pencilled note that "Frère Jacques,"

> represents finally the oneness of the universe itself: what Swedenborg called a sound like 'one . . . one . . .,' Plato, the Music of the Spheres. A simple little tune sung by children, with infinite variations, because the children grow up. (23:6, 36 verso)

Lowry hoped to capture the rhythm and unity of the universe by applying what he called, the "canon form" of "Frère Jacques" to his work. Thus, the stories in *Hear Us O Lord* repeat with variations the themes in "The Bravest Boat," and *Hear Us O Lord* as a whole repeats over and over the rhythm of withdrawal and return in "The Voyage That Never Ends." The motifs, even individual words (for example, "mirror," "reflection" and "Pleiades" from "The Bravest Boat"), recur like musical notes,[10] while the scale announcing "*Your weight and your destiny*" (14 and 15) echoes *October Ferry,* and Chaucer's "contrary winds" (22) recall both *Dark as the Grave* and *October Ferry.* Lastly, the "giant pinnacles, images of barrenness and desolation, upon which the heart is thrown and impaled eternally" (22), although they recur in "Through the Panama" (32), inevitably recall Geoffrey's Popocatapetl in *Under the Volcano*. In short, the motifs reinforce the unity of the book, heighten similarities among different stories, and forge links between *Hear Us O Lord* and the rest of Lowry's work.

The most important and beautiful passage in "The Bravest Boat" is the narrator's description of the trials encountered by the little boat, forced to begin its twelve-year voyage again and again:

> Ah, its absolute loneliness amid those wastes, those *wildernesses,* of rough rainy seas bereft even of sea birds, *between contrary winds,* or in the great *dead windless swell* that comes following a gale; and then with the wind springing up and blowing the spray across the sea like rain, like a *vision of creation,* blowing the little boat as it climbed the highlands into the skies . . . and then sank down into the *abyss,* but already was climbing again, while the whole sea crested with foam like lambs' wool went furling off to leeward, the whole vast moon-driven expanse like the pastures and valleys and snow-capped ranges of a Sierra Madre in delirium, in *ceaseless motion, rising and falling,* and the little boat rising, and falling into a *paralyzing* sea of white drifting *fire* and smoking spume by which it seemed overwhelmed: and all this time a sound, like a high sound of singing . . . as again the boat slanted onward. (22 [italics added])

Not only does Lowry establish here the background to "The Bravest Boat," but the punctuation and the rhythm of the passage capture the sensation of ceaseless, incremental withdrawal and return. The description counterpoints flow and stasis; the stasis of "the great dead windless swell" gives away to "ceaseless motion" and then again to "a paralyzing sea." The words "abyss" and "fire" remind us not only of specific moments in *Volcano* and *October Ferry* respectively, but also of the general spiritual and physical hells which Lowry repeatedly invisions in these terms. But to counteract these constant terrors there is the ever-present "vision of creation" (repeated in "Through the Panama," 74) and "a high sound of singing" (repeated in "The Forest Path," 271, where Lowry quotes Aiken) which serve as reminders of the significance and beauty of universal motion.

In "Through the Panama," the voyage proper begins with Sigbjørn Wilderness' exploration of hell. "Through the Panama," constantly echoing *Under the Volcano,* depicts a multi-faceted hell consisting of the southward journey to the infernal region of Mexico and the static containment of the ship in the locks.[11] The journey and the locks symbolize withdrawal, the descent of the protagonist within the abyss of self, and even more seriously, the loss of identity of the writer enmeshed in his own book.

"Through the Panama" consists of the journal entries of the writer, Sigbjørn

Wilderness, during a passage from Vancouver south to Panama and east to Europe. Wilderness, plagued by vague guilt, hatred, suspicion, and sinister coincidences (a fellow passsenger is called Charon) and tormented by the threat of separation from his wife, Primrose, sinks deeper and deeper into despair. His days are spent longing for the next aperitif and writing fragments of a novel about a novelist, Martin Trumbaugh, who becomes enmeshed in his own novel. By the time the boat encounters a dreadful storm in mid-Atlantic, the journal entries no longer distinguish between Sigbjørn and his character or between inner and outer reality. Gruesome as this sounds, "Through The Panama" is a delightful parody of Lowry's own problems, as a writer and as a man, in which he maintains a keen sense of the ridiculousness of the situation: "The signal of abandon . . . Couldn't hear it given in this noise" (97).

Lowry's narrative techniques, in particular the journal and the gloss from *The Ancient Mariner* create a temporal dislocation that reinforces the hellish possibilities of the story. With its dated entries, the journal serves as a reminder that calendar time is passing, but this relentless march of time becomes meaningless as the entries increasingly involve the subjective world of Sigbjørn's novel and Sigbjørn/ Martin's reflections on shipwreck. The more Sigbjørn withdraws into his private world and his novel, the more the temporal sequence becomes distorted and utterly useless as a gauge for external reality; in this inner timeless world, position reports and dates are irrelevant.

Lowry handles the *Ancient Mariner* passages brilliantly. On the one hand, the allusions underline the universal significance of Sigbjørn's state; on the other, the contrast in diction and tone is enough to remind the reader of Martin's ludicrous position: "Joyced in his own petard" (38). A short passage illustrates this well:

Martin woke up weeping, however, never before having realized that he had such a passion for the wind and the sunrise. Si, hombre, that is tequila (This now seems ridiculous to me, having risen early and washed a shirt.) —I am the chief steward of my fate, I am the fireman of my soul. Nothing can exceed the boundless misery and desolation and wretchedness of a voyage like this. (Even though everyone is so decent and it is the nicest crew one could have encountered, the best food, etc. And the Trumbaughs were of course having a hell of a good time, etc., etc.) (41)	The Mariner awakes, and his penance begins anew. He despiseth the creatures of the calm

More important, the use of the gloss breaks up the page spatially, forcing the reader to abandon the customary temporal reading sequence and thereby reinforcing the sensation of entrapment on the page, both for Sigbjørn and the reader. Furthermore, Coleridge's Mariner, in a manner analogous to the Lowry protagonist who is obliged to retell and relive his tale, is trapped in "his loneliness and fixedness" just as Sigbjørn/Martin is caught within the "fixity of the closed order" of perception—"death in short" (38). This "death-in-life" state will only end when the sinner perceives the beauty of life and allows his soul to flow outwards in blessing. Sigbjørn, like the Mariner, must overcome the destructive bounds of self, and the gloss reminds Sigbjørn and the reader that motion is salvation, for the Mariner "yearneth towards the journeying Moon, and the stars that still sojourn, yet still move onward" (38).

The long passages of paraphrase from Helen Nicolay's *The Bridge of Water* are also typographically juxtaposed with the main narrative. Although they contribute further to the spatialization of the page and the reader's sense of dislocation in time, the mock-serious tone and ironic jibes undercut the extremity of Sigbjørn's dilemma. The distinction between the historical account of the Panama Canal and Sigbjørn's reflections become blurred, so that as Sigbjørn reads Nicolay's book, external, factual reality merges with internal, felt reality until the former gives way to the latter and historical past merges with personal present. As Sigbjørn/Martin notes, only ships passing in the opposite direction through the Canal are in the Bergsonian flow of time—"Another ship from London, all going the other way steaming very swiftly as with the current. (Bergson.)"—whereas to Sigbjørn, the containment and immobility of his ship, as it is held by the locks, seems symbolic of his negative state.

Predictably, the Panama Canal strikes him as "something like a novel—in fact just such a novel as I, Sigbjørn Wilderness ... might have written myself—" (62). Sigbjørn, trapped within his novel about a novelist, is "Ortega's man" writing his life as he goes along; however, the distressing thought is that he is, perhaps, *only* a character in someone else's novel of life, and so on *ad infinitum*. The "celestial meccano" of the locks also parallels the containing layers of Sigbjørn's consciousness and the mind, like the canal, resembles Dunne's serial universe with a series of observers each sitting in control over a lesser observer. Worse still, past, present, and future seem to be fixed and unchanging within this serial universe where the "superlative general observer"[12] sitting "in *his* invisible control tower ... is able to see everything that is happening to me at every moment—and worse, everything that is *going* to happen—" (63).

The climax of the story occurs "Beyond and astern of time" (80) during a terrifying "STORM OVER ATLANTIS" (82) which threatens to destroy the ship. Both time and space are meaningless terms—unless one can salvage some hope from the fact that the ship is over the apocryphal city of Atlantis. At this point, Sigbjørn *is* Martin, position reports are pointless, and crew and passengers are awake day and night in the struggle to stay alive; the dilemma of the ship, caught "Amid the sea, betwexen windes two" (87) and steering "by dead reckoning" (89), parallels the Sigbjørn/Martin dilemma. As Sigbjørn notes, Martin "could not make anything move" (86). Wheels are utterly useless in this "descent into the maelstrom" (90) where everyone is isolated from everyone else:

—Martin took his ignorance of the nature of the crisis to heart, telling himself that it was because these Liberty ships were not like the old ships where you could see what was going on, that there was an almost Kafka-like occlusion, everything closed, ghastly ... but no matter what he told himself, it seemed all part and parcel of his wider isolation, and in fact like the ultimate ordeal of—(92).

The "ultimate ordeal" of "occlusion" (or death) is descent into hell, which Lowry always symbolizes by containment, timelessness, and stasis. Of course, buried beneath Lowry's narrative is the parallel with the "Voyage" and "The Ordeal of Sigbjørn Wilderness" where the protagonist does cross the boundary into death before being "reborn."

"Through the Panama" has the most emphatically circular form of all the stories in *Hear Us O Lord*. The circle, however, is not as tightly closed as in *Under the Volcano*, for Sigbjørn, like the Mariner, has his "vision of creation" and is able to bless. The ceinture around the boat, a beneficent circle, has brought the ship through the storm, and the engines no longer sing "*lamenti*na ... doom doom doom" (35). "Through the Panama" explores the hell of timelessness and loss of identity, but, as the title suggests, the ship comes "through," and Lowry maintains a delicate balance of parody and mock-seriousness for this slightly ridiculous ordeal.

The next three stories in *Hear Us O Lord*, "Strange Comfort Afforded by the Profession," "Elephant and Colosseum," and "Present Estate of Pompeii," develop the significance of the past—literary, personal, and historical. In "Strange Comfort" the past exists as both torment and comfort. The lonely protagonist, Sigbjørn Wilderness, a writer in Rome on a Guggenheim Fellowship, visits Keats' house then retreats to a bar. Meditating on the merciless display of the dead poet's letters, he studies his notebook only to discover notes made years before while visiting Poe's house and a draft of a letter from his own past in which he pleaded for help. These two entries disturb him because he had thought the notebook to be empty of any "destructive stoop, from the past" (110).

Two refrains running through the story clarify the meaning of the past. In his visit to Rome's Mamertine Prison, Wilderness had recorded in his notebook that "*The lower is the true prison*" (103). Likewise the draft letter is "from absolutely the lowest ebb of those low tides of his life"—the past is, then, the lower and true prison. But the past is not only a prison because the past represented by his notes on Poe also brings comfort—the strange comfort afforded by the literary profession. The second refrain, "descent into the maelstrom," is destined to become "Swinging the Maelstrom," while the knowledge that he is one of a long line of literary sufferers like Poe—"*And many others*" (103, 109)—brings a kind of relief. The story ends with an ambiguous cough-laugh as Sigbjørn realizes that the coincidence of finding his old letter has led him to a fuller realization of his affinity with Keats and Poe.[13] In a sense he is participating constructively in the law of series by repeating the artist's ordeal.

"Elephant and Colosseum," together with "Through the Panama" and "The Forest Path to the Spring," is crucial to the voyage theme of *Hear Us O Lord*. Here the withdrawal into the past yields insight into those coincidences and recurrences which disclose the significance of life and lead to faith and rebirth. It was one of Lowry's favourite stories, and he worked on it through several versions originally titled "Sooner or Later, or So They Say." With "Panama" and "Forest Path," it represents Lowry's most polished comic endeavour.

The protagonist of "Elephant and Colosseum," Kennish Drumgold Cosnahan, is an American writer of Manx origins with vague magical powers and the author of *Ark from Singapore* (a book reminiscent of *Ultramarine*). He is in Rome primarily to contact the Italian translators of his book. As he sits alone in the restaurant, terrified by the traffic, unable to move or write, he catches sight of his face reflected in the window and of his photograph on the back of his book. Neither these images nor the biographical blurb on the book dust jacket reassures him of his identity. To the contrary:

> Reading these later eulogies produced in Cosnahan a bizarre mental commotion as of some endless mirrored reduplication . . . for a moment he felt like an eternal writer eternally sitting in the eternal city, eternally reading precisely the same sort of notices. (119)

This sense of lost identity, intensified by his immobility, merges with a loss of the sense of time. Time stands still in the eternal city as Cosnahan's memories grow and the present reality of Rome fades.

Finally, disturbed by the waiter, Cosnahan rises to begin his long "circumambient operation" of crossing busy streets such as the "circolare Sinistra" in order to meet his publisher. His fear of crossing streets is significant. Like *Dark as the Grave,* where the phenomenon of crossing borders symbolized the movement of the protagonist from one level of consciousness or sphere of reality to another, "Elephant and Colosseum" is primarily about the "translation" of Cosnahan's consciousness across the barriers of memory and the confusion of immediate reality: "the very word 'translated' had a mystical tinge to him" (136). Typically, Lowry has used a word with a wide range of dictionary meanings. In addition to its literary significance, "to translate" can mean to interpret, to transform the nature of, to move from one place to another, to exalt, or enrapture, and to convey to heaven without natural death. Certainly, the sense of translation as conveyance to heaven without natural death suggests, however obliquely, that Lowry is again toying with the "threshold of death" idea from the "Ordeal."

Rome, the eternal city of crossroads where the visitor is sure to encounter someone (or something) he knows, is the ideal setting for Cosnahan's "translation." Once again Lowry is employing his concept of space, here the space of city streets, as a boundary that must be crossed if life is to have value. Seen positively, these boundaries are points of intersection, but one must have courage to cross these "awful and dangerous" (148) roads, and for Cosnahan this is a major ordeal. Consequently, during his walk, he escapes more immediate horrors by withdrawing into "contra-Proustian reveries" (151). When he finally arrives at the publisher's office, Cosnahan learns that he is unknown there, that his book is not being translated there, and that he is likely in the wrong city. However, if the *book* is not being translated in Rome, *Cosnahan* is, and he makes his way to the zoo where his "anagnorisis" (167) awaits him in Rosemary, the elephant heroine of his novel.

Cosnahan's meeting with Rosemary is fortunate in many ways because Rosemary provides testimony of Cosnahan's identity; she recognizes and remembers him. In this way, she provides external validation of a Cosnahan who exists in the present. Furthermore, the coincidence of meeting Rosemary indicates the importance of recurrence in temporal phenomena: "Naturam expellas pitch-fork, something or other recurret!" (126)[14] History, personal or social, moves in cycles. In the typed notes for "Elephant and Colosseum," Lowry explained that Horace's famous remark was "the main theme or motif of the story":

> The main theme of the story, thus—although an apparently light and humorous one—is to the highest degree intellectual. . . . For example, the apparition of Rosemary herself is an example of nature coming back again (and indeed in the zoo scene we even have the image of the pitchfork). The ancient idea of eternal recurrence which is the *form* of the story is another example. (24:13, 7a)

As in all his work, Lowry fuses the form and theme of this story into a narrative structure embodying a complex metaphysical concept in its perfect symbolic counterpart. The form of the story is a beneficent circle. Cosnahan's walk around Rome draws a circle in space while, by meeting Rosemary, he completes a temporal circle as well: "and so his earlier train of thought, like Cosnahan himself in his walk around Rome, came full circle—" (171).

By finding verification of his personal identity and gaining, through the coincidental encounter with Rosemary, crucial insight into the nature of time and space, Cosnahan escapes from the Rip Van Winkle state he experienced earlier in the day. The meeting with Rosemary restores peace, love, faith in the meaning of life, and, most important, his ability to write. His circular movement through time and space has led to his "translation":

> Indeed, Cosnahan had changed himself, was aware, quite apart from the extraordinary sense of well-being he felt, of one of those changes which, fiction to the contrary, it is given to very few to remark exactly when they take place, for the good reason, he thought, that maybe they take place in sleep. And Cosnahan felt that he'd woken up. (168-69)

By accepting change he has changed himself; therefore, seated confidently at his trattoria of the morning, he finds now that "the same ceaseless traffic" has "riches and peace and grace about the flow of it" (169). Because he has been "Translated —his mother's son at last—into a conscious member of the human race" (173), he knows he is one with Quayne, Quaggan, Quillish, and Illiam Dhone, and because his journey has brought him full circle to "one of those points where life and poetry meet" (172), he is ready to "begin again" (172).

"Present Estate of Pompeii," the third exploration of the past, is another treatment of withdrawal into pessimism. Although similar to "Through the Panama," the emphasis of the story is less on timelessness than on the fear of time running out. The title plays upon the significance of the fact that ancient ruins persist into present time, thereby bequeathing (estate as inheritance) their ruined condition (estate as condition in life) to future generations. Pompeii itself is an obviously ominous symbol. The protagonist bears the ambiguous name of Roderick (recalling Poe's unlucky Mr. Usher) MacGregor Fairhaven. Apparently, elements of disaster and safe-harbour (Fair-haven) co-exist within this unwilling traveller, who would prefer to be in his British Columbia home on Eridanus Inlet. Suffering from "a migraine of alienation" (177), Fairhaven withdraws into the "anonymity" of trains and dark Pompeiian restaurants, while his wife, Tansy, who is a born traveller, is at home in her "moving ever changing background" (178). Once again the Lowry protagonist, reflected this time "in a flawed mirror" (177), repeatedly escapes the present reality of their guided tour through the ruined city by withdrawing into memories of Eridanus.

The past, represented by Eridanus, counterpoints the present in Pompeii, and the two ways of life are thrown into contrast. To Fairhaven, the present survival of Pompeii seems more sinister than its destruction, and his memories of an evening at Eridanus with his neighbours, the Wildernesses, when he had read from Volney's *Ruins* bring the meaning of the "present estate" of Pompeii into sharp focus:

> Going through the forest that night with the bounding and whirling cat all at once it had seemed to him, as if he stood outside time altogether, that in

some way these cities of Volney's had not been exactly destroyed, that the ancient populations *had* been reproduced and perpetuated, or rather that the whole damned thing was happening now, at this moment, continually repeating itself. (194)[15]

The guide, Signor Salacci (a somewhat unsuccessful wag), interrupts these thoughts with details concerning Roman brothels and disease, for which a Yeatsian refrain, recalling "Through the Panama" and *Under the Volcano*, provides succinct comment: "The abomination of desolation sitting in the unholy place" (198).

In "Present Estate of Pompeii," the cycles of history—unlike the cycles of nature—appear negative and revolting, and the story ends on a note of cynicism. Man now, as in the past, lives in a dislocated relationship with his environment amidst the everpresent threat of ruin: "Partly it was as if man built with ruin in view" (199). Life unfortunately has *not* changed. Mankind has not been "translated." As Signor Salacci remarks of Vesuvius, "Yesterday she give-a the beeg-a shake!" (200); man always lives under a volcano.

"Gin and Goldenrod," although the shortest and least substantial of the stories, performs an important function within the overall voyage of *Hear Us O Lord*. Following the discouragement in "Present Estate of Pompeii," the story charts the penitential pilgrimage of Sigbjørn Wilderness through a limbo-like motionless landscape:

> It was a warm, still, sunless day in mid-August. The sky did not appear so much cloudy as merely a uniform pearly gray. . . . The sea, where they saw it through the motionless drooping trees, was gray too, the bay looking like a polished metal mirror in which the reflections of the lead-gray mountains were clear and motionless. (201)

Sigbjørn's penance is a true Lowry joke, for he is on his reluctant way to pay a bootlegger for a considerable quantity of gin. Consumed by "terror, fear, distrust, anger, anguish, and a hatred" (202), because of the infernal bourgeois suburb of Dark Rosslyn which lies between his Eridanus cabin and the bootlegger's home, Sigbjørn soon discovers that he is unsure of the way. "Nel mezzo del cammin di nostra vita mi ritrovai in" (115, and 158) seems most applicable here in this mock-Dantean journey. Sigbjørn, lost and despairing, wants to give up the search until his wife reminds him that he undertook the journey "to make a new start" (207). Largely owing to her persistence, they find the house, pay the bill, and leave.

On the way back, their lives appear to have been redeemed—they gather flowers, speak to a woman in her garden, and worry over an ambulance. No longer is Sigbjørn trapped in an abyss of hatred and self-absorption. Finally, the heavens move: "The rain began to fall, soft and gentle and cool, a benison"

(213), prefiguring the circles of raindrops in "The Forest Path to the Spring." Primrose Wilderness confesses that one bottle of gin has survived Sigbjørn's debauch and is hidden at home where they can celebrate the successful completion of their ordeal: "In the cool silver rainy twilight of the forest a kind of hope began to bloom again" (214). This return, if somewhat ironic, marks "a new start," as once more withdrawal is overcome and the Lowry voyager is free to move on into the cycle of "The Forest Path to the Spring."

The final story, "The Forest Path to the Spring," is Lowry's beautiful vision of paradise. It is written in eight parts, the last of which was to be the coda to "The Voyage That Never Ends." Lowry believed the story to contain "some of the best things [he had] ever done" (*Selected Letters*, 245):

> (. . . it is a story of happiness, in fact, roughly of our life here in the forest, exultant side of) entitled "The Forest Path to the Spring." So far as I know this is the only short novel of its type that brings the kind of majesty usually reserved for tragedy . . . to bear on human integration and all that kind of thing: though it isn't my final word on the subject by a damn sight, I'm mighty proud of it. (*Selected Letters*, 266)

"Forest Path," the story of an ex-jazz musician's life in a beach cabin on Eridanus Inlet, is a celebration of the beauty and ferocity of nature. The plot, if it can be called such, consists of a couple's daily activities — swimming, building, boating, helping neighbours and, most important, fetching water and finding a spring. Whether or not the story can be called a "short novel" is debatable. Douglas Day calls it, with the other stories in *Hear Us O Lord*, a "meditation,"[16] and it is certainly another statement of the Lowry myth. "Forest Path" is a quest, a journey in which the nameless protagonist endures withdrawal and return, twice confronts the hell of his past, succumbs to hatred and inertia, and finally voyages on with renewed insight to a temporary position of harmony, balance, and wisdom. In Lowry's words, "the story has no 'back to nature' or Rousseau-like message: there is no 'back' *permanently* to anywhere; the aim is harmony, so that the view is not intended to be sentimentalized" ("WP," Notes, A).

"Forest Path" repeats and resolves the conflict in *Hear Us O Lord*; it marks the full circle point for the voyage introduced in "The Bravest Boat" and begun in "Through the Panama," and it re-affirms Lowry's vision of a new-world Eden regained through marital bliss — the vision which haunts *Volcano* and towards which the couples of *Dark as the Grave* and *October Ferry* struggle.[17] Important motifs such as "Frère Jacques" and the fisherman's hymn, "Hear us O Lord from heaven Thy dwelling place," even key words such as "translate" recur. In fact, "Forest Path" is a positive serial structure reflecting or containing all the stories. Once again, the Lowry world of sea, ship, bells, and lighthouse (the lighthouse that invites the storm and lights it) appears in a natural setting of mysterious power, and the central symbol of the path ("Del cammin") links *Hear Us O Lord* with

Under the Volcano, Dark as the Grave, and *October Ferry*. The path parallels Achad's cabbalistic path in the Tree of Life and Ouspensky's Tarot path,[18] but by calling it the "Proteus" path in the story, Lowry emphasizes its metaphysical value as a symbol of movement, change, and potential flexibility:

> There has always been something preternatural about paths, and especially in forests . . . for not only folklore but poetry abounds with symbolic stories about them: paths that divide and become two paths, paths that lead to a golden kingdom, paths that lead to death, or life, paths where one meets wolves, and who knows? even mountain lions, paths where one loses one's way, paths that not merely divide but become the twenty-one paths [Achad's Cabbalistic paths] that lead back to Eden. (269)

The path in "The Forest Path to the Spring" is, then, the road that the Lowry voyager must travel in his multilevelled quest for the water of life and the season of rebirth.

On the level of psychological quest, the narrator must come to accept the past: "This much I understood, and had understood that as a man I had become tryannized by the past, and that it was my duty to transcend it in the present" (279). The past is like the ladder that the protagonist "salved" from the sea and up and down which his mind climbs "meaninglessly" (261). But only by transforming the past, or by confronting it without fear, as he confronts the cougar on the path, is the Lowry voyager able to create himself in the present and believe in the future. The success or failure of the psychological quest necessarily involves the social quest because by overcoming his withdrawal into the past, the narrator can overcome his misanthropy, which enables him, unlike Geoffrey Firmin, to enjoy communion with his wife and neighbours.

The hatred that nearly destroys him on the path, as it had destroyed the Consul on another forest path, arises from forgetting "nature's intolerance of inertia" (229). He wants to stop the ugly encroachments of civilization in order to maintain his pristine retreat from social, moral, and technological contamination, but unfortunately, he is overlooking the profound truth that, "One could not make a moment permanent and perhaps the attempt to try was some form of evil" (225). Because Lowry tended to describe all conflict in terms of opposites, particularly that of stasis and motion, the consuming problem of hatred that plagues the Lowry protagonist in his search for social identity is also portrayed in this light. In a remarkable image of forest fire, the "Forest Path" narrator describes his agonized hatred as a fiery inversion of the tidal rhythm of the inlet:

> But the movement of the forest fire is almost like a perversion of the movement of the inlet: flames run into a stand of dry inflammable cedar, yellow flames slice them down, and watching, one thinks these flames will roll over the crest of the hill like a tidal wave. Instead, perhaps an hour later, the wind

has changed, or the fire has grown too big for itself, and is now sucking in a draft that opposes its advance. So the fire doesn't sweep up the hill, but instead settles back to eat the morsels of the trees it felled during its first rush. So it seemed was this hatred behaving, turning inward and back upon myself, to devour my very self in its flames. (243-44)

The religious quest in *Hear Us O Lord*, despite the use of the hymn, is not a sectarian one. The Lowry protagonist is searching for faith and meaning which he finds in nature and in virtues that are fundamentally Christian, and "Forest Path" explores a religious crisis in which the narrator, diving into the brimming tides, feels "as though [he has] been baptized afresh" (270). Although the Lowry paradise comprises the sunrises, tides, and mountains which the *balanced* mind perceives as gifts from God, it is not without its warning, for despite a neighbour who is called "Kristbjorg," the colony of squatters is under perpetual threat of eviction. Thus, the narrator's greatest insight in the "Forest Path" is a recognition that "the joy and happiness of what we had known would go with us wherever we went or God sent us and would not die" (281). Paradise, then, is a hard-won state of mind sustained by the acceptance of change and by faith in the creative power of the past. The fact that Lowry more frequently depicted the past as a hellish abyss reveals how ambivalent, how tenuous, he considered the moment of faith to be.

The quest is also an aesthetic one. The narrator's friends bring him a cottage piano because they know that he must create in order to live, and in order to create, he must be able to act and escape the paralysing forces of hatred, doubt, guilt, and fear. Surrounded by the rhythm of the tides he realizes that what he creates — poem, prose, or jazz opera — must capture reality as does his cabin on the beach:

> It was not merely that the sunlight came in, but the very movement and rhythm of the sea, in which the reflections of trees and mountains and sun were counter-reflected and multi-reflected in shimmering movement within. As if part of nature, the very living and moving and breathing reflection of nature itself had been captured. (273)

Again and again in his notes and manuscripts, Lowry refers to the significance of his cabin and pier, and he held a particularly superstitious identification with the pier because he felt it magically embodied the rhythms of the universe. Therefore, for Lowry, pier and cabin typify truly realistic creations — unlike so-called realistic novels — because they are never finished or static. Certainly, *Hear Us O Lord,* with its changing scene and protagonists, is an attempt to create what Lowry understood as a realistic work of art, and by his own standard the book is a success, reflecting as it does his entire opus and completing yet another circle through time and space.

The metaphysical quest underlies, contains, and informs all other aspects of the journey. The insight Lowry found in Aiken, where he learned that "from the whole world, as it revolved through space, came a sound of singing" (271), and the ideas he discovered in Achad, Bergson, Ortega, Ouspensky, and Dunne are given artistic form in "The Forest Path to the Spring." The most dramatic symbol of this accumulated wisdom is the path itself, for during his trips to the spring for water, the narrator feels that the path is "shrinking at both ends" (268); the path seems to *move*. Moreover, the "Proteus" path is the place where, conscious and unconscious fears overcome, he experiences mystical illumination, "a wonderful and profound moment" that reveals the protean nature of reality. Recalling this indescribable moment in a dream, he likens it to the feeling that his "being had been transformed into the inlet itself" and the inlet is always one of Lowry's most positive symbols:

> But here in the inlet there was neither sea nor river, but something compounded of both, in eternal movement, and eternal flux and change, as mysterious and multiform in its motion and being, and in the mind as the mind flowed with it, as was that other Eridanus, the constellation in the heavens, the starry river in the sky. (234).

Man's greatest task, in Lowry's terms, is to live in harmony with this movement. Only by perceiving and understanding the nature of time and space can one know oneself, reality, or God. For Lowry, who was tormented by a Protestant system emphasizing sin, guilt, and fear, the search for metaphysical truth was an arduous personal ordeal which he could only conceive of as a never-ending quest in which man stands perpetually in jeopardy. Futhermore, if the universe were founded on a principle of eternal flow, then there would be no final absolute rest: "Punctum Indifferens: Skibet Gaar Videre." And the voice of the narrator in "Forest Path," speaking in the past tense, is enough to remind the reader that this position of beauty and vision has *already* been left behind.

"The Forest Path to the Spring" closes the circle of *Hear Us O Lord from Heaven Thy Dwelling Place*, but the voyage of withdrawal and return, the expansion and translation, never ceases. The circle, Lowry's symbol for tenuous order, is like the rain falling into the sea:

> Each drop falling into the sea is like a life, I thought, each producing a circle in the ocean, or the medium of life itself, and widening into infinity.... Each is interlocked with other circles falling about it.... Then we saw that the whole dark water was covered with bright expanding phosphorescent circles. ... They were perfect expanding circles of light, first tiny circles bright as a coin, then becoming expanding rings growing fainter and fainter, while as the rain fell into the phosphorescent water each raindrop expanded into a

ripple that was translated into light. And the rain itself was water from the sea . . . raised to heaven by the sun, transformed into clouds, and falling again into the sea. While within the inlet itself the tides and currents in that sea returned, became remote, and becoming remote, like that which is called the Tao, returned again as we ourselves had done. (282)[19]

And this is Lowry's message. Whether in terms of metaphysics or more simply in terms of everyday life, man must achieve faith in universal processes, he must embrace change within himself; most of all, he must live in harmony with nature. This vision of the rain falling into the sea at the close of "Forest Path" counterbalances Yvonne's interpretation of the bull's ordeal in *Volcano* as "like a life; the important birth, the fair chance . . . followed by disaster, capitulation, disintegration" (261), and Lowry hoped that "The Forest Path to the Spring," in which he described human happiness with the enthusiasm and high seriousness usually found in tragedy would "impress you as a direct impression of life in its universal flux and flow, agings and decays and renewals" (WP," Notes, E).

Conclusion

A conclusion to a study of Malcolm Lowry is inevitably something of a *punctum indifferens*, if for no other reason than because the pleasure of reading and re-reading, of discovery, will go on. But some points can be made with certainty. Most important is the need to see Lowry's work as a whole: "The Voyage That Never Ends" was more to him than a grandiose plan for a masterwork that he did not live to complete. Through its repetition and elaboration within each text, as well as from text to text in the "Voyage," the concept of never-ending voyage provides substantial unity for the unfinished novel cycle. An appreciation of the "Voyage," in turn, encourages a reconsideration of *Ultramarine, Lunar Caustic, Dark as the Grave,* and *October Ferry* which, as the preceeding chapters show, richly reward close examination. Furthermore, to see Lowry's masterpiece, *Under the Volcano,* as part of the "Voyage" is to see it from an important perspective—as a crucial stage in the Lowry process of withdrawal and return.

This rhythm, or process, of withdrawal and return characterizes all aspects of Lowry's work, from his magnificent wheeling prose and deliberately repetitive plots, to his understanding of man's artistic and spiritual relation to his world. And although he did not organize or formulate his views as, for example, Yeats did in *A Vision,* the principle of continuous voyaging structured through regular withdrawal and return represents his response to the terrifying antinomies of human existence, as well as the nexus of his own aesthetic and philosophic system. Thus, in Lowry's fiction, the protagonist must repeatedly withdraw from the present into the past, from happiness into the depths of despair, from a sense of community with others into the loneliness of self, from the recognition of an external reality into a terrifying inner world of hallucination, and if this individual, for whatever tragic or simply perverse reason, refuses to swing back, to return from the negative state of withdrawal, then he will be destroyed. However, if he continues to "strive upwards," he will escape Geoffrey Firmin's dead end, at least temporarily. But only by accepting the need for *continual* withdrawal and return can the Lowry protagonist heal the "immedicable horror of opposites" because, for Lowry, the controlled movement between a set of opposites creates psychic balance, and a balanced psyche, like that lost to Geoffrey Firmin but found by Ethan Llewelyn, indicates an individual at peace with himself, trusting in the future and living in harmony with nature. Undoubtedly the most terrifying aspect of this basic process, as it unfolds in Lowry's fiction, is the recurring need to withdraw. But Lowry nowhere implies that one can have the light without the dark: the other side of movement is stasis; to know harmony, one must know chaos; hell and heaven are the same place.

Although Lowry's protagonists toy with different methods for achieving balanced rhythmic movement between opposites, for Lowry himself harmony existed largely in his art; he needed to continue writing as much as he needed to maintain the delicate balance between his private life and his fiction, and for a writer terrified of "being written," the danger of withdrawing finally into his own work was only too real. Furthermore, his belief that fiction should mirror a reality that is itself in constant process of becoming placed an added burden on his art, and, as a result, the chief weakness of his writing is his tendency to overload his narrative, in part because of a desire to include everything and in part because of a fundamental unwillingness to bring sentence or subject to a close. His style, use of proliferating images and allusions, and choice of techniques to suggest shifting levels in his fiction all indicate this desire to create a continuous narrative-in-process. Similarly, his use of multiple point of view in *Volcano* and the self-reflexive "Voyage" narrator/protagonist, Sigbjørn Wilderness, convey a strong sense of a many-levelled personality or consciousness which attains increasing breadth and balance. Indeed, as Brian O'Kill and Ruth Perlmutter remark, one in terms of stylistics, the other in terms of semiotics, Lowry's use of narrators, or multiple point of view, creates the illusion of perceptual as much as perspectival movement.[1] Metaphorically, at least, Sigbjørn Wilderness, as writer of the entire "Voyage," can move beyond the closed perspective of his character, Geoffrey Firmin, whereas in *Volcano* the reader alone learns from his dramatic entrapment within four isolated views of the world, each one of which precludes understanding of the others, and in *October Ferry*, he shares in the process "of divesting oneself—by an arrangement, balancing them against their opposites—of unbalanced ideas" (169), as a single mind struggles toward equilibrium.

Many people have tried to describe Malcolm Lowry through his work and yet it is finally the protean quality of his fluctuating moods and constantly evolving fictions which has eluded, up to a point, the research of his biographer, Douglas Day, and even the cinematic impressionism of Donald Brittain.[2] However, the Canadian poet Al Purdy, who did not know him well but shared his love for language and gin, has captured the essential Lowry—chiefly by not trying to capture him at all. In the poem, "Malcolm Lowry," Purdy's tentative and incomplete remembering—"Not much reason/ to remember him on the beach"—evokes the image of "soused writer" and brilliant, ever-shifting coastal landscape without presuming to define either. Instead, the reader *sees* man, stones, trees, mountains, and water "slightly moving" in a world where "only/ the composition of colours must be/ much the same."[3]

Perhaps it requires another artist who also believes in the principle of continuous change, within nature as well as art—"I say the stanza ends/ but it never does"[4]—to appreciate the Lowry challenge and dilemma. In any case the basic philosophic and aesthetic affinity between Lowry and Purdy is but one instance of the larger context for Lowry's art.

National claims to Lowry are generally irrelevant because he remained legally and in other ways British, and what has been called his "Englishness" is apparent in his language—lexicon, idiom, nuance of voice—and use of a British literary tradition, a use which is echoed today by John Fowles.[5] Nevertheless, his work shares much with modern and contemporary Canadian writers, and he does "belong" spiritually to the country he loved. For example, one cannot read Canadian literature without confronting a peculiarly intense and pervasive awareness of what Robert Kroetsch calls "all the old dualities," for the country was founded upon dualities of language, race, religion, politics, and geography. Indeed the special concern for duality, for "seeing double" as Margaret Atwood describes it, is not only modern; many nineteenth-century Canadian writers presented the land and its culture in these terms. What makes Lowry appear so at home in the context of Canadian dualities is his need to balance and harmonize them instead of cancelling out one or the other.[6] It is a need felt by Hugh MacLennan, Sinclair Ross, Robertson Davies, Gabrielle Roy, Margaret Laurence, Robert Kroetsch, and Margaret Atwood. But of all these writers, or the others who could be mentioned, none has spoken with greater clarity or sympathy of this need for a harmonious process of balancing opposites than Sheila Watson. The characters in her classic, *The Double Hook,* experience a withdrawal into death, sterility, emptiness, and isolation and a return to life, fertility, ritual, and community. In the process they learn that life is cyclical, that darkness will recur only to be replaced with light because

> you can't catch the glory on a hook and hold onto it. . . .
> when you fish for the glory you catch the darkness too. . . .
> if you hook twice the glory you hook twice the fear.[7]

Lowry's fiction reveals how profoundly he knew that double hook.

Lowry also shares with Canadian writers an almost obsessive interest in a past that one cannot, indeed must not, escape, and a longing for what Northrop Frye describes as the "peaceable kingdom." As Margaret Laurence has claimed, Canadians must go home again if they are to know themselves and be able to develop in the future.[8] At the same time, the past can become a trap for the weak or self-indulgent because successful movement within memory depends upon the awareness that time should not be reified or hypostasized, that time is process. Thus, Lowry's characters like those of Laurence, Davies, or Alice Munro succeed in the search for self to the degree that they accomodate the past in the present and future. The dream of a "peaceable kingdom" which Frye identifies in much Canadian writing is closely associated with the desire to balance opposites and to overcome the separation between nature and culture.[9] Moreover, the "peaceable kingdom" is synonymous with a northern paradise, or first "home," which the

Canadian Adam and Eve must return to together; it is the kingdom Lowry celebrates in "The Forest Path to the Spring."

Lowry's obsession with temporal process, duality, and a northern paradise, however, does not link him solely with Canadian writing, and these concerns, central as they are, do not define Lowry's work. In many ways Lowry is recognizably a modernist—in his narrative strategies, his interest in time and space, and his exploration of the epistemological limits of language and fiction. Some of his writing can even be usefully compared with the metafiction of post-modernist writers. But on a fundamental level, Lowry retains ties with the nineteenth-century romantic moralists such as Coleridge and Carlyle, for his almost religious vision of self and world is passionately, personally expressed. The cool, ironic distance, the parody, the anti-realist foregrounding of language of Barth, Nabokov, or even Joyce are foreign to Lowry's work because the reader must respond with and to Lowry's writing emotionally. Of twentieth-century writers, his fictional world most resembles that of Conrad and Faulkner, a world of conspiracy, disaster, of fateful coincidence, moral terror, of a personal defeat that mirrors wider destruction, and yet of faith in man's ability to endure, perhaps prevail.

What these comparisons neglect is the largeness, the scope and complexity, of Lowry's writing, especially in *Under the Volcano*. Lowry's heir in this respect is Thomas Pynchon, particularly the Pynchon of *Gravity's Rainbow*. Both Lowry and Pynchon display stunning erudition in these many-levelled narratives which transform elements of traditional realism into symbol and parable. For both, character portrayal is of secondary importance, and language itself, in its sheer exuberance and power, receives first attention. At the centre of *Under the Volcano* and *Gravity's Rainbow* lies "The Word," *logos* and "Mene-Tekel-Peres." Similarities between the two works are many and striking, from their heroes—both of whom are twentieth-century men stalked by puritan ghosts—to the parallels between Lowry's hallucinatory Mexican landscape and the drugged nightmare of Pynchon's World War 2 "Zone." But most importantly, fictions such as *Volcano* and *Gravity's Rainbow* are encyclopaedic—containing, mirroring, mocking yet mourning contemporary systems and human madness. Encyclopaedic narratives, in Edward Mendelson's description, "attempt to incorporate representative elements of all the varieties of knowledge their societies put to use."[10] They are, as well, "polyglot books" commenting upon political systems and social and literary history, containing within themselves "images of their enormous scale" (in *Volcano,* of course, old "Popo" itself), and finally, prophesying upon actual historical events from a point in time just prior to those events. Characters in encyclopaedic fictions are not stable, three-dimensional individuals, and multiple point of view (such a striking feature in *Volcano*) is less an attempt to provide objectivity than to create an all-encompassing human consciousness,[11] the type of consciousness Lowry wanted to create in "The Voyage That Never Ends."

Generically, *Under the Volcano,* like *Gravity's Rainbow* and *Ulysses,* combines all four of Frye's prose fiction forms of novel, confession, anatomy, and romance, and it is the anatomy that links these fictions with encyclopaedism.[12] Where twentieth-century encyclopaedic narratives such as *Volcano* and *Gravity's Rainbow* differ from *Ulysses,* however, is in their intent. *Ulysses* is the quintessential modernist triumph because of its studied distance from the world, its monumental *ar*tificialty, but there is a strong ethical thrust to *Under the Volcano* (as there also is to *Gravity's Rainbow*) which attempts to close the emotional and imaginative gap between world and book, reader and text.[13] And it is precisely this desire to enter the reader's world, to warn, that epitomizes *Under the Volcano* and was to be focal in "The Voyage That Never Ends." *Volcano,* after all, is "passionate writing about things that will always matter," and the "Voyage" was to concern the struggle of the human spirit in the "ordeal" of life.

Lowry's vision and fiction, then, are best described as romantic and encyclopaedic—romantic in their emphasis upon unending voyage and Promethean desire to bring the word to the world, encyclopaedic in their style, themes, and formal scope. But Lowry's context, like critical comparisons, can only suggest ways of thinking about his art. His achievement finally resides in the fiction itself—in his masterpiece *Under the Volcano,* in the experiments with narrative form of *October Ferry to Gabriola* and *Hear Us O Lord from Heaven Thy Dwelling Place,* and in the philosophic, moral, and aesthetic interest of the "Voyage." Malcolm Lowry is one of the small number of writers who has tried to express what it means to be fully human and, therefore, his work continues to offer moving insight into the artistic, social, and spiritual dilemmas of twentieth-century life.

Appendix: Conrad Aiken

Conrad Aiken (1889-1973), American poet and novelist, was without doubt the major influence on Lowry, but for various reasons their literary relationship is less well known than it should be.[1] This may be partially because Aiken has been neglected by scholars until quite recently and partially because Lowry was slow to acknowledge his debt to the older writer. In fact, it was not until 1952, when *Wake* published a special Aiken issue, that Lowry commented publicly upon their friendship, and the extent of their relationship did not become clear until the publication of *Selected Letters* (1965) which included, at Margerie Lowry's timely insistence, a very few of the many letters which Lowry wrote Aiken from 1928 until shortly before his death. Over forty of Lowry's letters to Aiken, most of them unpublished, are in the Aiken collection at the Huntington Library and in them Lowry comments upon the copies of Aiken's work, such as *Brownstone Eclogues* (1942) and *Ushant* (1952), which Aiken had sent him, asks Aiken for help of various kinds, and reveals over and over again the influence Aiken's work, friendship, and conversation have had upon *Ultramarine, Under the Volcano,* and the later fiction. The influence was not entirely one-sided, however, and the story of this symbiotic relationship will not be complete until their correspondence is collected and published on its own.[2]

When he discovered Aiken's poem "House of Dust" (later a part of *The Divine Pilgrim*) in 1928, Lowry wrote its author, thereby beginning the friendship which Aiken summarized so accurately in 1971:

> *Blue Voyage* [Aiken's 1927 novel] he knew better than I did—he knew it by heart. Its influence on him was profound and permanent. . . . But though the influence was to continue even into the later work, a matter that was frequently and amusedly discussed between us, and was also to comprise a great deal that was said by me in conversation, it was much more compli-cated than that. The fact is that we were uncannily alike in almost everything, found instantly that we spoke the same language, were astonishingly *en rapport*.[3]

Although the influence of *Blue Voyage* on *Ultramarine* is now well known, the general impact on Lowry of Aiken's other work, including his views on art, are less well understood. But a familiarity with Aiken's philosophy and aesthetics certainly does illuminate the direction Lowry was taking.[4] Even a brief examination of Aiken's art, in particular *The Divine Pilgrim, Great Circle, Blue Voyage,* and *Mr. Arcularis,* reveals the influence and remarkable affinity of which Aiken speaks.

The central aim of Aiken's poetry and fiction is the investigation and development of consciousness—in particular, the self-consciousness of the writer. Speaking of fiction, Aiken writes that the "novel is the novelist's inordinate and copious lyric: he explores himself, and sings while he explores, like the gravedigger."[5] A long poetic sequence such as *The Divine Pilgrim* also explores the relationship between the universe and human consciousness in terms of the poet's mind, and Aiken presents the world as an inner landscape in elaborate metaphors of a city with winding streets, houses, stairs, windows and towers; landscape reflects the soul. Describing the projection of evanescent memories and dreams in which time and space appear to flow, merge, disintegrate, and reform, Aiken writes that, "the attempt has been made to relate these typical dreams, or vicarious adventures, not discreetly, but in flux."[6] What is more, because human identity is equally protean; the fragmented identity of the chief dreamer in *The Divine Pilgrim* represents different aspects of human consciousness.

To Lowry, who was to spend his life in the exploration of his own mind, the discovery of Aiken's poem was crucial, and the central problem of *The Divine Pilgrim* poems—the articulation of reality by an acutely self-conscious artistic mind—is reworked by Lowry in each of his novels. For Aiken, this articulation is of central importance because he had come to believe that language has a magic quality. Lowry also believed in the magical power of the word to represent the experience it names, and his habit of writing at great length and in energetic rushes reflects his belief that life and the flow of language are one.

Before turning to Aiken's prose, it is important to note that for the most part his poetry is deliberately presented as an interrelated series. In fact, Aiken's prose and poetry were intended to be interconnected and counterpointed much like Lowry's. For example, *Blue Voyage* and *Ushant,* the latter a continuation of the former, were intended to complement *The Divine Pilgrim* and *Preludes to Memnon,* which consist of several long poems exploring levels of reality and consciousness. Aiken conceived of both reality and consciousness as multi-levelled and the evolution of consciousness as a never-ending process: serial form, therefore, seemed the most viable way to present these ideas.[7]

Aiken's use of serial form and his concept of the evolution of consciousness are of particular interest with respect to Lowry. In a late preface (1965) to *Preludes for Memnon,* which he had started in 1927 after *Blue Voyage,* Aiken describes his use of serial form as "an attempt to find the ground for a new poiesis."[8] This poetic theory based on serialism (both musical and mathematical, according to Aiken) afforded great flexibility and replaced, to an extent, the beliefs, ethics, and gods destroyed by modern physics and psychoanalysis. Serial form also presented an excellent vehicle for portraying evolving consciousness.

In his 1948 preface to "House of Dust," the poem from *The Divine Pilgrim* that had so impressed Lowry in 1928, Aiken makes observations about consciousness that he must have discussed earlier with Lowry:

> Implicit in [the poem] . . . is the theory that was to underlie much of the later work—namely, that in the evolution of man's consciousness, ever widening and deepening and subtilizing his awareness, and in his dedication of himself to this supreme task, man possesses all that he could possibly require in the way of a religious credo.[9]

Lowry's "Voyage That Never Ends" is a re-statement of this "religious credo."

Aiken's short stories and novels, like the poems, begin and end in the mind of the chief protagonist, usually an erudite, cynical, failed writer or husband. Broken marriage is the recurrent theme which provides the focal issue in Aiken's stories, such as "Round by Round" and "The Fish Supper," and in the novel *Great Circle* (1933).[10] Starting with apparently straightforward domestic conflict, Aiken expands his theme through the protagonist's consciousness until he plumbs the depths of the past. The dilemma posed by a traumatic past is central to the novel, *Great Circle,* which both *Volcano* and *Dark as the Grave* resemble, and which Lowry had drawn upon closely for "The Last Address."[11]

Great Circle opens with a one-eyed university professor, Andrew Cather, on a train returning to Boston, ostensibly to surprise his wife, whom he suspects of betraying him with his best friend. As the train rushes into the future, he becomes increasingly obsessed with his past. In a present charged with dreadful expectations for the immediate future Cather finds himself reliving his childhood horror at finding his mother drowned with her lover, his uncle. As Cather staggers from a bar to his home, then out again to drink and finally to the home of a psychoanalyst friend, the point of the book becomes clear—the past must be understood before life can truly begin:[12] man must complete a great circle through time and space before he can move into the future.

Cather has a facility for interpreting external reality as symbol and portent. A coincidence, such as the authorities' search for a drowned man just as Cather crosses the river, becomes charged with significance, and the parallel here between Aiken's handling of the perceiving consciousness and Lowry's in *Volcano* is obvious. Furthermore, Aiken employs his favorite dream mechanism to recreate the summer during which Cather discovered his mother's adultery, but Aiken's handling of the dream is as obtrusive here as it is in *Blue Voyage.* When Lowry rewrote *Under the Volcano* in 1940-41, he dropped his original plan to use Laruelle's dream as a vehicle for recreating the past, and even in *Dark as the Grave* Lowry's use of dream is more subtle than Aiken's. Where Aiken overloads his narrative with Freudian analysis, Lowry avoids a cumbersome etiology in his fiction, particularly in *Volcano* and *October Ferry.*

Although commonly compared to *Ultramarine, Blue Voyage* is a veritable source book for techniques, images, even words (such as "horripilation" and "tintinnabulation") in *Under the Volcano* and the more striking resemblance between *Blue Voyage* and *Ultramarine* is largely a matter of technique. Lowry's protagonist and his use of the sea voyage owe more to Grieg's *The Ship Sails On* than to *Blue Voyage,* whose chief character, Demarest, is older and more sophisticated than Lowry's and Grieg's heroes, and the nature of the sea voyage, initiatory for Grieg and Lowry, is ironically repetitive for Aiken.

In *Blue Voyage,* Aiken explores Demarest's consciousness through the breakdown of time and space and the projection of personal identity upon all the other characters, male and female, old and young, who represent aspects of Demarest's psyche. Demarest spends his time composing monologues and never-to-be-sent letters — devices used by Lowry in *Ultramarine* and *Volcano* — and when he addresses his lost ideal lover, Cynthia, in his central dream-vision, the voice of Geoffrey Firmin can clearly be heard:

I would have given everything to have been able to wipe out my entire past . . . and all the countless minor episodes . . . constituted for me an inferno from which I seemed never destined to escape. Yes. Horrible. To come to the gateway in a rain of fire and looking through it to see the slopes of Purgatory; to guess, beyond, the Paradise. . . . What I am approaching is a profound psychological truth. It is my own nature, my character as patiently wrought by my character . . . from which I cannot move. *Why this is hell, nor am I out of it.*(83)

Probably Lowry was influenced in a more general way, and at second hand, by Aiken's reading. For example, had he not discovered Jung, Freud, and Bergson before his first meeting with Aiken, then under Aiken's influence he could not have missed them. Aiken had read *The Interpretation of Dreams* in 1915, and his use of dream clearly reflects Freud. Each of Aiken's protagonists, like Lowry's, achieves mental balance by reliving his past, but with Aiken the process is decidedly clinical and therapeutic whereas Lowry's characters, in addition to achieving psychological equilibrium through understanding and accepting the past, experience moments of vision into the nature of reality; reliving the past is more than therapy for early trauma. Both Aiken and Lowry employ Oedipal situations, but again Lowry places less emphasis than Aiken upon this Freudian theory, leaving it to suggest itself rather than allowing it to occupy a central position in his fiction. Aiken was also deeply impressed by Bergson, in particular by *Creative Evolution* (translated in 1931),[13] and intrigued as he was by questions of time, memory, and consciousness, Lowry certainly realized Bergson's relevance to his own work.

There is clearer evidence, however, of Jung's influence on Lowry. The protagonist of the "Voyage" was to be "man's unconscious" (*Selected Letters,* 331), and in his filmscript of *Tender Is the Night,* Lowry relates the sea voyage to Jung before he goes on to criticize Freud for setting up a tyrannous system and to approve Jung's more useful myth of the sea voyage (25:9, 306). But once more

Aiken's influence may have proved the more crucial one because Lowry was very familiar with Aiken's remarkable short story (later a play), *Mr. Arcularis*, which relates a man's imaginery sea voyage through time until he relives and comes to terms with his past before peacefully dying on an operating table.[14] Lowry could not have missed the striking parallel between Aiken's story and his own plan for Sigbjørn Wilderness' hospital experience which would frame "The Voyage That Never Ends." In fact, in an unpublished letter to Aiken written shortly after the fall from his pier on 14 July 1949, which sent him to hospital and precipitated his plans for "The Ordeal Of Sigbjørn Wilderness" (see chapter 1), Lowry describes his own hospital experience and remarks upon how close to the truth *Mr. Arcularis* comes.[15]

Notes

NOTES TO THE INTRODUCTION

1. Margerie Bonner was a novelist in her own right and published three works with Scribner's: *The Last Twist of the Knife* (1946), *The Shapes That Creep* (1946), and *Horse in the Sky* (1947). She wrote several successful radio scripts for the Canadian Broadcasting Corporation and collaborated with Lowry on a filmscript of F. Scott Fitzgerald's *Tender Is the Night*. The Lowry's notes for *Tender Is the Night* have now been published with an introduction by Paul Tiessen as, *Notes on a Screenplay for Tender Is the Night* (Bloomfield Hills, MI: Bruccoli Clark, 1976). For a further discussion of Bonner's work and her influence on Lowry, see my article, "Margerie Bonner's Three Forgotten Novels," *Journal of Modern Literature* 6, 2 (1977): 321-24.
2. From *Selected Poems of Malcolm Lowry*, ed. Earle Birney (San Francisco: City Lights Books, 1962), 78. Lowry's poems, most of them lyrics, are certainly less successful than his prose. A discussion of the poems is beyond the scope of this study, but poems quoted or mentioned in passing are from this collection unless otherwise indicated.
3. The best general discussion of Lowry's life to date is Douglas Day's *Malcolm Lowry: A Biography* (New York: Oxford University Press, 1973). Day's study is a well-written and interesting treatment of Lowry's life, with an excellent analysis of *Under the Volcano*. However, the rest of Lowry's work receives scant attention, and Lowry suffers from Day's determined Freudian approach. In *Malcolm Lowry: His Art and Early Life* (London: Cambridge University Press, 1974), Muriel Bradbrook argues that Lowry's early years, particularly those spent at Cambridge, provided him with material that he used throughout his life. Bradbrook clears up many questions surrounding Lowry's life in England, provides excellent biographical balance to Day, and is one of the first scholars to give serious attention to the post-*Volcano* work. The best general introduction to Lowry's work is still William New's *Malcolm Lowry* in McClelland and Stewart's Canadian Writers Subseries (Toronto, 1971). Richard Hauer Costa's *Malcolm Lowry* (New York: Twayne, 1972) offers many insights into Lowry and his work, most notably Lowry's attitude towards time and his affinity with Jung, and David Markson provides an exhaustive chapter by chapter analysis of Lowry's masterpiece in *Malcolm Lowry's Volcano: Myth, Symbol, Meaning* (New York: Times Books, 1978).
4. At the end of *Malcolm Lowry* (Erin, Ontario: Press Porcepic, 1973), Tony Kilgallin provides a list of one hundred writers whose work Lowry knew. It is an interesting but misleading list because only a few of these writers influenced Lowry's thought and art. The others are more accurately "kindred spirits," as Killgallin calls them, because Lowry was primarily attracted by their lives.
5. In *The Private Labyrinth of Malcolm Lowry* (New York: Holt, Rinehart and Winston, 1969), 4, Perle Epstein writes that the influence of Joyce on Lowry "is a critical commonplace." Costa offers a more closely argued explanation in "*Ulysses*, Lowry's *Volcano*, and the Voyage Between," *University of Toronto Quarterly* 36 (1967): 335-52. However, Lowry's key influences lie elsewhere. On 22 June 1946, for example, Lowry wrote his editor, Albert Erskine, regarding allusions and other matters in *Volcano*. Only part of the letter appears in *Selected Letters*, 112-14, and the accompanying notes are unpublished. Explaining Geoffrey's anguish in chapter 12, he writes:

   There are many influences here in the Consul's thought ... of contemporary ones Ouspensky is most drawn upon, though I seem to spot even a bit of beastly old Spengler at work in one section. ... Claude Houghton plays some part here. ... See Julian Grant Loses His Way, yet another novel about hell, where the author's method is just to throw in Swedenborg by the bushelful and leave it at that. (2:6, 12)

   And Lowry also points out that Ralph Bates' *The Fields of Paradise* (1940) suggested the Spanish-English dialogue and the use of the important word "Compañero."

   Lowry had read *The Art of the Novel* and seems to have taken the lessons of the master to heart. Following James' example, he concentrated on drama of consciousness, used an indirect narrator (with consummate skill in *Under the Volcano*), and recognized the need to show rather than to tell. In a reminiscence of Lowry, a Cambridge friend and editor of *Experiment*, Gerald Noxon, emphasizes Lowry's respect for the nineteenth century:

> Basically Malcolm was unwilling to repudiate the legacy which he had found awaiting him in the works of nineteenth-century novelists. While discarding the aridity of a purely realistic style, he was unwilling to adopt the kind of personal stenography which made the works of writers like Joyce and Faulkner superficially difficult for the reader but still insisting that his writing must be capable of carrying meaning at many different levels of intellectual and emotional communication which he discerned in Melville, for instance. ("Malcolm Lowry, 1930," *Prairie Schooner 37* [1963-64]: 318)

For Lowry's remarks on Melville see *Selected Letters*, 197. While never knowing Melville's fiction particularly well, he was moved by Melville's life.

6. For a discussion of the Lowry legend see Russell Lowry's "Preface: Malcolm — A Closer Look," in *The Art of Malcolm Lowry*, ed. Anne Smith (London: Vision Press, 1978), 9-27.

7. Day briefly describes "Work in Progess," dismissing it as "rather muddled" and as containing little "to gladden the heart of a publisher" (*Malcolm Lowry*, 426-27). But after seeing "Work in Progress," Random House offered Lowry a long-term contract, and Robert Giroux of Harcourt Brace believed that the new "Voyage" plan promised to be "the most important literary project of the decade" (*Selected Letters*, 455). In 1975 Albert Erskine sent me a complete copy of this impressive statement which expands upon the remarks Lowry made in his letters and clarifies his purposes. It is now on deposit in the Lowry collection at The University of British Columbia, Box 37.

NOTES TO CHAPTER ONE

1. "Ghostkeeper" was first published in *American Review* 17 (Spring, 1973): 1-34, and reprinted in *Psalms and Songs*, ed. Margerie Lowry (New York: Meridian, 1975), 202-27. All references are to *Psalms and Songs*. The story is an intriguing example of Lowry's type of metafiction. It moves from polished prose passages, to notes, to trial dialogue, as the protagonist, Bill Goodheart, writes his story within the story in which he is being written. "Ghostkeeper" recalls "Through the Panama" in style, but it is more interesting for Lowry's comments on life and art. For further discussion of the story see Barry Wood's, "Malcolm Lowry's Metafiction: The Biography of a Genre," *Contemporary Literature* 19 (1978): 1-25.

2. Dunne's book on serialism, *An Experiment with Time*, first published in 1927, enjoyed great popularity during the thirties, and Jones became a close friend who gave Lowry access to his library of mystic lore. The influence of Dunne and Jones is discussed in chapters 3 and 5. The influence of Ouspensky is diffuse and harder to assess, but see *A New Model of the Universe* (New York: Vintage Books, 1971), chapter 10, where he discusses the relationship of time, space, and consciousness within his holistic vision of an "eternally changing universe."

3. Lowry uses the term "churrigueresque" to describe *Under the Volcano* in *Selected Letters*, 82, 88. It is an architectural term describing the Spanish baroque style which reached its height in Mexico in the late seventeenth and early eighteenth centuries.

4. Brian O'Kill claims that Lowry typically avoids "the closed unit of the periodic sentence in favour of an open form with an almost infinite capacity for addition and reduplication" ("Aspects of Language in *Under the Volcano*," in *The Art of Malcolm Lowry*, 78).

5. *Dark as the Grave Wherein My Friend Is Laid* (New York: New American Library, 1968), 154. All further references are to this edition and are included in the text.

6. These are Mrs. Lowry's words quoting Lowry.

7. In his essay "Malcolm Lowry as Modernist," from *Possibilities: Essays on the State of the Novel* (London: Oxford Univesity Press, 1973), Bradbury remarks that "there lies, behind the experimental and modernist spirit, a deep vein of romanticism. . . . Lowry's essential assumptions about art thus tend to be purist romantic ones" (184). Lowry cannot be called an "anti-realist" even though he uses parody and explores the boundaries of fiction and life in "Ghostkeeper" and "Through the Panama." In "Notes on the Rhetoric of Anti-Realist Fiction," *Triquarterly* 30 (Spring, 1974): 3–50, Albert Guerard suggests some useful distinctions between American anti-realist fiction and fiction that imitates life and uses inherited forms.

8. *October Ferry to Gabriola* (New York: World Publishing, 1970), 61. All further references are to this edition and are included in the text.

9. Lowry's first oblique reference to the "Voyage" comes in an early letter to Conrad Aiken tentatively dated "Spring, 1940." Lowry closes thus: "Do send me news of you both and news too of the voyage that never ends" (*Selected Letters*, 25). Very likely Lowry and Aiken had already discussed the idea of never-ending voyage.

10. In his article "Lowry's Debt to Nordahl Grieg," *Canadian Literature* 64 (Spring, 1975): 41–51, Hallvard Dahlie examines the textual similarities of *Ultramarine* and *The Ship Sails On* in detail. It seems likely that Lowry was more impressed by Grieg's life and ideals than by his style. Grieg, an idealistic man from a disinguished family, sailed as a common seaman while young, spent a year at Oxford, and wrote essays, poetry, plays, and fiction. He held strong proletarian sympathies. In 1937 he went to Spain as a correspondent, and during 1936–37 he published the anti-fascist periodical *Vein Friem (The Road Ahead)*. During World War II he went to England where he read his poems of peace and patriotism for the BBC/Norway Broadcasts. These poems were published after his death as *War Poems of Nordahl Grieg* (1944). His plane was shot down over Berlin in 1943. Grieg was a restless, committed man of action and deep feeling, and he may well have provided the model for the best qualities that Lowry gave Hugh in *Under the Volcano*.

11. This outline appears on the title page of the statement. Further references to "Work in Progress" are included in the text as "WP," followed by the page number. David Miller's short monograph, *Malcolm Lowry and the Voyage That Never Ends* (London: Enitharmon Press, 1976) confuses the order of the sequence.

12. *Malcolm Lowry*, 419. Day goes on to suggest that Lowry began the "Ordeal" after the accident, but soon lost interest. This seems unlikely since the 1951 "Work in Progress" emphasizes its importance, and Lowry refers to the "Ordeal" later in a 1954 letter to David Markson (*Selected Letters*, 368)

13. In *Malcolm Lowry: His Art and Early Life*, 113–17, Muriel Bradbrook discusses the background and fictional transformation of the Fitte episode. She emphasizes the importance of Lowry's early years to his life's work. For further discussion of Lowry's part in the inquest into Fitte's death see the correspondence in the *Times Literary Supplement* for 26 April and 10, 13, 17, and 24 May 1974.

14. By this point in 1951, *October Ferry* had not developed into a major novel, and "La Mordida" completed the sequence. Sigbjørn's fears about his wife's scepticism parallel Margerie's reaction to Lowry's version of his back injury. She lost patience with his ramblings. As Lowry suggests, the "Ordeal" was to end much like the story, "The Forest Path to the Spring."

15. *Toward a Philosophy of History* (New York: W. H. Norton, 1941), 113. Ortega's ideas were most congenial to Lowry. A staunch Heraclitean, Ortega praised the dynamic of creativity and maintained that through memory man accumulates, possesses, and must use his past in order to create the future. This belief in memory and the past is a constant hope of the Lowry protagonist.

16. In "Malcolm Lowry's Metafiction," Wood offers a refreshing and important argument for re-evaluating Lowry's later fiction as metafiction instead of as failed novels. He is quite right in seeing "Ghostkeeper" as a paradigm of Lowry's inten-

tion and method, and I would agree with his speculation that the "Voyage" would have been metafictional.
17. Lowry describes the plot of "In Ballast" to David Markson in *Selected Letters,* 225ff.
18. In an important unpublished letter to Albert Erskine dated December, 1953, Lowry repeats this idea of the dead man forced to follow the live one. See discussion of this letter in chapter 5.
19. In *Mythology in the Modern Novel* (Princeton, NJ: Princeton University Press, 1971), 8, John White speaks of *Under the Volcano* and *Finnegans Wake* as "seeking to create a new myth." Lowry's myth is best understood in the terms of Robert Scholes and Robert Kellogg. They define *mythos* as "traditional story" which can be retold or recreated and myth as "a traditional plot which can be transmitted" ("The Narrative Tradition," in *The Novel: Modern Essays in Criticism,* ed. R. M. Davis [Englewood Cliffs, NJ: Prentice-Hall, 1969]).

NOTES TO CHAPTER TWO

1. The phrase "outward bound" is one of Lowry's nucleii of meaning referring to a ship's voyage from port and symbolizing the voyage of the soul or consciousness through life. It first appears in the early story, "June the 30th, 1934," which is discussed below, and it recurs throughout Lowry's work, most importantly in *Ultramarine* and *October Ferry*. As a character in "June the 30th, 1934" explains, the phrase comes from Sutton Vane's play, *Outward Bound* (New York: Boni and Liveright, 1924). In the play, all the characters on the boat are dead and outward bound for hell or heaven: "It's the same place you see." See chapter 5 for a further discussion of *Outward Bound*.
2. See the bibliography for a further list of Lowry's early stories. Suzanne Kim, in "Les oeuvres de jeunesse de Malcolm Lowry," *Etudes anglaises* 18 (1965): 383-94, offers a detailed discussion of Lowry's efforts at the Leys. I am concerned with four later stories dating from the late twenties and early thirties because they illustrate Lowry's growing appreciation of structure and his efforts to articulate his basic themes.
3. "Garden of Etla," *United Nations World* (June, 1950): 45-47.
4. "China," *Psalms and Songs,* 49-54. Further references are included in the text.
5. "Bulls of the Resurrection," dating from c. 1933, appeared in *Prism International* 5, no. 1 (1965): 5-11. Further references are included in the text.
6. "June the 30th, 1934." *Psalms and Songs,* 36-48. Further references are included in the text.
7. The "iron cross" is an allusion to Hermann Broch's *The Sleepwalkers: A Trilogy* (London: M. Secker, 1932), which Lowry admired. In Broch's book, the military iron cross worn by the aristocratic and romantic von Pasenow symbolizes the apparent substance of mankind's achievements, achievements which are, in fact, pathetic, destructive illusions. In the preceding paragraph of "June 30th, 1934" Lowry calls the train's passengers "somnambulists." This description, coupled with the reference to the iron cross, gives an ironic twist to Goodyear's vision of change.
8. The story was published under its new title (suggested by Aiken) in *The Best Short Stories of 1931,* ed. E.J. O'Brien (New York, 1931), 80-107. When Lowry incorporated the story into *Ultramarine,* he added a long passage in which Dana relives his last night in Liverpool. The "Skibet Gaar Videre" of the original title is from Grieg's *The Ship Sails On*. The story is also included in *Psalms and Songs*.
9. All references are to the 1962 Lippincott edition of *Ultramarine* and are included in the text. Pagination is identical in the 1963 Cape edition.
10. While many critics refuse to consider *Ultramarine* as of interest or value, a few have begun to examine the text seriously. Geoffrey Durrant in "Aiken and Lowry" and Hallvard Dahlie in "Lowry's Debt to Nordahl Grieg" argue

for the skill and complexity of the novel, while Ronald Binns in "Lowry's Anatomy of Melcancholy," claims that *Ultramarine* anticipates the open-ended, affirmative structure of *Dark as the Grave* and *October Ferry*. All three articles are in *Canadian Literature* 64 (Spring, 1975).

11. *Lunar Caustic*, edited by Earle Birney and Margerie Lowry, was first published in *Paris Review* 8 (1963): 12-72, and later re-issued by Jonathan Cape in 1968. All references are to the Cape edition. David Benham discusses the two versions in some detail in his article, "Lowry's Purgatory: Versions of *Lunar Casutic*," in *Malcolm Lowry: The Man and His Work. Lunar Caustic* is included in *Psalms and Songs*.

12. There may be several influences at work in Lowry's description of the puppet show, but one of particular interest is Robison's *Warning Shadows* (1922), which introduces the characters as shadows on a stage. Huge shadow hands take the characters away to emphasize the ominous sense of control. Several times Plantagenet is disturbed by the giant hand that snatches the puppets from the stage during the show (*Lunar Caustic*, 36-37).

NOTES TO CHAPTER THREE

1. *Selected Letters*, 201. Pethick was preparing a talk on *Volcano* for CBC.
2. The contemporary Black-American writer John A. Williams has cited Lowry as an influence; "In terms of form, my single influence has been Malcolm Lowry in *Under the Volcano*. I tried to emulate him in *Sissie* and improve on what he did with the telescoping of time. But I think I did much better in *The Man Who Cried I Am*" (*Interviews with Black Writers*, ed. John O'Brien [New York: Liveright, 1973], 233). Interestingly enough, David Markson, who knew Lowry well and wrote the first thesis on *Volcano*, also shows Lowry's influence in his novel *Going Down* (New York: Holt, Rinehart, Winston, 1970), particularly with regard to allegory and the excellent handling of time. According to William New, Lowry's influence is apparent in the work of New Zealand writer, Russell Haley. (See New's article, "Russell Haley's Lowry," in *Malcolm Lowry Newsletter* 4 [Spring, 1979]: 20-22, edited by Paul Tiessen, Wilfrid Laurier University). Among other writers to be influenced by Lowry's techniques or vision are French novelist, Tony Cartano, author of *Malcolm Lowry: Essai* (Henri Veyrier, 1979), Mexican writer Gerardo de la Torre whose story "Farolito" appears in *De los tres ninguno* (Federacion Editorial Mexicana, 1974) and Canadian novelist, poet, and critic, Robert Kroetsch, for whom Lowry is an inspiring kindred spirit.
3. To cite all those whose studies of *Volcano* have contributed to my understanding of the novel would be to repeat three-quarters of the bibliography, but since the publication of Day's biography in 1973 at least two other critics have attempted the *Gestalt* reading Day called for: Kristofor Dorosz in *Malcolm Lowry's Infernal Paradise* (Stockholm: University of Uppsala, 1976) and Barry Wood in his introduction to *Malcolm Lowry: The Writer and his Critics* (Ottawa: Tecumseh Press, 1980). The most exhaustive, and certainly invaluable, exegesis is David Markson's *Malcolm Lowry's Volcano: Myth, Symbol, Meaning*.
4. For a detailed discussion of Lowry's expressionism, see my article, "Malcolm Lowry and the Expressionist Vision," in *The Art of Malcolm Lowry*, 93-111. In "The Escape from Irony: *Under the Volcano* and the Aesthetics of Arson," *Novel* 10 (1977): 114-26, Charles Baxter refers to the "expressionistic framework" of *Volcano*, but he does not develop the idea.
5. For a detailed discussion of the Cabbala in *Under the Volcano*, see Perle Epstein's *The Private Labyrinth of Malcolm Lowry*. The Cabbala references Epstein discusses were a late addition for which the essential vision was already present. Yvonne's role is interestingly explained

by Epstein, however, who sees her as a *Shekinah* figure embodying God's feminine essence. From this perspective, Geoffrey's denial of Yvonne further emphasizes his spiritual isolation.

6. The two different manuscript versions with annotated carbon copies are housed in the Special Collections Division at the University of British Columbia. The manuscript version examined here is an annotated copy of the first complete novel version of the book (8:1-12). This annotated copy is marked, possibly in Margerie's writing, as "the draft refused by publishers in 1940 nearly complete." Several pencilled remarks on the typescript indicate Lowry's ideas for the eventual re-writing of the book.
7. *Under the Volcano*, 268. All references are to the Cape edition (London, 1947).
8. Martha Foley was a reader for Harcourt-Brace.
9. *An Experiment with Time* (London: Faber & Faber, 1969), 133. First published in 1927.
10. In his fine study, "*Under the Volcano:* A Reading of the Immediate Level," *Tulane Studies in English* 16 (1968): 63-105, Edmonds argues that the plot of *Volcano* functions very well and that events develop quickly and logically, one from the other.
11. Day, *Malcolm Lowry*, 332.
12. The term "spatial form" was used in the analysis of modern literature by Joesph Frank in *The Widening Gyre: Crisis and Mastery in Modern Literature* (New Brunswick, N.J.: Rutgers University Press, 1963). For other discussions of spatial form in *Volcano*, see Victor Doyen, "Elements Towards a Spatial Reading of Malcolm Lowry's *Under the Volcano,*" *English Studies* 50, no. 1 (1969): 56-61; Terence Wright, "*Under the Volcano:* The Static Art of Malcolm Lowry," *Ariel* 1, no. 4 (1970): 67-76; Sherrill Grace, "*Under the Volcano:* Narrative Mode and Technique," *Journal of Canadian Fiction* 2 (Spring, 1973): 56-61; and Markson argues that the mythic and symbolic materials of the novel "assume meaning only when seen spatially," *Malcolm Lowry's Volcano*, 9.

Todorov's discussion of narrative in *The Poetics of Prose,* trans. by Richard Howard (Ithaca, N.Y.: Cornell University Press, 1977), 120-42, is very useful when considering the narrative structure of *Volcano*. Todorov is analysing mediaeval quest literature in his essay, "The Quest of Narrative," but he points out that other forms of literature also contain both "horizontal" and "vertical" types of of organization: "There are two different kinds of interest, and also two kinds of narrative. One unfolds on a horizontal line: we want to know what each event provokes, what it *does*. The other represents a series of variations which stack up along a vertical line: what we look for in each event is what it *is*. The first is a narrative of contiguity, the second a narrative of substitutions" (135). Todorov's term horizontal "narrative of contiguity" corresponds to what I call the sequential, linear narrative pattern of *Volcano,* and his vertical "narrative of substitutions" corresponds to the reflexive narrative pattern, which is a major component of the novel's spatial form.
13. In his excellent study of style, "Aspects of Langauge in *Under the Volcano,*" O'Kill relates the verbal organization of the narrative to the overall construction and coherence of the text. He claims that Lowry's characteristic right-branching sentences (the dominant construction in the passage I am discussing) "mimic a kind of simultaneity," and I would argue that this quality of stylistic simultaneity is yet another factor contributing to the spatial form of the narrative.
14. The "Máquina Infernal" is a reference to Jean Cocteau's play of the same name which Lowry saw in Paris in 1934. Cocteau portrays the Oedipus story in terms of "une des plus parfaits machines construites par les dieux infernaux pour l'anéantissement mathématique d'un mortel" (*La Machine Infernal* [Paris; Bernard Grasset, 1934], 15).
15. Lowry, who had read Lewis Spence's *The Myths of Mexico and Peru* (London: Harrap, 1920), was aware of the ancient Mexican's obsession with time. The reason for Aztec ritualistic killing was to propitiate their gods; without human sacrifice the gods would allow time to stop and the cycles of life would not be renewed. According to Spence (77), the mountain Popocatepetl was sacred to the rain-god Tlaloc to whom regular sacrifices were made. Geoffrey's "sacrifice" is, then, a small positive sign that life will

continue, especially when it is remembered that the Pleiades were considered as the planets of hope (Spence, 44) by the ancient Mexicans. On the last day of the fifty-two year cycle all Mexicans watched for the culmination of a new cycle. In chapter 1, Jacques refers to the culmination of the Pleiades and, in chapter 11, Yvonne dies as the Pleiades rise; the suggestion is that time has been renewed and that the voyage will continue.

16. O'Kill, "Aspects of Language in *Under the Volcano*," 81-82.
17. Robert Scholes, *Structuralism in Literature* (New Haven: Yale University Press, 1974), 20. Jakobson was the first to make such large claims for these rhetorical processes in "The Metaphoric and Metonymic Poles," *Fundamentals of Language* (The Hague: Mouton, 1956), 76-82, and for this purpose he considers simile and metaphor together because they both operate analogically. In his study of metonymy in Proust, *Figures III* (Paris: Editions du Seuil, 1972), 41-63, Gerard Genette illustrates the complementary role of metaphor and metonymy in narrative discourse, and in *The Modes of Modern Writing: Metaphor, Metonymy, and the Typology of Modern Literature* (Ithaca, N.Y.: Cornell University Press, 1977), David Lodge applies Jakobson's theory brilliantly to twentieth-century fiction.
18. Stephen Spender was the first to recognize the importance of films in *Under the Volcano* in his introduction to the 1966 Signet edition, and since then Day, Costa, and Bradbrook have each commented upon its cinematic qualities. Kilgallin mentions many films that Lowry refers to, and one article has appeared on the subject: Paul Tiessen, "Malcolm Lowry and the Cinema," in *Malcolm Lowry: The Man and his Work*. Work has begun on Lowry's filmscript of *Tender Is the Night* with the publication by Bruccoli Clark of *Notes on a Screenplay for Tender Is the Night* (1976), and Ruth Perlmutter's article, "Malcolm Lowry's Unpublished Filmscript of *Tender Is the Night*," *American Quarterly* 27 (Winter, 1976): 561-74. Perlmutter argues convincingly for the similarity between Lowry's use of a narrator and the role of a camera.
19. Relatively few of the so-called classic German films of the twenties are examples of expressionism, but critics disagree as to which ones belong and which have only expressionist attributes in sets, acting, lighting, and so forth. *Caligari, From Morn Till Midnight, Raskolnikov, Waxworks* are obvious examples of the style with *The Student of Prague, The Hands of Orlac, Warning Shadows,* and *Sunrise* using expressionist techniques within a mixed style. See Eisner, *The Haunted Screen* (1969); Robson, *The Film Answers Back,* (1972); Kracauer, *From Caligari to Hitler* (1947); and Manvell and Fraenkel, *The German Cinema* (1971). For the titles of films important to Lowry, see the "Checklist of Films" in the bibliography.
20. Although this phrase, suggesting futile activity, is a delightful Lowry pun—a progression al-cohal—it is also a crude colloquialism about the anus.

NOTES TO CHAPTER FOUR

1. According to Mrs. Lowry (in a 1973 letter to me), Lowry studied the *I Ching* with Charles Stansfeld-Jones. The *I Ching* or *Book of Changes* is an ancient Chinese text, integral to Taoism, used as an oracle and a book of wisdom or right conduct and cosmic understanding. It is based upon the principle of change which assumes a cyclic form. The sixty-four Hexagrams of the *I Ching*, obtained by throwing the yarrow stalks, are configurations formed by chance. Both coincidence and individuality are of great importance to the philosophy of the book, as Jung explains in his introduction to the German translation: "The Chinese mind . . . in the *I Ching*, seems to be exclusively preoccupied with chance aspects of events. What we call coincidence seems to be the chief concern of this peculiar mind, and what we worship as causality passes almost unnoticed" (*The I Ching or Book of Changes*, 2 vols., trans. from the German by Cary F.

Baynes [London: Routledge and K. Paul, 1951], ii.).
2. *Dark as the Grave Wherein My Friend Is Laid* (New York: New American Library, 1968). There are three separate drafts of the novel in the Lowry Collection at the University of British Columbia, one of 172 pages, one of 148 pages, and one of 380 pages.
3. New, *Malcolm Lowry*, 44. Barry Wood discusses *Dark as the Grave* as a metafiction in some detail in "Malcolm Lowry's Metafiction."
4. Lowry is probably thinking of Pirandello's *Six Characters in Search of an Author*, which explores the identity of character and author through the equation of life and art. Lowry praises Pirandello's idea in *Selected Letters*, 210.
5. Woodcock, *Malcolm Lowry: The Man and his Work*, 69. Richard Cross repeats Woodcock's error when he claims that *Dark as the Grave* is "related in a linear chronological fashion" (*Malcolm Lowry: A Preface to his Fiction* [Chicago: University of Chicago Press, 1980], 70).
6. Keats dedicated his poem *Endymion* (1818) to Thomas Chatterton — one of Lowry's many kindred spirits. The parallels between *Endymion* and *Dark as the Grave* are many, even though they are not always well developed by Lowry.
7. In his article "Masks and the Man: The Writer as Actor," Matthew Corrigan recognizes the circular nature of experience in *Dark as the Grave* when he comments that the "trip through Mexico leading to Oaxaca . . . itself takes on a circulatory motion, duplicated visually in the vultures that gyre in the high sunlight, and on another level, duplicated in the circumlocution of the style" (*Shenandoah* 19 [1967–68]: 91).
8. The Banco Ejidal was an agrarian land bank set up by Cárdenas to restore the quality of farmland and to return it to the peasants. Ejidal riders were Cárdenas supporters who carried necessary funds to outlying villages.
9. Sigbjørn's refusal of entry into the United States at the British Columbia border town of Blaine echoes Lowry's refusal in 1939 as a person likely to be a public charge. Lowry had hoped to meet Margerie Bonner, with whom he had fallen in love, in Los Angeles, but when this trip failed, he wired her of his desperate state and she came to Canada to nurse him back to health. Typically, Lowry invested the mishap with tremendous significance and added it to his growing list of personal injuries.
10. Although the parallel is not clearly developed here, references to *The Fall of the House of Usher*, both Poe's story and Epstein's film, occur frequently in Lowry's work. The film, less well known than Poe's work, is a brilliant portrayal of artistic possession and evil; the implication is that Usher has captured his wife's soul in his painting. Visually the film is a spectacular example of double exposure, fantasy, *chiaroscuro*, and slow motion, all used to portray Usher's distorted perceptions and tortured psyche.
11. In the biography, Day describes Lowry as drunk or in hospital during most of his 1947 visit to Haiti. However, Lowry was at least familiar with the basic concepts and point of view of Voodoo: he admired the novels of the Haitian writer Thoby-Phillippe Marcelin and owned a copy of Milo Marcelin's *Mythologie Voodue*, 2 vols. (Haïti: Editions Haïtiennes, 1949), sent to him by the author early in 1951. In *Mythologie* Marcelin explains the foundation of Voodoo as the intersection of the supernatural and the natural via the rite of possession. The cross and the circle figure prominently in the diagrams used in the book. For Lowry's praise of Voodoo and of Marcelin's book, see *Selected Letters*, 235.
12. Maya Deren, *Divine Horsemen: The Living Gods of Haiti* (London: Thames and Hudson, 1953), 35.
13. Ibid, 37.

NOTES TO CHAPTER FIVE

1. *October Ferry to Gabriola* (New York: World Publishing, 1970); all references are to this edition. In her "Editor's Note," 335–36, Margerie Lowry explains her editorial task, but because the manuscripts of the novel do not fall into easily distinguishable drafts, it is difficult to assess how closely the published text

follows Lowry's plans. As a consequence, many critics (for example Day and Cross) have been reluctant to accept the work as it stands, and *October Ferry* has not been subjected to the kind of serious attention which has opened up *Under the Volcano*. Significant discussion of Lowry's later work began with William New's valuable 1972 article, "Gabriola: Malcolm Lowry's Floating Island" in *Articulating West*, 196–206, and continued in 1974 when Muriel Bradbrook published *Malcolm Lowry: His Art and Early Life*. In her 1978 article, "Intention and Design in *October Ferry to Gabriola*," in *The Art of Malcolm Lowry*, 144–55, Bradbrook offers one of the most sensitive readings of the novel to date. In her discussion she draws upon "Work in Progress" and the manuscripts and arrives at much the same conclusion about the novel's richness as I do, but where she contrasts the open and unfinished form of *October Ferry* with the more traditional "composite" form of *Hear Us O Lord*, I maintain that there is a deliberate, discernible, albeit open, "design" in *October Ferry* as well. Perhaps the most positive assessment of the novel is in Terence Bareham's "After the Volcano: An Assessment of Malcolm Lowry's Posthumous Fiction," in *Malcolm Lowry: The Writer and His Critics*, 235–49 (originally published in *Studies in the Novel* 6:3 [1974]: 349–62). According to Bareham, it is a "remarkable achievement" and its "central integrity is intact," 248.
2. According to *The New Catholic Encyclopedia*, 2:128, perichoresis is the interpenetration of the three Persons of the Trinity. Greek theology emphasizes the *activity* of union, a kind of "reciprocal irruption;" western theology emphasizes the state of "unicity."
3. During the forties Lowry had access to Charles Stansfeld-Jones' (Frater Achad) library on the occult, but he was particularly influenced by two of Achad's studies, *Q.B.L. or The Bride's Reception* (privately published in the twenties and reprinted, New York: Samuel Weiser Inc., 1972), and *The Anatomy of the Body of God* (Chicago: Collegium ad Spiritum Sanctum, 1925). References are to these editions and are included in the text.
4. The allusions to "Sunrise" and the mysterious refrain "Dweller on the Threshold" (111, 263, 296) are important. In his drafts of the novel Lowry had planned to incorporate his version of a Blake stanza:
He who bendeth to himself a green joy
Doth the winged life destroy
But he who embraceth the life as it flies
Doth live in eternity's sunrise. (16:11, 30)
Although the stanza does not appear in the published text, it clarifies Lowry's concern for movement; to possess is to invite death, whereas to "embrace the joy as it flies" is to *live*.

"Dweller on the Threshold" comes from Bulwer-Lytton's mystical romance *Zanoni* mentioned in Eino Railo's *The Haunted Castle* (London: Routledge, 1927), 209. Lowry's notes for *October Ferry* contain many references to and long quotes from *Zanoni*, which portrays the struggle of the Ideal and the Real via a gothic story of Italian passions. In his explanation of the novel, Lytton writes that the "Dweller on the Threshold" is "FEAR (or HORROR)" which may only be dispelled by "defiance and aspiration . . . whose Messenger and Instrument of reassurance is Faith" (*Zanoni* [New York: Little Brown, 1898], 538). *Zanoni* was important to Lowry, who saw Ethan as tormented by fears like Geoffrey and Sigbjørn but finally achieving faith at the end of his ordeal.
5. The film that Lowry is referring to was based upon E. Temple Thurston's play, *The Wandering Jew* (London: Putnam's, 1920), and was made in Britain in 1933, starring the famous expressionist actor, Conrad Veidt.
6. During my conversations with Mrs. Lowry in June, 1975, she recalled Lowry's tendency to make his own films, starting with an unusual shot or interesting detail in a film they were watching; he was later baffled to discover that he had not "seen" the same film as she.
7. Lowry took much of his information on fires and other "supernatural" happenings from Charles Fort, who rejected rational explanations of the universe and believed that "all existence is a flux and reflux" within a pattern of "infinite serialization"; see *The Books of Charles Fort* (New York: Holt, 1941), 313. Lowry's copy of *Charles Fort*, now in the Lowry Collection, was given him by Margerie in December 1953. Eino Railo's *The Haunted Castle* is the

source for the "Wandering Jew" passages in chapter 20 and the Spenser stanza (155).
8. Sutton Vane, *Outward Bound* (New York: Boni & Liveright, 1924), 63. Further references are included in the text. In his "Introduction" to *Mr. Arcularis, A Play* (Cambridge, MA: Harvard University Press, 1957), v–vi, Conrad Aiken remarks with interest that Diana Hamilton, the Englishwoman who first tried to stage Aiken's story in the forties, was Sutton Vane's widow. The subterrranean links between *Mr. Arcularis* and "The Ordeal of Sigbjørn Wilderness" are touched upon in the Appendix, and it is entirely possible that Aiken and Lowry were both influenced by Vane's popular play.
9. In a typescript of this passage Lowry has a marginal note paraphrasing Achad:
   "NB An image   Kether is then the Junction of these two Infinites, that particularly represents the concentration of the Light to a point on its way to the Infinitely Small, while Malkuth, — the 10th Sephira & Sphere of the elements — which the Cabbalists say is one with Kether — is the substance which is ever expanding, &, so to speak, gradually filling up the nothingness of the Ain-Suph-Aur (Limitless Light of Chaos)." (16:12, 16)
10. *King Lear*, Act 4, sc. 7, ll. 45–48.
11. New, *Articulating West*. In "Death in Life: Neo-Platonic Elements in 'Through the Panama,'" from *Malcolm Lowry: The Man and his Work*, Geoffrey Durrant sees another of Lowry's voyages as based upon the neo-Platonic myth of the soul's journey through the world of matter on its way back to God. The parallel is interesting for *October Ferry* and "Through the Panama," with the distinction that, unlike the neo-Platonists, Lowry is not concerned about a timeless goal; it is the voyage that is of value.
12. Three boxes (nos. 19, 20, 21) of *October Ferry* manuscripts now at The University of British Columbia were received from Harold Matson in the spring of 1973.
13. In his study of the "lyrical novel," Ralph Freedman describes such novels as emphasizing formal design instead of event and employing passive characters who mirror a world perceived solipsistically. In addition, the "lyrical novel" usually creates a strong sense of spatial form; details, images, and other aspects are presented in juxtaposition in order to be perceived as a poetic whole (*The Lyrical Novel: Studies in Hesse, Gide, and Woolf* [Princeton, NJ: Princeton University Press, 1963]). *October Ferry* conforms to Freedman's description of a "lyrical novel" in some ways, but Lowry never aims to present a timeless static poetic unit in his work. As with any effort to categorize Lowry's writing, the term "lyrical" must be applied to *October Ferry* with restraint.
14. This remark by Aiken is quoted in Jay Martin's study, *Conrad Aiken: A Life of His Art* (Princeton, NJ: Princeton University Press, 1962), 76, and is discussed further in the Appendix.
15. Lowry's reference is to the end of Goethe's *Faust*, II. His words, however, are a paraphrase of Santayana's in *Three Philosophical Poets* (Cambridge, MA: Harvard University Press, 1927), 193. Lowry knew Santayana's book well, and Santayana's interpretation of *Faust*, as well as his theory of the romantic journey, influenced Lowry's concept of voyage.

NOTES TO CHAPTER SIX

1. This is a fragment of a poem from the notes for "Present Estate of Pompeii" (24: 17, 1d).
2. *Hear Us O Lord from Heaven Thy Dwelling Place* (London: Jonathan Cape, 1962). See "Publisher's Note." All references are to this edition and are included in the text. "The Bravest Boat" and "Strange Comfort Afforded by the Profession" were published separately during Lowry's lifetime.
3. In his biography, Day states that according to the "Work in Progress," "Eridanus" was "to consist of the stories in *Hear Us O Lord*, the poems in *The Lighthouse Invites the Storm*, a play . . .

in short, everything not of novel length that was lying about the shack" (426). A more careful reading of "Work in Progress" makes clear that *Hear Us O Lord* was a separate and parallel work to the "Voyage." In his "Notes" on "Forest Path" ("WP," B), Lowry envisions the end of the "Voyage," the last part of "The Ordeal of Sigbjørn Wilderness 2," as "approximating to the end of this story."
4. The story "In the Black Hills" was published as "Kristbjorg's Story: In the Black Hills," in *Psalms and Songs* — Kristbjorg being a neighbour on the beach in "The Forest Path to the Spring." The story is a slight account of a lonely German miner from the Black Hills of South Dakota who drinks himself to death, but Kristbjorg's voice — a storyteller within a story — and the fate of the German would have set up interesting reverberations in *Hear Us O Lord*.
5. See Dale Edmonds, "The Short Fiction of Malcolm Lowry," *Tulane Studies in English* 15 (1967): 70, and Day, 446.
6. In "Malcolm Lowry's Other Fiction," *Cunning Exiles: Studies in Modern Prose Writers*, eds. Don Anderson and Stephen Knight (Cremone, Sydney: Angus and Robertson, 1974), 62-80, Creswell provides a thoughtful and convincing discussion of Lowry's neglected fiction. She considers the reservations and criticisms held by some critics, but she has high praise for *Hear Us O Lord* and concludes that Lowry's "whole canon warrants greater recognition." New's remark is in *Malcolm Lowry*, 13, where he uses *Hear Us O Lord* as an introduction to the design of Lowry's intended masterwork.
7. In *Malcolm Lowry: A Preface to his Fiction*, Richard Cross notes Norman J. Fry's explanation that the Old Norse word *bjarn* "has been used in all Germanic dialects as a euphemism for totemic appeasement in place of the original Indo-European word for 'bear' seen in Latin *ursus* and Greek *árktos*." Cross goes on to remark that Lowry's awareness of the totemic overtone is uncertain, but I find the implicit contrast between *Sigbjørn* and the Latin word in "The Bravest Boat" to be effective, even if not deliberately so. I would like to thank my colleague, Gernot Wieland, for explaining that the High German "Sig/fried," like the Old Norse "Sig/urd," comes from the Germanic root "Sig/ward," which means "guardian of victory."
8. New maintains that the "I" in "Forest Path" is Lowry, *Malcolm Lowry*, 13, but Day is probably correct in saying that the "I" is "none other than Wilderness" (444).
9. In *Notes on a Screenplay for F. Scott Fitzgerald's Tender Is the Night*, Lowry goes to considerable lengths to explain why the simple canon "Frère Jacques" should be used in the film of *Tender Is the Night* to suggest a ship's engines. First, he explains, the repetition must be varied or "free" despite the fact that it is a contradiction to speak of a canon as free form. The justification for this *"hot* canon" is its rhythm. As Lowry goes on to explain, referring to Aristotle, O'Neill, and the films, *M* and *Citizen Kane*:

> A film — or any other work of narrative art — would not hold together without something of the sort [rhythm]; for it is related to momentum, and it is certainly a serious explanation why so many novels fall apart. (50)

Rhythm, then, was essential to Lowry, and it is safe to say that he was always conscious of rhythms in his writing — nowhere more so than in *Hear Us O Lord*. It was particularly jazz rhythms such as those of Lang, Venuti, and Beiderbecke that, he believed, could "convey a seriousness, an anguish, of mood" and "in the next breath . . . convey exuberance, fury" (54). *Under the Volcano* can also be seen as embodying both the anguish and the exuberance Lowry speaks of, not only thematically or even in the rich convoluted prose, but in the rhythm of the chapters and the speed with which time moves. Indeed, one could go so far as to liken the four main characters of *Volcano* to four instruments, each playing its own unique variation upon the themes of failure, loneliness, love, and hope. Although it is difficult to analyse Lowry's writing in musical terms, he certainly thought of his writing and its rhythms this way — especially in *Volcano* (see *Selected Letters*, 68–69, 76, 80), *October Ferry*, and *Hear Us O Lord*.
10. References to Schoenberg and Berg

suggest that Lowry was aware of the twelve-tone technique developed by Schoenberg and popularly called "serial music." The very name "twelve-tone" and "serial" would be sufficient to intrigue his correspondence-oriented imagination. Whether he applied the principle of twelve-tone techinque (the arbitrary arrangement of twelve tones in a series which may be repeated only after the entire series has been used) in his writing is unlikely, but the concept of repeated series is, of course, basic to his thought (see also, *Selected Letters*, 265).

11. In "Death in Life: Neo-Platonic Elements in 'Through the Panama,'" from *Malcolm Lowry: The Man and his Work*, Geoffrey Durrant offers a convincing argument for Lowry's use of the neo-Platonic myth of the soul. The myth helps to account for Lowry's use of *The Ancient Mariner* and his use of the south as an infernal region.

12. In *An Experiment With Time*, 196, Dunne allows for a God-like final observer, although how this is consistent with a serial universe is unclear.

13. In "A Note on Romantic Allusions in *Hear Us O Lord*," *Studies in Canadian Literature* 1 (Winter, 1976): 130–36, William New discusses the importance of Coleridge and Keats to Lowry's use of form and language "as an associative phenomenon."

14. Lowry's notes for "Elephant and Colosseum" show that he gleaned this quotation from Arnold Toynbee's "Russia's Byzantine Empire," *Horizon* 15 (August, 1947): 82. The Latin quote, "*Naturam expellas furca, tamen usque recurret*," is also a motif in *October Ferry*.

15. Lowry is referring to Constantine F. Chasseboeuf de Volney's *Ruins; or, Meditation on the Revolutions of Empires* (Boston: Gaylord, 1835), a heavily moralistic tract supporting historicism and rationalism.

16. "Once again, we are liable to feel that nothing is happening, that no one *does* anything; that properly speaking, these are not stories at all. . . . Suppose we say that *Hear Us O Lord* is a collection not of short stories, but of *fictional meditations:* reflective pieces, more or less autobiographical in nature, on a common theme" (Day, 446).

17. In *Malcolm Lowry: A Preface to his Fiction* (101–2), Cross comments upon Lowry's non-American choice of marriage as the ideal North American edenic state. As he rightly points out, the American Adam regains paradise alone (or at most, if Fiedler is correct, with a male Indian soul-mate). However, it is common in the Canadian tradition, at least from Isabella Valancy Crawford's "Malcolm's Katie" (1884) on, to find Adam and Eve sharing paradise; such otherwise different contemporary novels as Jack Hodgins' *The Invention of the World* (1977), Robert Kroetsch's *What the Crow Said* (1978), Sheila Watson's *The Double Hook* (1959), or even Margaret Atwood's more problematic *Surfacing* (1972), come to mind.

18. In *A New Model of the Universe*, 203, Ouspensky describes the Fool of the Tarot thus:

> Weary and lame he dragged himself along a dusty road, across a lifeless plain beneath the scorching rays of the sun.
>
> Gazing stupidly sideways with fixed eyes, with a half-smile, half-grimace frozen upon his face, he crawled along neither seeing nor knowing whither, plunged in his own chimerical dreams, which moved eternally in the same circle.
>
> The fool's cap and bells was on his head back to front. His clothes were torn down the back. A wild lynx with burning eyes leaped at him from behind a stone and drove its teeth into his leg.
>
> He stumbled nearly falling, but dragged himself ever further, carrying over his shoulder a sack full of unnecessary, useless things, which only his madness forced him to carry.
>
> In front the road was cleft by a ravine. A deep precipice awaited the crazy wanderer . . . and a huge crocodile with gaping jaws crept out of the abyss.

In "Forest Path" the protagonist learns "to accept myself as a fool again" (284), and the stages of the Fool's journey, as described by Ouspensky, clearly correspond to stages in Lowry's "Voyage" — the mountain lion in "Forest Path" recalls Ouspensky's lynx. And in "No Still Path" from *Selected Poems*, 50, Lowry laments: "Alas, there is no still path in my soul, / I being evil, none of memory."

19. Barry Wood's "The Edge of Eternity," *Canadian Literature* 70 (Autumn, 1976): 51-58, is one of the best discussions to date of the mystical aspects of "Forest Path." Wood examines Lowry's handling of opposites through the circle symbolism of the story, especially as it compares with the Chinese concept of the Tao.

NOTES TO THE CONCLUSION

1. Brian O'Kill, "Aspects of Language in *Under the Volcano*," *The Art of Malcolm Lowry*, 72-92; Ruth Perlmutter, "Malcolm Lowry's Unpublished Filmscript of *Tender Is the Night*," *American Quarterly* 28, 5 (1976): 561-74.
2. The National Film Board of Canada documentary, *Volcano: An Inquiry into the Life and Death of Malcolm Lowry* (1977) was narrated by Donald Brittain and produced by Brittain and Robert Duncan.
3. Douglas Day describes Purdy's 1953 visit to Lowry in *Malcolm Lowry*, 431-34. Purdy's poem, "Malcolm Lowry," appears in *The Cariboo Horses* (Toronto: McClelland and Stewart, 1965), 9-10.
4. Purdy, "Postscript," *The Cariboo Horses*, 11.
5. In "The Englishness of Malcolm Lowry," *Journal of Commonwealth Literature* 11 (December, 1976): 134-49, Tony Bareham argues for this "Englishness" by pointing to Lowry's non-American attitudes such as his respect for Cárdenas and the fact that his questing heroes, unlike American heroes, must return home. Not only do Bareham's questionable assumptions about the United States vitiate his argument, but also his ignorance of the Canadian tradition leads him to suggest that Lowry's sensitive fusion of opposites, such as his treatment of the beauty and horror of British Columbia, is uniquely British. I suspect that a valid defence of Lowry's "Englishness" would rest upon the way he uses the language, which is quite distinct from either Canadian or American English.

   Fowles, like Lowry, refuses to reject "the great tradition of the English novel" in favour of an empty modernism (see the interview with Fowles in *Counterpoint*, interviewer, Roy Newquist [New York: Rand McNally, 1964], 220). Fowles discusses his affection for Victorian fiction, as well as his struggle with reality, realism, and the limitations of the *nouveau roman* at greater length in "Notes on an Unfinished Novel" from *Afterwords: Novelists on their Novels*, ed. Thomas McCormack (New York: Harper & Row, 1969), 161-75. Here Fowles' comments are reminiscent of Lowry's claim that he would not write "silly ass style and semicolon technique," but attempt to start "another Renaissance" (*Selected Letters*, 80). For further discussion of this point, see note 5 to the Introduction. pp. 129-30
6. In *Among Worlds: An Introduction to Modern Commonwealth and South African Fiction* (Erin, Ontario: Press Porcepic, 1975), 119-21, William New considers Lowry's exploration of duality as his chief link with Canadian writers such as Watson, Davies, and Kroetsch.
7. Sheila Watson, *The Double Hook* (Toronto: McClelland and Stewart, 1959), 61.
8. Although Margaret Laurence has frequently spoken of the need to return "home," she best dramatizes that need in *The Diviners* (Toronto: McClelland and Stewart, 1974). A useful distinction could be drawn here between Laurence and Lowry's treatment of the past and William Faulkner's. Although he influenced both writers, and Lowry's style and intensity have much in common with Faulkner's, Faulkner's main characters (especially in *The Sound and the Fury* and *Absalom, Absalom!*) haunt a lost past and are uninterested in living fully in the present.
9. See Frye's "Conclusion to a *Literary History of Canada*" in *The Bush Garden: Essays on the Canadian Imagination* (Toronto: Anansi, 1971), notably 246-49. In "Malcolm Lowry and the Northern Tradition," *Studies in Canadian Literature* 1 (Winter, 1976): 105-14, Hallvard Dahlie

suggests that Lowry "provided an initial example" of the literary treatment of a northern paradise which is important to contemporary writers like Atwood, Kroetsch, and Rudy Wiebe.
10. Edward Mendelson, ed., "Introduction," *Pynchon: A Collection of Critical Essays* (Englewood Cliffs, NJ: Prentice-Hall, 1978), 9.
11. Although O'Kill does not call Lowry an encyclopaedic writer, his analysis in "Aspects of Style in *Under the Volcano*" clarifies the degree to which Lowry's "cumulative" sentences contribute to the encyclopaedic nature of the text. He also points out that Lowry's object in characterization is "to create a composite, inclusive or collective consciousness with unlimited resources of learning, memory, and language" (76); *Volcano's* characters all have the same rhetorical style. In "Lowry's Anatomy of Melancholy," *Canadian Literature*, 64 (Spring, 1975): 8–23, Ronald Binns does describe Lowry as encyclopaedic, and he draws general comparisons with Rabelais, Burton, and Sterne. It should be noted, as well, that *October Ferry* shows signs of becoming encyclopaedic, and the "Voyage" would certainly have comprised a vast compendium of materials.
12. Frye discusses prose fiction forms and encyclopaedism in his fourth essay, "Rhetorical Criticism: Theory of Genres," in *Anatomy of Criticism* (New York: Atheneum, 1968), 303–26. Frye concludes that *Ulysses* "is a complete prose epic with all four forms employed in it" (314), and I would argue that *Gravity's Rainbow* and *Under the Volcano* are equally complete in Frye's terms, although in my view the former emphasizes anatomy and the latter romance. In "The Form of Carnival in *Under the Volcano*," *PMLA*, 92, 3 (1977): 481–89, Jonathan Arac describes the novel as an example of Menippean satire, but what Arac has done is to single out one generic approach to the text. Interestingly, the form he chooses is the one Frye sees as leading directly into anatomy and encyclopaedism (*Anatomy of Criticism*, 311–12), but because *Volcano* is such a successful blend of all four forms, it is better served by a *Gestalt* approach than by a narrow generic one.
13. Mendelson draws a similar distinction between *Ulysses* and *Gravity's Rainbow*. See his "Introduction," pp. 10–11.

NOTES TO THE APPENDIX

1. The first Lowry scholar to emphasize and describe the importance of Aiken was Richard Hauer Costa, who claims that "Aiken's tutorship . . . was crucial" in *Malcolm Lowry* (New York: Twayne, 1972), 29. Although, in my view, Costa overestimates the influence of Joyce on Lowry via Aiken (28–44), he also discusses the biography of their friendship, as Aiken reveals it in *Ushant* (52–57), and touches upon their shared "messianic" views of art and experience (59–60).
2. Parts of this correspondence have been published in *Selected Letters of Conrad Aiken*, ed. Joseph Killorin (New Haven and London: Yale University Press, 1978) and in Lowry's *Selected Letters*. I am thankful for the opportunity to examine Lowry materials in the Aiken collection at the Huntington Library, San Marino, California in the fall of 1981. Among several interesting unpublished letters is one from Aiken to Lowry, dated 16 October 1945, in which Aiken asks Lowry for advice on the *Collected Poems* and states that he values Lowry's advice above all others. In another letter, dated 17 April 1947, to John Davenport (a mutual friend), Aiken comments on Lowry's debt to him and remarks that Lowry found it difficult to acknowledge this debt because Aiken was not famous.
3. "Malcolm Lowry: A Note," *Malcolm Lowry: The Man and His Work*, 101–2. For Lowry's views on Aiken, see *Selected Letters*, 3–16 and 270–79, where he writes that Aiken's work "slammed down upon my raw psyche like the lightening slamming down on the slew at this moment."
4. Day gives an account of the years when Aiken served "*in loco parentis*" for Lowry, and Durrant's article, "Aiken and Lowry," offers an excellent analysis of the Aiken influence with particular attention to *Blue Voyage* and *Ultramarine*.
5. Quoted in Jay Martin, *Conrad Aiken:*

A Life of His Art (Princeton, NJ: Princeton University Press, 1962), 76.
6. Quoted from the preface to part two of *The Divine Pilgrim*, entitled "The Jig of Forslin," *The Jig of Forslin: A Symphony* (Boston: The Four Seas, 1916), 8.
7. Jay Martin describes *Landscape West of Eden* (1934), which is a continuation of *Preludes*, as an attempt to create a myth, based upon motion, of the development of consciousness: "In his narrative . . . Aiken continuously shifts from one level of consciousness to another; for at no point can we say: Here we arrive at awareness. Theoretically the poem can have no end, for consciousness has had none" (*Conrad Aiken*, 141).
8. *Preludes* (New York: Oxford University Press, 1966), vi.
9. *Collected Poems* (New York: Oxford University Press, 1953), 102.
10. *The Short Stories of Conrad Aiken* (Freeport, NY: Books for Libraries Press, 1950), and *Three Novels* (London: W.H. Allen, 1965). Further references are included in the text.
11. In an unpublished letter to Aiken in the Huntington Aiken collection, dated 6 September 1940, Lowry writes that he is reworking "The Last Address" and cutting the passage of dialogue which he had borrowed from *Great Circle*. That Lowry borrowed heavily from this novel is also apparent from Aiken's discovery, in 1960, of *Ultramarine* mss. in which Lowry had carefully copied out an entire page of Aiken's text. See *Selected Letters of Conrad Aiken*, 307.
12. In *The Coming Forth By Day of Osiris Jones* (1931), Aiken uses the Osiris myth from *The Egyptian Book of the Dead* to explore the concept of reliving the past in order to understand it, because without understanding there can be no forgiveness.
13. I am grateful to Professor Martin who confirmed Bergson's importance to Aiken in a letter.
14. *Mr. Arcularis* was first written as a story in the early thirties and included in *Among the Lost People* (1934). It went through some important changes before Aiken published it as a play in 1957 and these are outlined by Aiken in his introduction and by Jay Martin, who also discusses its relationship to *Great Circle*, in *Conrad Aiken*, 117-19.
15. Lowry's undated letter is in the Huntington Aiken collection and consists of two small note-pad pages covered with cramped writing. Lowry explains his accident, his injury, and his visions in the hospital, and then comments upon *Mr. Arcularis*. Gerald Noxon's radio adaptation of the play was broadcast on Andrew Allan's CBC programme, "Sunday Matinee," on 28 November 1948, and Lowry, who had heard the production, was full of praise for it.

Selected Bibliography

The following bibliography of primary and secondary material is a selection of those works central to this study of Lowry. For a complete primary bibliography, see *Canadian Literature* 8 (Spring, 1961): 81–88, 11 (Winter, 1962): 90–93, and 19 (Winter, 1964): 83–86. William New's *Malcolm Lowry: A Reference Guide* (Boston: G. K. Hall, 1978) provides a comprehensive, annotated Lowry bibliography of primary and secondary material from 1927 to 1976. Complete references for Lowry's reading and other secondary materials are included in the notes. A short film checklist is appended.

PART I: MALCOLM LOWRY'S PUBLISHED WORK

"Bulls of the Resurrection," *Prism International* 5, 1 (Summer, 1965): 5–11.
China and Kristbjorg's Story: In the Black Hills. New York: Aloe Editions, 1974. Also in *Psalms and Songs.*
Dark as the Grave Wherein My Friend Is Laid. New York: New American Library 1968.
"Economic Conference, 1934." *Arena* 2 (Autumn, 1949): 49–57.
"Garden of Etla." *United Nations World* 4 (June, 1950): 45–47.
"Ghostkeeper." *American Review* 17 (Spring, 1973): 1–34. Also in *Psalms and Songs.*
"Goya the Obscure." *The Venture* 6 (1930): 270–78.
Hear Us O Lord from Heaven Thy Dwelling Place. London: Jonathan Cape, 1962.
"Hotel Room in Chartres." *Story* 5 (September, 1934): 53–58. Also in *Psalms and Songs.*
"In Le Havre." *Life and Letters* 10 (July, 1934): 642–66.
"June the 30th, 1934." *Psalms and Songs,* pp. 36–48.
Lunar Caustic. London: Jonathan Cape, 1968. Also in *Psalms and Songs.*
Notes on a Screenplay for F. Scott Fitzgerald's "Tender Is the Night."
   Bloomfield Hills, Mich.: Bruccoli Clark, 1976. The Lowrys prepared these "Notes" as well a complete filmscript of the novel together.
October Ferry to Gabriola. New York: World Publishing, 1970.
"On Board the West Hardaway." *Story* 3 (October, 1933): 12–22. Also in *Psalms and Songs.*
"Port Swettenham." *Experiment* 5 (February, 1930): 22–26.
"Preface to a Novel." *Canadian Literature* 9 (Summer, 1961): 23–29.
Psalms and Songs. New York and Scarborough, Ont.: New American Library, 1975. Contains selected stories, reminiscences, and criticism.
"Punctum Indifferens Skibet Gaar Videre." *Experiment* 7 (Spring, 1931). Published in *Best British Short Stories of 1931,* ed. E. J. O'Brien, as "Seductio ad Absurdum." New York, 1931, pp. 80–107.
Selected Letters of Malcolm Lowry. Edited by Harvey Breit and Margerie Bonner Lowry. Philadelphia: J. B. Lippincott, 1965.
Selected Poems of Malcolm Lowry. Edited by Earle Birney. San Francisco: City Lights Books, 1962.
Ultramarine. Revised edition. Philadelphia: Lippincott, 1962.

"Under the Volcano." *Prairie Schooner* 37, (Winter, 1963-64): 284-300. Also in *Psalms and Songs*. *Under the Volcano*. London: Jonathan Cape, 1947.

PART 2: LOWRY CRITICISM

Aiken, Conrad. *A Heart for the Gods of Mexico*. London: M. Secker, 1939.
_____. "Malcolm Lowry: A Note." *Canadian Literature* 8 (Spring, 1961): 29-30.
_____. *Ushant: An Essay*. London: W. H. Allen, 1963.
Arac, Jonathan. "The Form of Carnival in *Under the Volcano*." *PMLA* 92 (1977): 481-89.
Bareham, Terence. "After the Volcano: An Assessment of Malcolm Lowry's Posthumous Fiction." *Studies in the Novel* 6 (1974): 349-62; reprinted in *Malcolm Lowry: The Writer and his Critics*, edited by Barry Wood.
Bareham, Tony. "The Englishness of Malcolm Lowry." *Journal of Commonwealth Literature* 11 (December, 1976): 134-49.
Barnes, Jim. "The Myth of Sisyphus in *Under the Volcano*." *Prairie Schooner* 42 (Winter, 1968-69): 341-48.
Baxter, Charles. "The Escape from Irony: *Under the Volcano* and the Aesthetics of Arson." *Novel* 10 (1977): 114-26.
Benham, David. "Lowry's Purgatory: Versions of *Lunar Caustic*." *Malcolm Lowry: The Man and his Work*, edited by George Woodcock, pp. 56-65.
Binns, Ronald. "Lowry's Anatomy of Melancholy." *Canadian Literature* 64 (Spring, 1975): 8-23.
Bradbrook, Muriel. "Intention and Design in *October Ferry to Gabriola*." In *The Art of Malcolm Lowry*, edited by Anne Smith, pp. 144-55.
_____. *Malcolm Lowry: His Art and Early Life*. Cambridge: Cambridge University Press, 1974.
Bradbury, Malcolm. *Possibilities: Essays on the State of the Novel*. London: Oxford University Press, 1973.
Corrigan, Matthew. "Malcolm Lowry: The Phenomenology of Failure." *Boundary II* 3, 2 (1975): 407-42.
_____. "Masks and the Man: The Writer as Actor." *Shenandoah* 19, 4 (1968): 89-93.
_____. "The Writer as Consciousness: A View of *October Ferry to Gabriola*." In *Malcolm Lowry: The Man and his Work*, edited by George Woodcock, pp. 71-77.
Costa, Richard Hauer. "Lowry's Forest Path: Echoes of Walden." *Canadian Literature* 62 (Autumn, 1974): 61-68.
_____. *Malcolm Lowry*. New York: Twayne World Authors Series, 1972.
_____. "*Pietà, Pelado*, and 'The Ratification of Death': The Ten-Year Evolvement of Malcolm Lowry's *Volcano*." *Journal of Modern Literature* 2 (September, 1971): 3-18.
_____. "*Ulysses*, Lowry's *Volcano*, and the *Voyage* Between." *University of Toronto Quarterly* 36, 4 (1967): 335-52.
Creswell, Rosemary. "Malcolm Lowry's Other Fiction." In *Cunnning Exiles: Studies of Modern Prose Writers*, edited by Don Anderson and Stephen Knight. Sydney & London: Angus & Robertson, 1974, pp. 62-80.
Cross, Richard K. *Malcolm Lowry: A Preface to his Fiction*. Chicago: University of Chicago Press, 1980.
Dahlie, Hallvard. "Lowry's Debt to Nordahl Grieg." *Canadian Literature* 64 (Spring, 1975): 41-51.
_____. "Malcolm Lowry's *Ultramarine*." *Journal of Canadian Fiction* 3, 4 (1975): 65-68.
_____. "Malcolm Lowry and the Northern Tradition." *Studies in Canadian Literature* 1, 1 (1976): 105-14.
Day, Douglas. *Malcolm Lowry: A Biography*. New York: Oxford University Press, 1973.
_____. "Of Tragic Joy." *Prairie Schooner* 37 (1964): 354-62.
Dodson, Daniel B. *Malcolm Lowry*. New York: Columbia Essays on Modern Writers, 1970.
Dorosz, Kristofer. *Malcolm Lowry's Infernal Paradise*. Stockholm: University of Uppsala, 1976.
Doyen, Victor. "Elements Towards a Spatial Reading of Malcolm Lowry's *Under the Volcano*." *English Studies* 50, 1 (1969): 65-74.
Durrant, Geoffrey. "Aiken and Lowry." *Canadian Literature* 64 (Spring, 1975): 24-40.
_____. "Death in Life: Neo-Platonic Elements in *Through the Panama*." In *Malcolm Lowry: The Man and his work*, edited by George Woodcock, pp. 42-55.

———. "Heavenly Correspondences in the Late Work of Malcolm Lowry." *Mosaic* 11, 3 (1978): 63–77.
Edmonds, Dale. "The Short Fiction of Malcolm Lowry." *Tulane Studies in English* 15 (1967): 59–80.
———. "*Under the Volcano:* A Reading of the Immediate Level." *Tulane Studies in English* 16 (1968): 63–105.
Epstein, Perle. *The Private Labyrinth of Malcolm Lowry: Under the Volcano and the Cabbala.* New York: Holt, Rinehart & Winston, 1969.
Garnett, George Rhys. "*Under the Volcano:* The Myth of the Hero." *Canadian Literature* 84 (Spring, 1980): 31–40.
Grace, Sherrill. "Malcolm Lowry and the Expressionist Vision." In *The Art of Malcolm Lowry,* edited by Anne Smith, pp. 93–111.
———. "Outward Bound." *Canadian Literature* 71 (Winter, 1976): 73–79; reprinted in *Malcolm Lowry: The Writer and his Critics,* edited by Barry Wood, pp. 6–14.
———. "The Creative Process: Time and Space in Malcolm Lowry's Fiction." *Studies in Canadian Literature* 2, 1 (1977): 61–68.
———. "*Under the Volcano:* Narrative Mode and Technique." *Journal of Canadian Fiction* 2 (Spring, 1973): 57–61.
Heilman, Robert H. "The Possessed Artist and the Ailing soul." In *Malcolm Lowry: The Man and his Work,* edited by George Woodcock, pp. 16–25.
Hirschman, Jack. "Kabbala/Lowry, etc." *Prairie Schooner* 37 (1964): 347–53.
Kilgallin, Anthony. *Lowry.* Erin, Ont.: Press Porcepic, 1973.
Kim, Suzanne. "Les Oeuvres de jeunesse de Malcolm Lowry." *Etudes anglaises* 18 (1965): 383–94.
Leech, Clifford. "The Shaping of Time: *Nostromo* and *Under the Volcano.*" In *Imagined Worlds,* edited by Maynard Mack and Ian Gregor. London: Methuen, 1968, pp. 323–41.
Markson, David. *Malcolm Lowry's Volcano: Myth, Symbol, Meaning.* New York: Times Books, 1978.
———. "Myth in *Under the Volcano.*" *Prairie Schooner* 37 (1964): 339–46.
New, William. *Among Worlds: An Introduction to Modern Commonwealth and South African Fiction.* Erin, Ont.: Press Porcepic, 1975.
———. "A Note on Romantic Allusions in *Hear Us O Lord.*" *Studies in Canadian Literature* 1, 1 (1976): 130–36.
———. "Gabriola: Malcolm Lowry's Floating Island." In *Articulating West.* Toronto: New Press, 1972, pp. 196–206.
———. "Lowry, the Kabbala, and Charles Jones." In *Articulating West.* Toronto: New Press, 1972, pp. 189–95.
———. "Lowry's Reading." In *Malcolm Lowry: The Man and his Work,* edited by George Woodcock, pp. 125–32.
———. *Malcolm Lowry.* Toronto: McClelland & Stewart, 1971.
———. "Russell Haley's Lowry." *Malcolm Lowry Newsletter* 4 (Spring, 1979): 20–22.
Noxon, Gerald. "Malcolm Lowry: 1930." *Prairie Schooner* 37 (1964): 315–20.
O'Kill, Brian. "Aspects of Language in *Under the Volcano.*" In *The Art of Malcolm Lowry,* edited by Anne Smith, pp. 72–92.
Pagnoulle, Christine. *Malcolm Lowry: Voyage au fond de nos abimes.* Lausanne: Editions l'Age d'Homme, 1977.
Perlmutter, Ruth. "Malcolm Lowry's Unpublished Filmscript of *Tender Is the Night.*" *American Quarterly* 28 (1976): 561–74.
Smith, Anne, ed. *The Art of Malcolm Lowry.* London: Vision Press, 1978.
Spender, Stephen, "Introduction." *Under the Volcano.* New York: Lippincott, Signet Edition, 1965.
Tiessen, Paul G. "Introduction" to Malcolm and Margerie Lowry's *Notes on a Screenplay for F. Scott Fitzgerald's Tender Is the Night.*
———. "Malcolm Lowry and the Cinema." In *Malcolm Lowry: The Man and his Work,* edited by George Woodcock, pp. 133–43.
Veitch, Douglas W. *Lawrence, Greene and Lowry: The Fictional Landscape of Mexico.* Waterloo, Ont.: Wilfrid Laurier Univesity Press, 1978.
Wood, Barry. "Malcolm Lowry's Metafiction: The Biography of a Genre." *Contemporary Literature* 19 (1978): 1–25.

———, ed. *Malcolm Lowry: The Writer and his Critics.* Ottawa: Tecumseh Press, 1980.
———. "The Edge of Eternity." *Canadian Literature* 70 (Autumn, 1976): 51–58.
Woodcock, George. "Four Facets of Malcolm Lowry." In *Odysseus Ever Returning.* Toronto: McClelland & Stewart, 1970, pp. 56–75.
———, ed. *Malcolm Lowry: The Man and his Work.* Vancouver: University of British Columbia Press, 1971.
Wright, Terence. "*Under the Volcano:* The Static Art of Malcolm Lowry." *Ariel* 1 (October, 1970): 67–76.
Yakoubovitch, Roger I. "Cassure, canal. baranquilla." *Les lettres nouvelles* 2-3 (May-June, 1974): 184–204.

PART 3: A FILM CHECKLIST

The following list of films by title, director, and year, represents only those films that have been discussed in the text as important to Lowry. Further information can be found in Paul Rotha, *The Film Till Now: A Survey Of World Cinema* (London: Vision Press, 1960), and Lotte Eisner, *The Haunted Screen* (London: Thames and Hudson, 1969).

Cabinet of Dr. Caligari, The	Robert Weine	1919
Fall of the House of Usher	Jean Epstein	1928
From Morn till Midnight	Karl Martin	1920
Hands of Orlac, The	Robert Weine	1924
(with Conrad Veidt)		
Isn't Life Wonderful	D.W. Griffith	1924
Looping the Loop	Arthur Robison	1928
Mad Love	Karl Freund	1935
(with Peter Lorre)		
Outward Bound	Meyrick Milton	1930
Student of Prague, The	Henrik Galeen	1926
Sunrise	Fred Murnau	1927
Wandering Jew, The	Maurice Elvey	1923
(with Matheson Lang)		
Warning Shadows	Arthur Robison	1922

Index

Achad, Frater. *See* Stansfeld-Jones, Charles
"After Publication of *Under the Volcano*,"
  Selected Poems of Malcolm Lowry, xiv
Aiken, Conrad, 97, 123–27
  Blue Voyage, 123, 125–26
  The Divine Pilgrim, 124–25
  Great Circle, 125, 143
  letters to and from Lowry, 131, 142–43
  and Lowry, 3, 20, 102, 116
  Mr. Arcularis and the "Voyage," 127, 138, 143
  and serialism, 124
Arac, Jonathan, 142
Atwood, Margaret, 120, 142

Banco, Ejidal, 68, 136
Bareham, Terence, 137
Bareham, Tony, on Lowry's "Englishness," 141
Bates, Ralph, 130
Berg, Alban, 139–40
Bergson, Henri, and Aiken, 126, 143
  and Lowry, 2, 20, 49, 59, 60, 61, 107, 116
Besant, Annie, 2, 9
Binns, Ronald, 142
Birney, Earle, 29, 34
Blake, William 137
Blue Voyage. See Aiken, Conrad
Bonner, Margerie. *See* Lowry, Margerie
Bradbrook, Muriel (M.C.), 9, 129, 131, 137
Bradbury, Malcolm, on Lowry as modernist, 5, 131
Bridge of Water, The. See Nicolay, Helen
Brittain, Donald, 119, 141
Broch, Hermann, *The Sleepwalkers,* 132
"Bulls of the Resurrection," 21–22, 132

Cabbala, 37, 76–77, 78–80, 92, 94–95, 96–98, 133–34, 138. *See also* Stansfeld-Jones, Charles
Cabinet of Dr. Caligari, The, Robert Weine
  and *Lunar Caustic,* 31
  and *Under the Volcano,* 35, 46, 55, 56. *See also* Expressionism
"Canadian Turned Back at the Border, The,"
  and *Lunar Caustic,* 70
Cape, Jonathan, and Lowry's letter about *Under the Volcano,* 6, 36–38

Chaucer, Geoffrey, 60, 104
"China," 21
Cinema. *See* Film
Circle, symbolism, xv
  in *Dark as the Grave,* 70–73
  in early stories, 21–24
  in *Hear Us O Lord,* 102, 108, 110–11, 112, 113, 116–17, 141
  in *October Ferry,* 93–94
  in *Ultramarine,* 25–29
  in *Under the Volcano,* 43–47, 58
Cocteau, Jean 134
Coleridge, Samuel Taylor, 3, 92, 106–7, 121, 140
Conrad, Joseph, 121
Corrigan, Matthew, 136
Costa, Richard Hauer, 129, 142
Creswell, Rosemary, 101, 139
Cross, Richard, 136, 139, 140

Dahlie, Hallvard, 131, 141–42
Dark as the Grave Wherein My Friend Is Laid
  manuscripts of, 61–63, 65, 70, 72, 136
  and the "Voyage," 9, 14
Dark Journey, The. See Green, Julian
Day, Douglas
  editor of *Dark as the Grave,* 61
  Malcolm Lowry: A Biography, 76, 119, 129, 130, 131, 133, 136, 138–39, 142
  on *Hear Us O Lord,* 113, 140
  on *Under the Volcano,* 35, 42
Demian. See Hesse, Hermann
Deren, Maya, *Divine Horsemen: The Living Gods of Haiti. See* Voodoo
Divine Pilgrim, The. See Aiken, Conrad
Doppelgänger, 12, 37, 76, 82
Double Hook, The. See Watson, Sheila
Dunne, J.W., 2, 20, 65, 102, 107, 116, 130, 140.
  See also Serialism
  influence on
  Under The Volcano, 40–41
Durrant, Geoffrey, 138, 140, 143

Edmonds, Dale, 41, 134
Eliot, T.S., 25
Encyclopaedism, 18, 121–22, 142
Epstein, Jean. *See Fall of the House of Usher*
Epstein, Perle, 129, 133–34, 136

"Eridanus," and the "Voyage," 8, 15
Erskine, Albert, 1, 8, 76, 90, 129, 130
  and Lowry's unpublished letter about *October Ferry,* 76–77, 90, 95, 97, 98, 132
Expressionism, 36, 55–57, 82, 86, 92, 133, 135. See also Film; and titles of specific films
Fall of the House of Usher, film by Jean Epstein, 71, 136
Faulkner, William, 121, 141
Faust. See Santayana, George
Film, the influence of, 54–57, 88–89, 135, 139. See also Expressionism; and titles of specific films
Fitzgerald, F. Scott, *Tender Is the Night,* the Lowrys' filmscript of, 129, 135, 139
"flowering past, The," *Selected Poems of Malcolm Lowry,* xii
Foley, Martha, 40, 134
Fort, Charles, 3, 89, 137
Fowles, John, 120, 141
Freedman, Ralph, 97, 138
"Frère Jacques," Lowry's use of, 104, 139
Freud, Sigmund, 126
Frye, Northrop, 120–21, 122, 142

Galeen, Henrik. See *The Student of Prague*
"Garden of Etla," 20
"Ghostkeeper," 1–2, 5, 130
Giroux, Robert, praise for the "Voyage," 18
Gravity's Rainbow. See Pynchon, Thomas
Great Circle. See Aiken, Conrad
Green, Julian, *The Dark Journey,* 63–64
Grieg, Nordahl, *The Ship Sails On,* 7, 20, 126, 131

Hands of Orlac, The, Robert Weine, 55, 56. See also Expressionism
Haunted Castle, The. See Railo, Eino
Hear Us O Lord from Heaven Thy Dwelling Place
  genesis of, 100–101
  and the "Voyage," 1, 16, 99, 100, 113
Hesse, Hermann, *Demian,* 87, 95–96
Horace, quoted in "Elephant and Colosseum," 110, 140
Houghton, Claude, 129

I Ching, Lowry's interest in, 60–61, 135
"In Ballast to the White Sea," 6–7, 132
"In the Black Hills." See "Kristbjorg's Story: In the Black Hills"
Isn't Life Wonderful, D.W. Griffith, 88, 89

Jakobson, Roman, theory of metaphor and metonymy, 52, 135
James, Henry, Lowry's knowledge of, 130

Jazz, Lowry's interest in, 104, 139
Joyce, James, influence on Lowry, 129
  Ulysses, 35, 121, 122, 142
"June the 30th, 1934," 22–24, 132
Jung, C.G., 102, 126, 129, 135

Keats, John, *Endymion* and *Dark as the Grave,* 65–66, 136
  and *Hear Us O Lord,* 108–9, 140
Keyserling, Hermann, 2
Kilgallin, Tony, 129
Kim, Suzanne, 132
King Lear, William Shakespeare, 93–94, 97, 138
"Kristbjorg's Story: In the Black Hills," description of, 139
  and *Hear Us O Lord,* 100
Kroetsch, Robert, 120, 133

"La Mordida"
  manuscripts of, 59–61
  and the "Voyage" 8, 9, 15–16
"Last Address, The" and *Lunar Caustic,* 29–30
Laurence, Margaret, 120, 141
"Le caustique lunaire." See "Swinging the Maelstrom"
Looping the Loop, Arthur Robison, 46, 88
Lowry, Malcolm. See also Myth; Opposites; Reality; Serialism; Style; Withdrawal and Return; Works, See specific titles
  aesthetics of, 4–6. See also Expressionism, Metafiction, Realism
  alcoholism, xiii, 35
  biography, xiii–xv, 136
  evolving consciousness, concept of, 3, 102–3, 119. See also Sigbjørn Wilderness, persona of
  letters to Aiken, 143
Lowry, Margerie, xiii, 8, 29, 61, 74, 89, 100, 123, 129, 131, 135, 136, 137
Lowry, Russell, xv, 130
Lunar Caustic
  analysis of, 29–33
  and the "Voyage," 13–14
Lytton, Edward George Earle Bulwer-*Zanoni,* 137

Mad Love. See *The Hands of Orlac*
Marcelin, Milo. See Voodoo
Markson, David, 75, 129, 133
Martin, Jay, 142–43
Melville, Herman, 30, 130
Mendelson, Edward, 121, 142
Metafiction, and Lowry's fiction, 5, 13, 121, 130. See also Wood, Barry
Mr. Arcularis. See Aiken, Conrad
Murnau, Fred. See *Sunrise*

Myth, Lowry's concept of, 19, 37, 58, 113, 132. *See also* Spence, Lewis; and Durrant, Geoffrey
Myths of Mexico and Peru, The. See Spence, Lewis

New, William, on Lowry and Canadian writers, 141
 on Lowry's works, 62, 96, 101, 129, 133, 137, 139, 140
Nicolay, Helen, *The Bridge of Water* and *Hear Us O Lord*, 107
"No Still Path," *Selected Poems of Malcolm Lowry*, 141
Noxon, Gerald, on Lowry's style, 130

October Ferry to Gabriola
 critical reception of, 137
 genesis of, 74–75
 unpublished letter about. *See* Erskine, Albert
 and the "Voyage," 16–18
O'Kill, Brian, 44, 51, 119, 130, 134, 142
O'Neill, Eugene, 36
Opposites, Lowry's concept of, 3, 118–19, 141
 in *Hear Us O Lord*, 101, 114, 141
 in *October Ferry*, 97
 in *Ultramarine*, 26
"Ordeal of Sigbjørn Wilderness, The"
 and *Mr. Arcularis*, 127, 138
 and the "Voyage," 9–11. *See also* Sigbjørn Wilderness, persona of
Ortega y Gasset, José, influence on Lowry, 2, 12, 102, 107, 116, 131
Ouspensky, P.D., influence on Lowry, 2, 3, 20, 22, 54, 59, 102–3, 114, 116, 129, 130, 140–41
Outward Bound, the film, 81, 88. *See also* Vane, Sutton
Outward Bound, the play. *See* Vane, Sutton

Perichoresis, concept in *October Ferry*, 78, 137
Perlmutter, Ruth, 119, 135
Pethick, Derek, Lowry's letter to, 34–35
Pirandello, L., 7, 63, 136
Plomer, William, criticisms of *Under the Volcano*, 36
Poe, Edgar Allan, 30, 37, 71, 76, 104, 108–9, 111, 136. *See also Fall of the House of Usher*
"Punctum Indifferens Skibet Gaar Videre." *See* "Seductio ad Absurdum"
Purdy, Alfred, 119–20, 141
Pynchon, Thomas, *Gravity's Rainbow*, 35, 121–22, 142

Railo, Eino, *The Haunted Castle*, 89, 137–38

Realism, Lowry's attitude toward, 5–6, 13, 36, 88, 115, 121. *See also* Reality
Reality, Lowry's concept of, 1–3, 88–89, 96, 115–16, 119. *See also* Realism
Robison, Arthur. *See Looping the Loop;* and *Warning Shadows*

Santayana, George, interpretation of *Faust*, 138
Schoenberg, Arnold, concept of "serial music," 139–40
Scholes, Robert, quoted on Roman Jakobson, 52
"Seductio ad Absurdum," 24
Serialism, in Lowry's fiction, 20, 40–41, 57, 62–63, 66, 70–71, 81, 93, 102, 107, 113, 140. *See also* Aiken, Conrad; and Dunne, J.W.
Shakespeare, William. *See King Lear*
Ship Sails On, The. See Grieg, Nordahl
"Sigbjørn," etymology of, 102, 139
Sigbjørn Wilderness, persona of, 12–13, 63, 69, 102–3, 119. *See also* "The Ordeal of Sigbjørn Wilderness"
Sleepwalkers, The. See Broch, Hermann
Sonnenaufgang. See Sunrise
Spatial form, xv–xvi, 134, 138
 in *Dark as the Grave*, 66
 in *Hear Us O Lord*, 106–7, 108
 in *October Ferry*, 86–88, 96
 in *Under the Volcano*, 40, 42, 47–51, 53, 56, 58
Spatialize. *See* Spatial form
Spence, Lewis, *The Myths of Mexico and Peru*, Lowry's knowledge of, 134–35
Stansfeld-Jones, Charles, 2, 54, 114, 116, 130, 135, 137, 138. *See also* Cabbala
 influence on *October Ferry*, 78–80, 91, 92, 93, 96
Stasis. *See* Spatial form
Student of Prague, The, Henrik Galeen, 37, 55, 76, 88, 92. *See also* Expressionism
Style, aspects of Lowry's 119, 134
 in *Hear Us O Lord*, 105
 in *October Ferry*, 83–85
 in *Under the Volcano*, 44–45, 51–52
Sunrise, Fred Murnau, 46, 55, 56–57, 88. *See also* Expressionism
"Swinging the Maelstrom," and *Lunar Caustic*, 29–30
"[Symbols of tenuous order]," unpublished Lowry poem, 99, 138

Tender Is the Night, F. Scott Fitzgerald, the Lowrys' filmscript of, 129, 135, 139
Thurston, E. Temple. *See The Wandering Jew*
Todorov, Tzvetan, 42, 46, 134

UFa (Universum Film-Aktiengesellschaft), 36
Ultramarine, analysis of, 24-29
   and the "Voyage," 8, 19, 29
Ulysses. See Joyce, James
Under the Volcano, discussion of the 1940
   manuscript, 38-41, 43, 134
   and the letter to Cape, 36-38
   and the "Voyage," 8, 14, 58

Vane, Sutton, *Outward Bound,* 89-90, 132, 138
Veidt, Conrad
   in *The Hands of Orlac,* 55
   in *The Wandering Jew,* 137
Volney, Constantine F. Chassebeuf de. See
   Volney's *Ruins*
Volney's *Ruins,* Constantine F. Chassebeuf de
   Volney, 111-12, 140
Voodoo, imagery in *Dark as the Grave,* 72-73
   in Milo Marcelin's *Mythologie Voodue,* 136
"Voyage That Never Ends, The," Lowry's plans
   for, 6-9

Wagner, Richard, 37, 86, 90, 102
Wandering Jew, The, E. Temple Thurston, 81,
   88-89, 137

Warning Shadows, Arthur Robison, and *Lunar*
   Caustic, 133
Watson, Sheila, *The Double Hook,* 120
Weine, Robert. See *The Cabinet of Dr. Caligari;*
   and *The Hands of Orlac*
Williams, John A., Lowry's influence on, 133
Withdrawal and Return
   Lowry's concept of xv-xvi, 118
   in *Dark as the Grave,* 63, 64, 67-69, 71, 73
   in *Hear Us O Lord,* 103, 105, 109, 111, 113
   in "La Mordida," 15-16, 60-61
   in *Lunar Caustic,* 32-33
   in *October Ferry,* 75, 82, 95, 98
   in *Ultramarine,* 29
   in *Under the Volcano,* 45, 47
   in the "Voyage," 12, 18-19
Wood, Barry, on Lowry's metafiction, 13,
   131-32, 140
Woodcock, George, 64, 136

Yeats, William Butler, 112, 118

Zanoni, Lytton, Edward George Earle Bulwer-,
   137